AWESOME ALMANAC™ ILLINOIS

SEAL OF THE STATE OF ILLINOIS
NATIONAL UNION SOVEREIGNTY STATE GOVERNMENT
AUG. 26TH

Created by
Jean F. Blashfield

Compiled and Written by
Jean F. Blashfield

B&B Publishing, Inc.

B & B Publishing, Inc.
P. O. Box 393
Fontana, Wisconsin 53125

Editor – **Nancy Jacobson**
Photo Researcher – **Margie Benson**
Computer Design and Production Manager – **Dave Conant**
Computer Specialist and Indexer – **Marilyn Magowan**
Cover Design – **Gary Hurst**

Publisher's Cataloging in Publication

Blashfield, Jean F.
    Awesome almanac—Illinois / Jean F. Blashfield.
    p. cm.
    Includes index.
    Preassigned LCCN: 92-074707
    ISBN 1-880190-04-4

1. Illinois—Miscellanea. 2. Illinois—History. 3. Almanacs,
American—Illinois. I. Title.

F539.B53 1993

                       977.3'003
                       QBI92-20123

ATTENTION SCHOOLS AND BUSINESSES:
    This book is available at quantity discounts with bulk purchases for educational, busi-
    ness, or sales promotional use. For information, please write to B&B Publishing, Inc.,
    P.O. Box 393, Fontana, WI 53125

DISTRIBUTOR TO THE BOOK TRADE:
    Publishers Distribution Service, 6893 Sullivan Road, Grawn, MI 49637

TABLE OF CONTENTS

The Capitol Building, Springfield

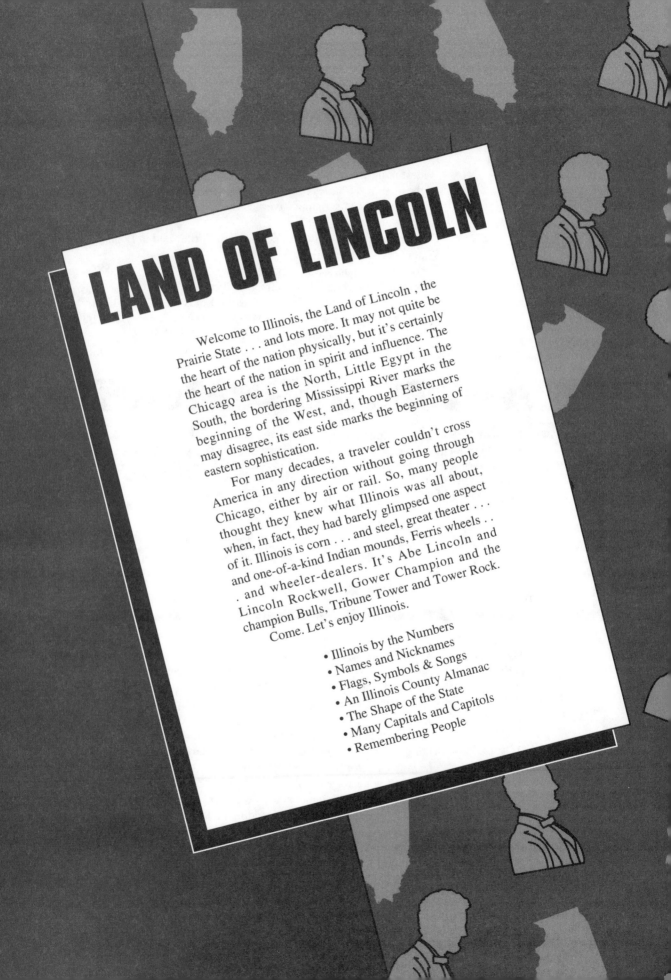

LAND OF LINCOLN

Welcome to Illinois, the Land of Lincoln, the Prairie State . . . and lots more. It may not quite be the heart of the nation physically, but it's certainly the heart of the nation in spirit and influence. The Chicago area is the North, Little Egypt in the South, the bordering Mississippi River marks the beginning of the West, and, though Easterners may disagree, its east side marks the beginning of eastern sophistication.

For many decades, a traveler couldn't cross America in any direction without going through Chicago, either by air or rail. So, many people thought they knew what Illinois was all about, when, in fact, they had barely glimpsed one aspect of it. Illinois is corn . . . and steel, great theater . . . and wheeler-dealers. It's Abe Lincoln and Lincoln Rockwell, Gower Champion and the champion Bulls, Tribune Tower and Tower Rock.

Come. Let's enjoy Illinois.

ILLINOIS BY THE NUMBERS

The land
Land area – 55,645 square miles (24th largest state)
Longest point from north to south – 385 miles
Widest point from east to west – 218 miles
Highest point – Charles Mound in Jo Daviess County at 1,235 feet
Lowest point – Mississippi River in Alexander County at 279 feet
Average elevation – 600 feet
Geographic center – 28 miles northeast of Springfield in Logan County
Water area – 700 square miles
Largest lake – manmade Carlyle Lake in Clinton County, 26,000 acres
Climate – Temperate—hot summers and cold winters
Highest temperature – 117° F., in East St. Louis on July 14, 1954
Lowest temperature – -35° F., at Mount Carroll on January 22, 1930
Date of entry into the Union – December 3, 1818 (20th state)
The chief of state is the governor, who is elected to a 4-year term.

THE PEOPLE

1990 Resident Census Population
11,430,602 (6th largest state)

Gender
Female – 5,878,369   Male - 5,552,233

Age
Under 18 – 25.8%
65 & over – 12.6
Median age – 32.8

Race
White – 8,952,978 (78.3%)

Black – 1,694,273 (14.8%)

Asian or Pacific Islander –
285,311 (2.5%)

Hispanic – 904,446 (7.9%)

Native American (American Indian,
Eskimo or Aleut) – 21,836 (0.2%)

Illinois's government
The state legislature is called the General Assembly. It consists of an upper house, the Senate, with 59 members, and a lower house, the House of Representatives, with 117 members.

Senators are elected for 4-year terms and representatives for 2-year terms.

Illinois is the only state that elects its representatives by cumulative voting. This means that each voter has three votes. These may be cast one vote each for three candidates; three votes for one candidate; or one and a half votes for each of two candidates.

Illinois has 2 senators and 20 representatives in the U.S. Congress (down 2 from the 1980 census), adding up to 22 electoral votes.

The court system
There are three kinds of courts in the state: Circuit courts hear all lower-court cases. The judges are elected to 6-year terms. Appellate (or appeals) courts have 34 judges, each elected to 10-year terms. Illinois Supreme Court consists of 7 judges, each elected to a ten-year term.

NAMES AND NICKNAMES

The name "Illinois" was given the area by Sieur de La Salle, who sailed along the river he named in 1679. It is derived from an Algonquin word Inini, meaning "the men" and "accomplished." The French twisted the sound into "Illini" and added the ois ending, which makes the name mean "the tribe of accomplished (or superior) men."

The meaning of the name "Illinois"

At various times Illinois has been given different nicknames. It has been known as the **Garden of the West**, **Prairie State**, **Corn State**, and **The Hub of the Nation**. One nickname, **Crossroads of America**, was borrowed by its neighbor to the east, Indiana. The official nickname, **Land of Lincoln**, has been emblazoned on its license plate since 1955.

The southern part of the state, along the Ohio River, has often been called **Little Egypt** because of the town of Cairo, which, like its namesake in Egypt, is low-lying along a major river.

It has even been called a "sucker." The origin of the term **Sucker State** is uncertain. The seemingly insulting term may have originated in the small crawfish holes that held fresh water, from which early travelers could suck up water. A scout would announce the presence of such a hole by shouting "A sucker!"

Nicknames

When the first settlers arrived in Illinois, half of the land was forest and the rest was prairie, which is open, rolling land covered primarily with perennial grasses. Much of Illinois was tall-grass prairie, with grasses growing waist high. Illinois's was the first land area on which pioneers encountered prairie, although other states have even more, so Illinois became known as "The Prairie State."

In 1989, Illinois adopted big bluestem, also called turkeyfoot grass, as the official state prairie grass. It grows taller than a person on horseback and is generally found nowadays only in state preserves.

"The Prairie State"

POPULATION

Census Year	Illinois	United States
1990	11,430,602	248,709,873
1980	11,427,409	226,542,203
1970	11,110,285	203,302,031
1960	10,081,158	179,323,175
1950	8,712,176	151,325,798
1940	7,897,241	132,164,569
1930	7,630,654	123,202,624
1920	6,485,280	106,021,537
1910	5,638,591	92,228,496
1900	4,821,550	76,212,168
1890	3,826,352	62,979,766
1880	3,077,871	50,189,209
1870	2,539,891	38,558,371
1860	1,711,951	31,443,321
1850	851,470	23,191,876
1840	476,183	17,063,353
1830	157,445	12,860,702
1820	55,211	9,638,453
1810	12,282	7,240,000

Graph shows the population of Illinois as a percentage of the United States population.

The first governor

Shadrach Bond, originally from Maryland, was the first delegate to the U.S. House of Representatives from Illinois Territory from 1812 to 1814. In 1813 he sponsored a "preemption" law that allowed the first residents of a territory to buy the land they settled on. This made moving west more attractive to ordinary people. When Illinois became a state in 1818, Bond was elected governor without opposition, and he served from 1818 to 1822. Bond's grave, now a state memorial, is in Chester. If you've ever wondered who the Achsah Bond of the Adler Planetarium's address is, she was Shadrach's wife.

Lt. governor by finagling

Pierre Menard, a settler from Canada, became so popular that when Illinois was made a state, the men attending the constitutional convention made special rules that were fit just for him. The governor had to have been a citizen for 30 years, but the lieutenant governor only had to be a citizen and have lived in Illinois for two years. Menard was elected the state's first lieutenant governor. His plantation-style home at Kaskaskia is part of Fort Kaskaskia State Park.

Illinois was a shrimp

Illinois is the smallest state ever admitted to the Union—by population, that is. Laws required that a territory have a population of 60,000 in order to apply statehood. But young Daniel Pope Cook, the editor of the only newspaper, began to urge statehood on the people, and the territorial legislature followed his lead. In Washington, Cook's uncle, Nathaniel Pope, the territorial delegate, petitioned for statehood, even though he knew that Illinois didn't have enough people. Congress wanted a census to prove that Illinois had at least 40,000 people. Territorial governor Ninian Edwards took charge of the census and, with a tug at the truth here, a totally outrageous guesstimate there, and even some outright fraud, Illinois camee up with a count of 40,258. Congress accepted the figure, though it acknowledged later that Illinois probably had not had more than 34,000 inhabitants when it became a state.

FLAGS, SYMBOLS, AND SONGS

The making of a flag

The Illinois General Assembly adopted the first official state flag in 1915. Somehow, it didn't really dawn on anyone that the name "Illinois" wasn't on it. The name was added to the flag in 1969 at the suggestion of Chief Petty Officer Bruce McDaniel from Waverly. Mrs. Sanford Hutchinson from Greenfield submitted a new design, which was adopted July 1, 1970. The white field with the word "Illinois" has an exact copy of the state seal, though the seal doesn't have its outer border.

In 1907, Illinois schoolchildren were given the awesome responsibility of choosing the State Flower and State Tree by ballot. The children chose the violet and the oak, choices made official on July 1, 1908. Gradually it became clear that "oak" was not specific enough, and in 1973, children voted to change to the white oak. The State Flower is the "native violet," probably the bird's-foot violet.

The procedure was repeated to select a State Bird. The children's selection, the cardinal, was officially adopted on June 4, 1929. Other favorites have been added in recent years:

State Insect—monarch butterfly (1975)
State Animal—white-tailed deer (1982)
State Fish—bluegill (1987)
State Prairie Grass—big bluestem (1989)

The State Mineral is fluorite (or fluorspar or calcium fluorite), declared in 1965. The mineral is important in production of enamels, aluminum, steel, and chemicals. Illinois is the nation's biggest producer.

The state's motto appears on the Great Seal. It says "State Sovereignty—National Union." It was adopted on March 7, 1867.

State symbols

"Illinois"

*Words by C.H. Chamberlain,
Music by Archibald Johnston*

From a wilderness of prairies,
Straight thy way and never varies,
Till upon the inland sea,
Stands thy great commercial tree, turning all the
world to thee.

(Refrain)
By thy river gently flowing, Illinois, Illinois
O'er thy prairies verdant growing, Illinois, Illinois,
Comes an echo on the breeze,
Rustling through the leafy trees, and its mellow
tones are these, Illinois, Illinois.
And its mellow tones are these, Illinois

When you heard your country calling,
Where the shot and shell were falling,
When the southern host withdrew,
Pitting Gray against the Blue, There were none more
brave than you. (Refrain)

Not without thy wondrous story,
Can be writ the nation's glory,
On the record of thy years,
Abraham Lincoln's name appears, Grant and Logan,
and our tears. (Refrain)

Who was Logan?

Several people are mentioned in the State Song. Grant and Lincoln were, of course, presidents of the United States, but who was Logan? He was John A. Logan, born on February 9, 1826, in Jackson County. He served as an Illinois congressman from 1859 to 1861, when he resigned his seat to join the Union Army. He was for a while Comman-der of the Army of the Tennessee. He helped to found the GAR, Grand Army of the Republic. As their commander in chief in 1868, and at the request of his wife, he founded Memorial Day by asking the members to decorate the graves of the fallen.

AN ILLINOIS COUNTY ALMANAC

Illinois Counties – 102

Largest by population – Cook, 5,105,067 (the second largest county in the U.S.)

Smallest by population – Hardin, 5,189

Largest in area – McLean, 1,173 square miles

Smallest in area – Putnam, 166 square miles

ILLINOIS COUNTIES

COUNTY	1990 POP.	COUNTY SEAT	SQ. MILES	FOUNDED	NAMED FOR
Adams	66,090	Quincy	852	1/13/1825	President John Adams
Alexander	10,616	Cairo	236	3/4/1819	Wm. Alexander, settler
Bond	14,991	Greenville	377	1/4/1817	Gov. Shadrach Bond
Boone	30,806	Belvidere	282	3/4/1837	Daniel Boone
Brown	5,836	Mt. Sterling	306	2/1/1839	Jacob Brown, a military officer
Bureau	35,688	Princeton	869	2/28/1837	Pierre Bureo, a French trade
Calhoun	5,322	Hardin	250	1/10/1825	John C. Calhoun
Carroll	16,805	Mt. Carroll	444	2/22/1839	John Carroll
Cass	13,437	Virginia	374	3/3/1837	Lewis Cass, territorial governor
Champaign	173,025	Urbana	998	2/20/1833	Champaign Co., OH
Christian	34,418	Taylorville	710	2/15/1839	Christian Co., KY
Clark	15,921	Marshall	506	3/22/1819	George Rogers Clark
Clay	14,460	Louisville	469	12/23/1824	Henry Clay
Clinton	33,944	Carlyle	472	12/27/1824	Gov. DeWitt Clinton of NY
Coles	51,644	Charleston	509	12/25/1830	Gov. Edward Coles
Cook	5,105,067	Chicago	958	1/15/1831	Cong. Daniel Pope Cook
Crawford	19,464	Robinson	446	12/31/1816	Sen. Wm. Crawford of GA
Cumberland	10,670	Toledo	346	3/2/1843	Cumberland Road
De Kalb	77,932	Sycamore	634	3/4/1837	Johann De Kalb of Am. Revolution
DeWitt	16,516	Clinton	397	3/1/1839	Gov. DeWitt Clinton of NY
Douglas	19,464	Tuscola	417	2/8/1859	Stephen A. Douglas
DuPage	781,666	Wheaton	337	2/9/1839	DuPage River
Edgar	19,595	Paris	623	1/3/1823	John Edgar, a settler
Edwards	7,440	Albion	223	11/18/1814	Gov. Ninian Edwards
Effingham	31,704	Effingham	478	2/15/1831	Thomas Howard, Earl of Effingham

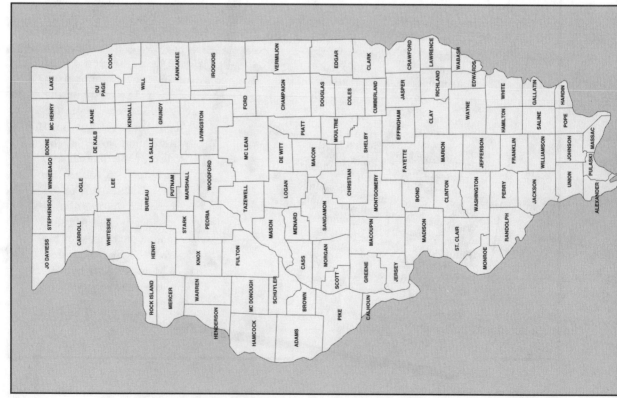

COUNTY	1990 POP.	COUNTY SEAT	SQ. MILES	FOUNDED	NAMED FOR
Fayette	20,893	Vandalia	709	2/14/1821	Marquis de la Fayette
Franklin	40,319	Benton	414	1/2/1818	Benjamin Franklin
Ford	14,275	Paxton	486	2/17/1859	Gov. Thomas Ford
Fulton	38,080	Lewistown	871	1/28/1823	Robert Fulton, inventor
Gallatin	6,909	Shawneetown	325	9/14/1812	Albert Gallatin, Sec. of Treasury
Greene	15,317	Carrollton	543	1/20/1821	Nathanael Greene
Grundy	32,337	Morris	423	2/27/1841	Attorney General Felix Grundy
Hamilton	8,499	McLeansboro	436	2/8/1821	Alexander Hamilton
Hancock	21,373	Carthage	796	1/13/1825	John Hancock
Hardin	5,189	Elizabethtown	181	3/2/1839	Hardin Co., KY
Henderson	8,096	Oquawka	373	1/20/1841	Henderson Co., KY
Henry	51,159	Cambridge	824	1/13/1825	Patrick Henry
Jackson	61,067	Murphysboro	590	1/10/1816	Andrew Jackson
Jasper	10,609	Newton	496	2/15/1831	Wm. Jasper of Am. Revolution
Jefferson	37,020	Mt. Vernon	570	3/26/1819	Thomas Jefferson
Jersey	20,539	Jerseyville	373	2/28/1839	State of New Jersey
Jo Daviess	21,821	Galena	603	2/17/1827	Joseph H. Daveiss, attorney
Johnson	11,347	Vienna	346	9/14/1812	Richard M. Johnson, killed Tecumseh
Kane	317,471	Geneva	524	1/16/1836	Sen. Elias Kent Kane
Kankakee	96,255	Kankakee	679	2/11/1853	Kankakee Indians
Kendall	39,413	Yorkville	322	2/19/1841	Amos Kendall, journalist
Knox	56,393	Galesburg	720	1/13/1825	Henry Knox, Sec. of War
Lake	516,418	Waukegan	454	3/1/1839	Lake Michigan
LaSalle	106,913	Ottawa	1,139	1/15/1831	Explorer Sieur de la Salle
Lawrence	15,972	Lawrenceville	374	1/16/1821	James Lawrence, ship commander
Lee	34,392	Dixon	725	2/27/1839	Sen. Richard H. Lee of VA
Livingston	39,301	Pontiac	1,046	2/27/1837	Sen. Edward Livingston of LA
Logan	30,798	Lincoln	619	2/15/1839	Dr. John Logan, pioneer
McDonough	35,244	Macomb	590	1/25/1826	Thomas Macdonough, naval hero
McHenry	183,241	Woodstock	606	1/16/1836	William McHenry, pioneer
McLean	129,180	Bloomington	1,185	2/25/1830	Sen. John McLean
Macon	117,206	Decatur	581	1/19/1829	Sen. Nathaniel Macon of NC
Macoupin	47,679	Carlinville	865	1/17/1829	Indian word: white potato
Madison	249,238	Edwardsville	728	9/14/1812	Pres. James Madison
Marion	41,561	Salem	573	1/24/1823	"Swamp Fox" Francis Marion
Marshall	12,846	Lacon	388	1/19/1839	US Chief Justice John Marshall
Mason	16,269	Havana	536	1/20/1841	Mason Co., KY
Massac	14,752	Metropolis	241	2/8/1843	Fort Massac
Menard	11,164	Petersburg	315	2/15/1839	Lt. Gov. Pierre Menard
Mercer	17,290	Aledo	559	1/13/1825	Hugh Mercer, soldier
Monroe	22,422	Waterloo	388	1/6/1816	Pres. James Monroe
Montgomery	30,728	Hillsboro	705	2/12/1821	Richard Montgomery, soldier
Morgan	36,397	Jacksonville	568	1/31/1823	Daniel Morgan, soldier
Moultrie	13,930	Sullivan	325	2/16/1843	Gov. Wm Moultrie of SC
Ogle	45,957	Oregon	759	1/16/1836	Joseph Ogle, pioneer
Peoria	182,827	Peoria	621	1/13/1825	Illini Indians
Perry	21,412	Pinckneyville	443	1/29/1827	Oliver Perry, naval hero
Piatt	15,548	Monticello	439	1/17/1841	James Piatt, settler
Pike	17,577	Pittsfield	830	1/31/1821	Explorer Zebulon Pike
Pope	4,373	Golconda	374	1/10/1816	Nathaniel Pope, congressman
Pulaski	7,523	Mound City	103	3/3/1843	Polish Count Casimir Pulaski
Putnam	5,730	Hennepin	160	1/13/1825	Israel Putnam, soldier
Randolph	34,583	Chester	583	10/5/1795	Attorney Gen. Edmund Randolph
Richland	16,545	Olney	360	2/24/1841	Richland Co., OH
Rock Island	148,723	Rock Island	423	2/9/1831	Rock Island
St. Clair	262,852	Belleville	672	4/27/1790	Arthur St. Claire, territorial gov.
Saline	26,551	Harrisburg	385	2/25/1847	Salt springs in area
Sangamon	178,386	Springfield	866	1/30/1821	Indian word: good hunting place
Schuyler	7,498	Rushville	436	1/13/1825	Sen. Philip J. Schuyler of NY
Scott	5,644	Winchester	251	2/16/1839	Scott Co., KY
Shelby	22,261	Shelbyville	747	1/23/1827	Gov. Isaac Shelby of KY
Stark	6,534	Toulon	288	3/2/1839	John Stark, soldier
Stephenson	48,052	Freeport	564	3/4/1837	Delegate Benjamin Stephenson
Tazewell	123,692	Pekin	650	1/31/1827	Sen. Littleton Tazewell of VA
Union	17,619	Jonesboro	414	1/2/1818	Baptist union revival meeting
Vermilion	88,257	Danville	900	1/18/1826	Vermilion River (from red clay)
Wabash	13,111	Mt. Carmel	224	12/27/1824	Wabash River
Warren	19,181	Monmouth	543	1/13/1825	Dr. Joseph Warren, soldier
Washington	14,965	Nashville	563	1/2/1818	George Washington
Iroquois	1,118	Watseka		2/16/1833	Iroquois Indian
Wayne	17,241	Fairfield	715	3/26/1819	"Mad" Anthony Wayne
White	16,522	Carmi	497	12/9/1815	State Sen. Leonard White
Whiteside	60,186	Morrison	682	1/16/1836	Politician Samuel Whiteside
Will	357,313	Joliet	844	2/12/1836	Assemblyman Conrad Will
Williamson	57,733	Marion	427	2/28/1839	Williamson Co., TN
Winnebago	252,913	Rockford	516	1/16/1836	Winnebago Indians
Woodford	32,653	Eureka	527	2/27/1841	Woodford Co., KY

THE SHAPE OF THE STATE

Determining the boundaries

The final shape of Illinois was determined over a number of years and events, starting in 1783 when the treaty, signed by the new United States of America and Great Britain at the end of the Revolutionary War, provided for the land north of the Ohio River to be turned over to the new nation. That land, called the Northwest Territory, was everything north of the low-water mark on the Ohio River and extending to the Mississippi River on the west.

1787

1800

1805

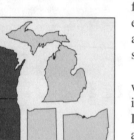

1809

1818

1787 - Congress tentatively broke the Northwest Territory into five future states and established rules for when an area could become a state.

1800 - The Northwest Territory was split in half, called Ohio and Indiana. Indiana included all of the future Indiana, Illinois, Michigan, and Wisconsin.

1805 - Michigan Territory was separated from Indiana Territory, though it did not qualify for statehood until 1837.

1809 - Illinois Territory, the area west of the Wabash River (which still included Wisconsin), was broken off from Indiana Territory. Kaskaskia was named the territorial capital.

1818 - Illinois became a state (see below), leaving Wisconsin to rejoin Michigan.

The man who made the state bigger

The original statehood papers called for Illinois to have its northern border at the southern tip of Lake Michigan, leaving the territory farther north for Wisconsin. However, Illinois's congressional delegate, Nathaniel Pope, recognized that Illinois would probably never amount to much unless it had access to the Great Lakes. He persuaded Congress to amend the Statehood Act to give the state an additional 51 miles on the northern end, thus opening the state to settlement by people coming from New England through the Erie Canal. The addition of the land on the lake, with the state's focus shifting to northern industry, probably kept the state from becoming a slave state in later years.

But part of Illinois is in Missouri

The Mississippi is a fickle river. It tends to move around a lot, playing musical river beds. Because of that, one small piece of Illinois is actually in Missouri. Old Kaskaskia, where much of Illinois history started, was flooded by the shifting waters of the river, which left a chunk of it above the floodwaters but on the west side of the river. Called Kaskaskia Island, it has a tiny population, which can reach the mainland only by a bridge that goes into Missouri.

MANY CAPITALS AND CAPITOLS

When Illinois because a state in 1818, Kaskaskia was the capital because it had been the capital of Illinois Territory since 1809. Within a year, however, it was moved to the neighboring town of Vandalia. The site of the first capital at Kaskaskia is now under the waters of the Mississippi River. The waters had been slicing away at the town for many years, but the last pieces slipped under the water in 1909.

**Kaskaskia—
The first capital**

The General Asembly first met in Vandalia on December 4, 1820. Illinois's first state capitol building was a quickly constructed two-story wooden structure, 30 by 40 feet. The House met on the first floor and the Senate on the second, until it was destroyed by fire in 1823.

A second building was constructed using the walls of a bank building that had burned the previous January. The new building was used until 1836. That year, the second capitol building was torn down and the materials from it used in constructing a new capitol building, which, the citizens hoped, would keep the General Assembly from moving the capitol elsewhere. It was used from 1836, to July 4, 1839. But ultimately the Vandalians' plan didn't work.

When Vandalia was the capital

The delegates to the General Assembly from Sangamon County included Abraham Lincoln. They were referred to as the "Long Nine" because they were all tall (collectively, 54 feet). These nine were responsible for engineering the compromise that made Springfield the capital of Illinois. The other towns in the running—Alton, Peoria, Jacksonville—were granted internal improvements if they would cast their votes for Springfield. Lincoln himself moved to the new capital before it started functioning. State records were moved to the new capital in July 1839.

**Compromise:
The essence of government**

The cornerstone of the new capitol building was laid in a ceremony held on the July 4, 1837. It was not completed for 16 years. The building (now called the Old State Capitol) opened in 1840. It was used by both the legislature and the Illinois Supreme Court until the newer building was available in 1876. Since that time, it has been used as the Sangamon County Courthouse. In 1961, the State of Illinois bought the building back from the county and began its reconstruction as an historical site. Inside the beautiful limestone outer walls and the magnificent Doric columns is a totally brand new building that reproduces the chambers as Lincoln knew them.

The new capitol building at Springfield

Ground was broken for a new capital building on March 11, 1868. The supervising architect was Alfred Piquenard. It was no easy task getting it finished. It took twenty years of controversy and delay. When John C. Cochrane, a Chicago architect, was awarded $3,000 for the winning design, his partner, George Garnsey, claimed the money, saying he'd done most of the work. After construction began in 1868, a dispute over materials halted construction. A constitutional amendment-put a $3.5 million ceiling on costs, and 1871 passed without more funds being appropriated.

Several cities, disgusted with the slow pace of Springfield, wanted to move the state capital. Chicago said the legislature could move there at no cost to the state, but the Great Fire of 1871 stopped Chicago's serious bid. Unskilled prison laborers were used to cut stone for the building, which caused further delays. When voters twice rejected additional funding, contruction was stopped for eight years and didn't begin again until 1884. Finally, in 1888, at a cost of $4.5 million, the state capitol building was completed.

The capitol is shaped like a cross on a circular foundation that supports the huge dome. The walls of the dome at ground level are 17 feet thick. The building is 405 feet tall to the top of the flag pole.The stained glass replica of the state seal, located in the interior dome, had a misspelled word in the motto: "State Sovereignity, National Union."

The Executive Mansion

The Executive Mansion in Springfield is the third oldest continuously occupied governor's mansion in the country. Built for $45,794, its first occupant was Governor Joel A. Matteson, who served from 1853 to 1857 and moved into the house at midterm.

REMEMBERING PEOPLE

Who should be a statue?

After the House of Representatives was moved into a new wing of the U.S. Capitol in Washington in 1864, each state was invited to send two statues to the new Statuary Hall formed out of the old House. Illinois first sent a bronze statue of General James Shields sculpted by Leonard Wills Volk, unveiled in 1893. Shields was a brigadier general in the Mexican and Civil wars, governor of Oregon territory, and a senator. The carving on his statue calls him "Warrior, Jurist, Statesman."

Actually, because the hall was not big enough for a hundred or more statues, only one statue from each state actually stands in Statuary Hall. Shields is located in the Hall of Columns. The Illinois statue in Statuary Hall depicts Frances E. Willard, founder of the Women's Christian Temperance Union (see page 69), a major force behind Prohibition. Willard's marble statue, sculpted by Helen Farnsworth Mears, was unveiled in 1905. It was the first statue of a woman sent by any state.

The Poles donate a state holiday

The first Monday in March is celebrated as the birthday of General Casimir Pulaski. An outcast Polish general who left Poland because he had been falsely suspected of trying to murder the king, Pulaski ran across Benjamin Franklin in Paris and was enticed into coming to America to help George Washington stage a revolution.

NATURAL SETTING

Four times during the last hundred thousand years, glaciers descended from the north and covered much of Illinois, gradually giving it the shape we know today. Most of the state was covered by the third glacier, which has come to be called the Illinoian. It reached down almost to the southern tip of the state. The last glacier, the Wisconsinan, which retreated about 15,000 years ago, covered only the north and east. Between them, these two glaciers flattened the land and pulverized enough rock to create a deep, fertile layer of soil.

Equally important to Illinois's land is the large number of rivers that have shaped it, too. Almost surrounded by waterways and with new waterways opened throughout it, Illinois became the gateway to the West.

But development has threatened Illinois's original natural setting. There's little prairie left. The list of endangered species is long. But there are people now at work doing something to restore Illinois's natural heritage.

Come in and look at the land and its life.

- Prairies and Wetlands
- Rivers and Canals
- Bridges to Cross
- Trees and Forests
- Parks for Pleasure
- Weather and Worse
- Wildlife
- Endangered Species
- Tending the Environment

Home of the Great Spirit

According to the Illinois Indians, Manitou, or the Great Spirit, resided in a large cave on the Ohio River. Called Cave-in-Rock, the cavern is 200 feet deep, with an opening 55 feet wide and 20 feet high. When the country was being settled, Cave-in-Rock was used by river pirates and gangsters. For the convenience of river travelers it even had a liquor store it in for a while. The cavern was featured in the film *How the West Was Won.*

PRAIRIES AND WETLANDS

The Prairie State

A traveler in Illinois early in its statehood, Captain Basil Hall exclaimed in writing over the magnificent prairies. Hall described the life cycle of the prairie during a summer, starting with low flowers such as violets, the State Flower, which appeared in early spring. They then gave way to a succession of wonderful plants ending in the tall blue-stem prairie grass that turns yellow like wheat in autumn.

Hall wrote, "While the grass is green those beautiful plains are adorned with every imaginable variety of color. It is impossible to conceive of a greater diversity." Untouched except by the occasional grass fire set by lightning, the prairie developed dense, nearly impenetrable roots that almost defeated settlers until plows were invented that could convert the land to farms. Today, environmentalists are trying to convert as much land as possible back to the original prairie.

Dickens wanted no part of it

Novelist Charles Dickens visited his brother in St. Louis in 1842. Having heard tales of the great Illinois prairie, he asked to be shown the "paroarer" (as he wrote the word in his journal). A coach took him to open land near Belleville. He was not impressed. He wrote, "It was lonely and wild, but oppressive in its barren monotony."

Restoring the prairie

Only 0.01 percent of Illinois's original landscape remains, but the state is leading the nation with innovative land-restoration projects. Volunteer seed gatherers comb the last remaining prairie areas, usually along railroad tracks or other undisturbed locations, to collect and preserve native plants. In 1991, volunteers from the Illinois Nature Conservancy collected over 51 kitchen-size garbage bags of seeds representing 80 prairie plant species.

Atoms and prairie grasses

An experimental prairie growing on the land enclosed by the proton accelerator ring at Fermi National Accelerator Laboratory in Batavia has been studied for 15 years to determine how to best restore the state's prairie land to its original beauty (see page 88). Scientists have learned that big bluestem grass, Indiana grass, and yellow cone flowers should be planted first to get the soil ready for more colorful flowers such as shooting stars. In order to thrive, these restored prairies must also be burned every few years so that nutrients can be released in the soil and unwanted plants die out. In 1992, there were more than 200 different prairie sites being restored around Illinois, from a small cemetery in Peoria to the huge Illinois Dunes State Park.

Butterfly haven

One of the sights that greeted the wondering eyes of pioneers was the millions of black, white, and orange butterflies that fluttered across the tall prairie grasses. Called gorgone checkerspot butterflies, they disappeared along with the prairie. The Illinois Nature Conservancy acquired a 700-acre prairie site, called Nashusa Grasslands, near Dixon, to which naturalists are bringing rare checkerspots—when they can be found—back to the prairie. Unlike most prairie species, the checkerspot was never able to adapt to the rough grasslands that usually replaced prairies. It needs a specific plant, the prairie sunflower, in order to survive. There is also a move afoot to reintroduce buffalo to the refuge by the year 2000.

Settling of the Bottom

The American Bottom is the low-lying floodplain between the Mississippi River and the bluffs near Kaskaskia. Because bottomland is very fertile, the region was used for agriculture by the earliest Indians. It was also the main area of Illinois to be settled by the early white settlers, who came into the state from the South. The name was used early to distinguish it from the floodplains on the other side of the Mississippi, which were owned by the Spanish. More recently, much of the bottomland has been drained by cutting special ditches and channels.

Ancient wetlands of Little Egypt

Thousand-year-old trees grow from the wet soil of the swamps of southern Illinois. Considered the oldest living things east of the Mississippi River, the prehistoric cypress trees are being preserved in 500 acres of the Cache River wetlands owned by the Nature Conservancy. The endangered Indiana bat nests there.

Wetlands provide necessary habitat for 40 percent of Illinois's endangered or threatened species, as well as breeding grounds for fish and waterfowl. When Illinois became a state, there were 8.2 million acres of wetlands. All but 0.9 million acres are gone. H.L. Kiner, author of *History of Henry County, Illinois,* described how the draining of the Green River marshes changed things. "Time was when the fusillade of shotguns along the Green River marshes north of Atkinson and 'way up to north of Mineral, was like a battle royal at sundown in the Spring and Fall. Now there's an occasional pop, lonely and isolated, like a bad egg bursting in a sour hen's nest on a hot midnight. . . ."

RIVERS AND CANALS

Rivers shape lives and towns

In 1805, the old town of Kaskaskia was swept away by a Mississippi River flood. The river also changed its course and a part of Illinois was left on the west side of the river by Missouri.

In 1937, the Ohio River flooded, covering most of Gallatin County with about ten feet of water. When the waters reached the second floor of the main bank in Shawneetown, many residents, having been through this before, decided that it was time to do something drastic. An entirely new town was constructed on the hills above the old town.

Keeping Jolliet's promise—canals

In 1673, explorer Louis Jolliet portaged across the low land between the Des Plaines River and the parallel Chicago river, and observed that the two rivers should be joined by a canal. Later, other people saw that Chicago needed to be connected directly with the Mississippi River. A system of canals was the result.

In 1900, the Sanitary and Ship Canal (**2**) connected Lake Michigan with the Des Plaines River at Lockport, reversing the flow of the Chicago River (**1**). It is now known as the Chicago Drainage Canal.

On April 10, 1848, the Illinois and Michigan Canal (**3**), connecting Chicago and Peru, opened. Along its length such new Illinois cities flourished as Lockport, Joliet, LaSalle, Marseilles, Utica, Morris, Seneca, and Ottawa. The canal did its job well until all traffic on the I & M stopped in 1933 when the Illinois Waterway (**5**) was completed. (See also page 22.)

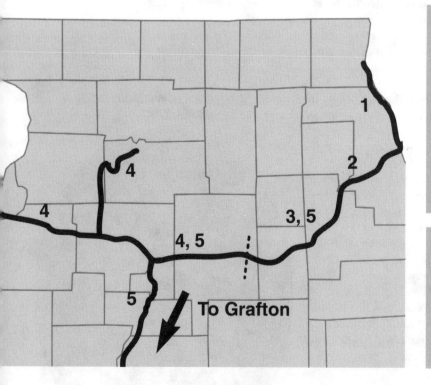

In 1907, the Illinois and Mississippi Canal opened, connecting the Illinois and the Mississippi rivers a considerable distance north of where the two rivers actually join. Now called the Hennepin Canal (**4**), the 95.7-mile-long waterway closed in 1951 to commercial navigation. The paths alongside it now form the Hennepin Canal State Trail.

On June 22, 1933, the Illinois Waterway (**5**), connecting the Great Lakes with the Gulf of Mexico, was finally completed. The waterway has been called the single most important factor in the development of Illinois.

The graveyard in the Mississippi

Steamboats were of critical importance on the Mississippi River from about 1817, when Zebulon Pike brought one up to St. Louis, until diesel engines took over in the twentieth century. However, the roaring river was not always placid, and steam engines themselves were dangerous. A 1867 study of the river between Cairo and St. Louis found an area called the Graveyard to contain 133 sunken steamboats.

Chicago is cut by two branches of the Chicago River, running north and south, parallel to the lakeshore. In the 1850s, as Chicago grew, the city fathers began planning a city-wide sewer system. Unfortunately, the swampy subsoil in the area kept them from burying pipes, so, instead, the engineers chose to raise the streets to cover the pipes. In doing so, many residents found their front entrances cut off, and they had to build steps to the second floor.

However, the pipes just ran out into the lake, pumping out sewage only half a mile from where drinking water was drawn. The *Chicago Tribune* reported that the water "was not only black, with a shocking odor, it was greasy to the touch." The 1889 session of the Illinois General Assembly recommended construction of a "new river" which would turn the Chicago River around, sending sewage downstream to the Illinois River and finally to the Gulf of Mexico. So locks were built at the mouth of the river, and the Sanitary and Ship Canal (now also called the Chicago Drainage Canal) was dug by 8,000 men in eight years—at a cost of over $3 million.

The river that flows backward

BRIDGES TO CROSS

There are seven natural stone bridges in Illinois, all in the southern part of the state. The one at Pomona, in the Shawnee National Forest, is 90 feet long and 25 feet high at its highest point over the river valley. It is only 6 feet across at its narrowest point, though legend says that, in the past, people drove wagons over it.

Bridges built by nature

In 1855, engineers for the Rock Island Railroad built the first bridge across the Mississippi River, between Rock Island in Illinois and Davenport in Iowa. Only two weeks after it was opened to railway traffic, an incompetent steamer pilot hit one of the piers, causing a major span to collapse. In a lawsuit, Abraham Lincoln represented the railroad. The counsel for the steamer line spent two hours summing up his case for the jury. Lincoln spoke for only one minute . . . and won.

Brevity from Lincoln

The only suspension bridge in Illinois crosses the Kaskaskia River by Carlyle. Constructed in 1859, it was 180 feet long, with a 10-foot-wide deck. Stone towers supported heavy wire rope cables. When car traffic increased, it was replaced by a steel bridge just downstream, and the suspension bridge was left to deteriorate. When architecture historians found it in the 1950s, the state restored it to a pleasantly swinging 6-foot-wide walkway. In 1953, it was renamed the William F. Dean Bridge, for a Congressional Medal of Honor winner from the area.

The bridge that honors a POW

Protecting a covered bridge

Built in 1863, the Red Covered Bridge near Princeton is one of five original covered bridges still standing in Illinois. Users of the bridge must obey the old posted sign: "Five dollars fine for driving more than 12 horses, mules or cattle at any one time or for leading any beast faster than a walk on or across the bridge."

The wrong kind of submersion

It was a warm, beautiful spring day in 1873. Over 200 people had gathered on a bridge crossing the Rock River at Dixon to witness a submersion baptism in the river. But before the ceremony was over, the bridge collapsed, killing 42 people and injuring more than 100.

The bridge people wouldn't cross

Engineer James B. Eads, who had built the ironclads used on western rivers by the Union Army during the Civil War, became enamored with the project of building a bridge across the Mississippi River at St. Louis. He decided to use the steel-truss method, which had never been used on an American bridge. The project took seven years to complete, producing a bridge 6,222 feet long, in three spans.

However, there had been so many tales spread of odd incidents during the construction that people did not trust the structure. To demonstrate that the bridge was safe, on July 2, 1874, Eads had 14 heavy locomotives cross the bridge several times. When nothing happened, people began to use it. The Eads Bridge was officially opened two days later.

TREES AND FORESTS

The man who started Arbor Day

J. Sterling Morton, a New Yorker-turned-Nebraska-settler-and-politician, avidly believed that the land must be reforested as settlers moved West, cutting trees as they opened new land. He encouraged the state of Nebraska to set aside a special day for planting trees. Nebraska was the first state to recognize Arbor Day, which it holds each year on April 22, Morton's birthday. Illinois celebrates Arbor Day on the last Friday of April each year. Morton Arboretum in Lisle, which has no relationship to Morton Grove—named for Levi Parsons Morton, who was vice president under Benjamin Harrison—was created by J. Sterling's son, Joy, in 1922.

A moment's wind destroys 180 years

One of the great sights of Illinois was the state's tallest tree, an eastern cottonwood. It stood for more than 180 years near Morris in Grundy County . . . until high winds felled it on June 17, 1992. The tree was 138 feet high, with a trunk circumference of 32 feet 6 inches, crown 90 feet 6 inches, and bark 6 to 8 inches thick. Some branches were 3 feet thick and 90 feet long. Because the trunk was hollow 30 feet above the ground, wind gusts simply broke it off like a toothpick. For 20 years the tree had been listed as the largest eastern cottonwood in the U.S. Parts of the fallen tree are being preserved in museums.

Illinois has only one national forest—Shawnee National Forest, which runs from the Ohio River on the east to the Mississippi River on the west, through most of the southern tip of the state. Unlike most of the state, it is rugged territory filled with the rocks and hills and quiet valleys of the Shawnee Hills. The national forest itself is about a quarter of a million acres in size. Notice was given in 1933 when it was founded that the federal government would buy up considerably more land in the future. Headquarters of the forest are at Harrisburg. A major recreational trail, the Ozark-Shawnee Trail, goes from Grand Tower to Battery Rock on the Ohio. The forest is an important resting spot on the Mississippi Flyway, along which millions of birds migrate. The photo shows Burden Falls within the forest.

Illinois's only national forest

The Sinnissippi farm

Frank Lowden, a Chicago trial lawyer and a governor of Illinois, along with his wife, daughter of railroad magnate George Pullman, moved to the Rock River Valley in 1900. They bought up over a dozen farms, and named their holdings "Sinnissippi" from an Indian word meaning "troubled waters" or "rocky river." Lowden built a large home, The Oaks, raised cattle, and worked on maintaining his forested land. Some historians say he planted as many as 500,000 seedlings on his land. Lowden was known for his experimental farming and land management practices. Once he wanted to clear 300 acres, so he chose an environmentally sound method: he bought 500 angora goats and set them to nibbling.

In June 1992, Illinois purchased 1,196 acres of Lowden's Sinnissippi for a new state forest. The riverfront land has old pines and oaks rising to a height of 100 feet. The area purchased by the state was owned by Lowden's grandson, Warren Miller and his wife. Since the Millers have no heirs and didn't want the area turned into a subdivision, they decided to sell it to the state.

The Department of Conservation now has a fund derived from a tax on computer software to purchase land for state parks and forests. In 1820, Illinois had 13.8 million acres of forest. Today, 90 percent of the remaining 4.26 million acres are privately owned and most of those are small areas. About 25 areas of 1,000 acres or more remain in the entire state. The newly purchased Sinnissippi (see above) is the only state forest in northern Illinois. There are only four other state forests:

State forests

- Sand Ridge at Forest City in Mason County - 7,500 acres
- Trail of Tears at Jonesboro in Union County - 5,100 acres
- Big River at Oquawka in Henderson County - 3,000 acres
- Hidden Springs at Strasburg in Shelby County - 1,200 acres

PARKS FOR PLEASURE

The smallest national park

The Mississippi was dredged during President Grant's administration and cleared of hazardous rocks. Only Tower Rock, which stands 60 feet high and almost touches Missouri, was left because someone thought "it might some day form a natural foundation for a bridge." That never happened, but the rock is protected by the federal government, which calls it the "smallest national park in America."

The canal that turned into a new kind of park

By 1963, the old Illinois and Michigan Canal had been abandoned for 30 years. However, the Open Lands Project began to look at it as a piece of history and open space that should be rescued. The first fifteen miles of the canal had disappeared under an expressway, but they were successful in preserving the sixty miles between LaSalle and Joliet and turning it into a state park. They didn't give up on the remainder, either, even though it was enclosed by heavy industry. Instead, they got the National Park Service, the state, and businesses to look at the area in a new way. The result: the Illinois and Michigan Canal National Heritage Corridor. It includes the canal, numerous natural areas that were worth preserving, and a variety of Indian and other historical sites, in a "park" 120 miles long. In 1984, it became the first such park in the nation.

Garden of the Gods

Located within Shawnee National Forest is a region of ancient rock formations that have been weathered into a variety of fascinating shapes. Formations within the Garden of the Gods have such names as Buzzard's Roost, Camel Driver and Wife, Dinosaur, Noah's Ark, and Needle's Eye—sometimes requiring much imagination to see such shapes. The colorful rocks mark the southernmost limit of the glaciers that scraped much of North America clean in prehistoric times. On the other side of the state, but still within the forest, is a similar, colorful set of rock formations called Giant City State Park.

The first state park

Fort Massac, on the Ohio River near Metropolis, was originally a French trading post which was converted into a fort and named for the French minister in charge of colonization, not long before the French lost Illinois to the British. Although it burned at the time it was taken over (those were not necessarily related events), it was rebuilt by General "Mad" Anthony Wayne in 1794. The Daughters of the American Revolution bought the site in 1903 and restored it. In 1908, it was designated the first state park in Illinois.

Venturing underground

Beneath the bottomland at Burksville are the Illinois Caverns, the only major cave open to the spelunking (that's cavern-exploring) public in the state. About six miles long, the cavern (really only one, though its name is plural) dips to about 100 feet below ground. It drew visitors from the St. Louis World's Fair when they became bored across the river. Other caverns nearby are privately owned. The other three state caverns are closed because they are inhabited by the endangered Indiana bat.

Illinois has 57 state parks, as well as many other memorials and recreation areas to draw people. Many of them offer hiking, biking, and cross-country skiing trails. Some of the parks and their features include:

A plethora of parks

- Castle Rock at Oregon, with deep ravines, rugged rock formations
- Chain-O-Lakes at Spring Grove, with more lakes than the rest
- Ferne Clyffe at Goreville, featuring a 100-foot waterfall
- Dixon Springs near Golconda, once a health spa
- Matthiessen at Utica, with rough canyon lands
- Siloam Springs at Clayton, with healing springs
- Prophetstown, where a major Indian village once stood
- Jubilee College at Brimfield, 19th-century college site
- Lowden State Park at Oregon, with the Black Hawk statue
- Gebbard Woods at Morris, along the Michigan and Illinois Canal
- Pere Marquette at Grafton, featuring the Lincoln Fold of rock strata

White Pines State Park at Mount Morris has the southernmost stand of virgin white pine in the Midwest.

WEATHER AND WORSE

Illinois includes three plant hardiness zones, according to the U.S. Department of Agriculture. Most of the state is in Zone 5; plants should not be put out until at least April 15, and there the winters get to minus 10 to minus 20 degrees below zero. However, the southern fourth of the state is in Zone 6, with spring planting between March 15 and May 15. A little notch scooped out of the north central border is Zone 4, which may get to 30° below, but planting time is the same as for Zone 5.

When to plant

Alcoholic Dorothy Mae Stevens Anderson was discovered passed out in an alley on the night of February 1, 1951. Chicago's temperature had dipped to -11° F. that night, and the woman's blood, legs, and eyeballs were frozen solid. Her body temperature was 64.4° F., heart rate 12, respiration rate 3, and blood pressure nonexistent. In a hospital, she regained consciousness within 24 hours. Instead of losing her life, Mrs. Anderson lost both legs and lived until 1971.

Amazing alcoholic

On May 26, 1917, two giant cloud masses met over Mattoon, and in the collision, a tornado was spawned that destroyed 500 houses and killed 53 people. Another 38 were killed in Charleston, where more than 220 homes were destroyed. The twister wiped out a path 293 miles long, the longest continuous tornado path ever recorded. Mattoon was left with $2.5 million damage to buildings and property and 101 dead. The whole northern part of the town was completely leveled.

When giants collide

Awesome Illinois weather:
The coldest day on record - minus 32 ° F, on January 22, 1930
The hottest day on record - 117° F, on July 14, 1954
Normal annual average temperature - 52°
Most precipitation - 16.54" at East St. Louis, on June 14, 1957
Average precipitation per year - 38 inches

America's worst twister

🍁 The deadliest tornado outbreak in U.S. history struck Illinois and surrounding states in 1925. There were none of the characteristic warnings in the sky. Instead, observers saw what appeared to be a "rolling fog." Within the fog, chaos struck. In DeSoto, 118 people were killed, many of them children in a local school that exploded when hit. The tornado went through the heart of Murphysboro, destroying 1,200 buildings in 152 blocks. It killed 234 there and left 8,000 people without homes. West Frankfort was devastated, with 1,127 people left dead and almost a thousand houses destroyed.

A statue to a heroine

🍁 Not many towns can brag about having a monument to a female teacher, let alone a monument sculpted by the great Lorado Taft.

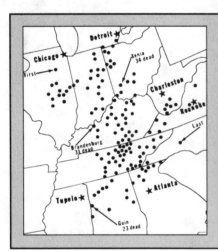

Most tornadoes ever

The largest recorded outbreak of tornadoes in U.S. history occurred after midnight on April 4, 1974. One tornado appeared in northern Illinois, and then 147 more dropped out of a massive storm system, killing 315.

However, the town of White Hall had a special teacher in Annie Louise Keller. When, on April 19, 1927, a tornado approached White Hall, she moved the kids under their desks and placed her body in the doorway of the school between the storm and the children. Annie Keller's tattered body was later pulled from the shattered bricks and boards. None of the children were killed. In grateful thanks, the town commissioned the statue by one of the world's most famous sculptors.

WILDLIFE

Fossil hunters, take note!

🍁 One area near Braidwood known as Fossil Ridge has produced numerous fossils, found in the waste when strip mines uncovered the ground. Called Mazon Creek fauna, after the nearby river, they include about 700 species of prehistoric plants and animals.

The Tully monsters

🍁 In 1955, an amateur archeologist from Joliet, Frank J. Tully, discovered the fossil remains of some tube-like invertebrates that have come to be called the Tully monsters, though they are only about a foot long and hardly monstrous. The creatures lived 280 to 340 million years ago in what was once the Sea of Illinois. More than 100 specimens have been found in Will, Fulton, Kankakee, and Grundy counties. The Tully Monster is the State Fossil.

Prisoners and wildlife

🍁 Crab Orchard National Wildlife Refuge is located near Marion, where it borders on the well-fenced grounds of the federal maximum security prison. Covering 43,600 acres, the refuge gets about 2 million birds, especially waterfowl, visiting it each year. Unlike the prisoners, they leave again on their way north or south. About 10 percent of the refuge is untouched. Wild turkeys are making a comeback.

The Mark Twain National Wildlife Refuge is a collection of 12 different areas totalling 30,000 acres of bottomland, plus another 86,000 acres, making it one of the main waterfowl migration refuges in the nation. 16,579 acres of the refuge are in Illinois. It spreads for 250 miles along the Mississippi Flyway in Illinois, Missouri, and Iowa. At least 200 species of birds stop in the area to feed and rest during their spring and autumn migrations. Wood ducks actually nest in the refuge. The headquarters of the refuge are at Quincy. The federal government acquired most of the land when the U.S. Army Corps of Engineers was building locks to assist the passage of barges.

Another national wildlife refuge, called the Upper Mississippi River National Wildlife and Fish Refuge, extends from Rock Island northward into Minnesota. 3,300 acres are in Illinois. The refuge, an important area for bald eagles, was instigated by Will Dilg of Chicago, founder of the Izaak Walton League. After his son drowned in the Mississippi in 1929, he started the move to create the refuge. Prominent among the visitors to the refuge are numerous canvasback ducks.

National wildlife refuges within Illinois include:

Chautauqua - 6,446 acres
Cypress Creek - 2,975 acres
Meredosia - 2,141 acres
Mississsssippi River - 20,120 acres

Mark Twain lives —in three states

Solving a pest problem

When Griggsville developed a serious mosquito problem, the enterprising townspeople used their location to their advantage. The town's position is along the migration route of the purple martin, North America's largest swallow and mosquito-eater. The townspeople built a 40-foot tower with 504 nesting units in the middle of the business district to encourage the purple martin to take a break from its migration. The idea worked and today thousands of the insect-eating birds summer in Griggsville. Needless to say, mosquitoes are no longer much of a problem to this community. It now justifiably calls itself the "Purple Martin Capital of the World."

In 1902, a hunter (or perhaps an ornithologist named Ridgeway) captured a pair of albino squirrels and brought them to Olney. The squirrels were released and the area soon became famous for large numbers of white squirrels. A city ordinance passed in 1925 made it illegal to kill a squirrel or take one out of town. The squirrels became a matter of state legislation when, in 1943, a law was passed prohibiting the "taking" of white squirrels. They even have the right of way on Olney streets.

The ornithologist was Robert Ridgeway, who was born in Mount Carmel in 1850. In 1906 he founded a bird sanctuary at Olney, named Bird Haven, where he later was buried. Ridgeway, the founder of the American Ornithologists' Union in 1883, was curator of birds at the Smithsonian for much of his life. Ridgeway helped create the official checklist of North American birds, which all bird watchers use.

White squirrels, birds, and Olney

King Kong's competition

For many years, an important resident of the Lincoln Park Zoo in Chicago was Bushman, one of the few gorillas brought into the United States in the first half of the century. The animal was captured as a baby in the French Cameroons after his mother was killed by hunters, and he was brought to Chicago in 1930. Called "the most outstanding animal in any zoo in the world" by the organization of zoo directors, he was the zoo's most popular exhibit, even after the "brawny but dumb" gorilla (who reached almost 600 pounds and 6 feet 2 inches) inadvertently hurt some people and had to be kept completely caged. When he died in 1951, Bushman was stuffed and continued to be on display at the Field Museum of Natural History.

Lincoln Park Zoo, located along the waterfront in Chicago, has greater attendance than any other zoo in the nation. More than 4.5 million visitors each year come to see the 2,000 species in about 35 acres. For many years its director was Marlin Perkins, who hosted "Zoo Parade" and then "Wild Kingdom" on television.

ENDANGERED SPECIES

Welcome back, snake

Settlers knew the eastern ribbon snake, especially if they frequented the swampy areas of southern Illinois. However, it hadn't been found in Illinois for 80 years, until 1986 when it was rediscovered, though in very limited quantities, in Johnson County.

Illinois's "pack rat" endangered

The eastern wood rat is the largest of America's rats and mice. Wood rats are called pack rats because they collect all sorts of things such as old bones, bottle caps, shotgun shells, and pieces of foil and glass. This photo shows one in its messy nest. The eastern wood rat is found in rocky wooded areas of ten southeastern states, but the Illinois wood rats are isolated from other known populations. They are found only in some cliffs and bluffs of Union County, though they once lived throughout the Shawnee Hills. The Illinois wood rat population is now very low; the count in 1990 was only about 20 animals. These rats do not hibernate, and harsh winter weather is a big reason for their decline. Predation and human activity have kept wood rat populations from rebuilding after extremely cold and snowy winters.

ILLINOIS'S ENDANGERED ANIMALS

Illinois used to be covered with forests, wetlands, and prairies but as settlers came west all that changed. Most endangered species in Illinois have lost their habitat to farming, cities, and roads. Effective December 3, 1991, all state and local units of government involved in construction of any kind must go through a review process to see how building will impact endangered species. Maybe it won't be too late for the following animal species endangered in Illinois (there are also 296 species of plants on the list). Those with an asterisk (*) by the name are on the federal list of animals protected by the Endangered Species Act.

Mammals
Southeastern myotis
*Gray bat
*Indiana bat
Rafinesque's big-eared bat
River otter
Eastern wood rat
White-tailed jackrabbit

Birds
Pied-billed grebe
Double-crested cormorant
American bittern
Least bittern
Great egret
Snowy egret
Little blue heron
Black-crowned night heron
Osprey
Mississippi kite
*Bald eagle
Northern harrier (marsh hawk)
Sharp-shinned hawk
Cooper's hawk
Red-shouldered hawk
Swainson's hawk
*Peregrine falcon
Greater prairie chicken
Yellow rail
Black rail
Purple gallinule
Sandhill crane
*Piping plover
Upland sandpiper
Wilson's phalarope
Common tern

Forster's tern
*Least tern
Black tern
Barn owl
Long-eared owl
Short-eared owl
Bewick's wren
Swainson's warbler
Backman's sparrow
Clay-colored sparrow
Yellow-headed blackbird

Fish
*Pallid sturgeon
Northern brook lamprey
Bigeye chub
Pallid shiner (chub)
Pugnose shiner
Bluehead shiner
Weed shiner
Cypress minnow
Greater redhorse
Northern madtom
Western sand darter
Eastern sand darter
Bluebreast darter
Harlequin darter

Reptiles and amphibians
Silvery salamander
Dusky salamander
Illinois mud turtle
Spotted turtle
River cooter
Broad-banded watersnake
Eastern ribbon snake

Invertebrates
Rattlesnake master moth
Hine's bog skimmer (dragonfly)
Arogos skipper butterfly
*Iowa Pleistocene snail

Mussels
Spectacle case
Slippershell
Salamander
Rabbitsfoot
*White wartyback pearly
*Orange-footed pearly
*Fanshell
Clubshell
*Rough pigtoe
Kidneyshell
Fanshell
*Ring pink
Round hickorynut
Scaleshell
*Fat pocketbook
Purple lilliput
Rayed bean
Rainbow
Little spectacle case
Wavy-rayed lamp
*Higgins' eye pearly
*Pink mucket pearly
Leafshell
Found combshell
Tennessee riffleshell
*White cat's paw pearly
Sampson's pearly
*Tubercled-blossom pearly
Snuffbox
*Cracking pearly
5 amphipods
4 crayfish
1 isopod

The boomers are almost gone

The greater prairie chicken is found only in very small areas of Marion, Washington, Wayne, and Jasper counties. Once large in numbers, the bird was hunted for food. The males are known for "booming" during mating season, when large orange air sacs inflate on their necks to attract females. They stomp their feet, long neck feathers become erect, and they make crashing, whooping noises across the booming ground. Farming has destroyed the prairie chickens' open habitat. Ringneck pheasants have taken over their territory.

Nature and computers

In the 1970s, under the leadership of John White, the state of Illinois prepared a Natural Areas Inventory, which compiled all the information known about 1,080 natural areas making up various ecosystems in Illinois, their inhabitants, their makeup, and their condition. The Nature Conservancy, an international nonprofit group that purchases land for the preservation of habitat, based their Heritage Program on the Illinois system. The Heritage Program is the world's most complete database on endangered or threatened living things in each state.

TENDING THE ENVIRONMENT

Reclaiming the land

An area around Fulton County, centered in Canton, is the world's largest coal strip-mining area. In all, 250,899 acres of Illinois land have had the surface removed so that coal deposits could be reached. For many decades, the waste was piled indiscriminately around, and the opened ground was left to fend for itself after all the coal was removed. However, in 1962, the state of Illinois passed the first reclamation law, requiring that strip-mined areas be returned as closely as possible to their previous state. Most land is prepared for agricultural use after the mining is complete.

Twentieth-century effigy mounds

Buffalo Rock State Park is a unique example of creativity in land reclamation. The area, now occupied by the 243-acre park, was a surface coal mine between 1934-42, covered with huge piles of mine spoil averaging 25 feet high. When the mining stopped in 1942, the land was an eyesore for 43 years—no reclamation laws existed or were enforced.

In 1985, a unique reclamation and land sculpture project turned the wasteland into a cultural, recreational, and environmental jewel. Michael Heizer designed the Effigy Tumuli Sculpture—five huge earthen figures (frog, catfish, turtle, water strider, snake) made to look like prehistoric Indian burial grounds. The acid was removed from the area and over 400,000 cubic yards of mine spoil was regraded and shaped into the earthen sculptures. The once-dead area is now full of plant and animal life.

❦ Illinoisans use 14 billion gallons of water every day, or about 1,250 gallons per person. That's 31st in water use in the country. Fortunately, less than 1 percent of that is used for agriculture because of the fairly predictable amount of rainfall the state receives.

The water users

❦ Illinois drivers drive 78,483,billion miles per year, which is about 6,800 miles per person. For 61 percent of those miles, single commuters drive in their cars alone. Only 18 percent carpool to get to work, and only 12 percent take public transportation.

Commuters

Potatoes for the environment

A division of Warner-Lambert Company in Rockford produces a number of biodegradable packaging products made from potato starch pellets. The packaging doesn't require CFCs in its production. Chlorofluorocarbons are chemicals that are depleting the protective ozone layer around the Earth. The products aren't plastic, so the packaging "peanuts" you receive in boxes shipped through the mail won't just sit forever in landfills, not degrading. Instead, they dissolve into safe, organic materials. The same people produce potato-starch golf tees that will disintegrate in rain. No trees to cut down!

AWESOME

❦ Illinois citizens and industry generate about 15 million tons of solid waste each year. The state ranks 6th in the nation in per capita waste: 1.293 tons. Most of it goes into landfills, in which there is only enough space to last another 5 to 10 years. The situation won't get better soon because state waste-recycling goals call for a reduction of only 25 percent, with no target year, and the goals apply only to counties with populations greater than 100,000, which means only 18 counties.

This too, too, solid waste

❦ At Fairview, in western Illinois, a huge hole is being specially constructed—the only landfill under construction in the state. Scheduled to become the largest landfill in the state, it opens to start receiving Chicago's solid waste in early 1993. Although only 80 acres is currently scheduled, the landfill could eventually be 995 acres in size, all built on waste, strip-mined land. The hole itself goes only about 50 feet into the ground, where it is lined with a 10-foot-deep layer of compacted clay that should prevent leachate (runoff liquid) from seeping into the groundwater. Initially, the landfill, constructed by Gallatin National Company, will be able to take in only a thousand tons of garbage a day, though that amount will rise. As it does, so will the hill of garbage.

Digging a special hole

No fishing, but it's coming back

For six years the residents of Waukegan were not allowed to fish in their own harbor because it was contaminated with PCBs (polychlorinated biphenyls), which are complex chemicals often used in industrial lubricant. Outboard Marine of Waukegan had used a hydraulic fluid containing PCBs from 1961-72. It wasn't until the late 1960s that the compound was found to be toxic and cancer-causing; it was banned in the mid-1970s. Two million pounds of PCBs were found in the drainage ditches, on land, and in Waukegan Harbor. In 1982, the harbor was placed on the Superfund list of the most polluted places in the country. In 1992, the harbor was dredged, and more than 19,000 gallons of the chemical were removed from the sediment at the bottom of the harbor. A new high-temperature process call Taciuk was used to separate PCBs from the soil and harbor sediment. The hazardous waste site will eventually become a grassy knoll. By fall, the health department had removed the "No Fishing" signs that had been in place for so long. Outboard Marine paid $21 million toward the cleanup costs.

Hazardous waste sites to be cleaned up

Superfund sites are locations where toxic materials have accumulated in the environment and have become a major danger to the health of people in the area. The federal government has put such sites on a list of places to be cleaned up as quickly as possible, using federal funds and money from the companies that dumped the hazardous material—if they can be found. Waukegan Harbor (see above) was one such site. The aim of the U.S. Environmental Protection Agency is to get the sites off the list as quickly as possible. Unfortunately, that's not very quick, and there are many more sites that can replace them. Superfund sites within Illinois include:

Antioch - H.O.D. Landfill
Belvidere - Amoco Chemicals (Joliet Landfill)
    Belvidere Municipal Landfill
    Lenz Oil Service Inc.
    MIG/Dewane Landfill
    Parsons Casket Hardware Co.
    Byron - Byron Salvage Yard
    Carterville - Sangamo Electric/Crab
    Orchard National Wildlife
    Refuge
DuPage County - 3 Kerr-McGee locations
East Cape Girardeau - Ilada Energy Co.
Galesburg - Galesburg/Koppers Co.
Granite City - NL Industries/Taracorp Lead
    Smelter
Greenup - A & F Material Reclaiming, Inc.
Joliet - Joliet Army Ammunition Plant
    (2 separate areas)
LaSalle - LaSalle Electric Utilities
Marshall - Velsicol Chemical
    Corp.
Morristown - Acme Solvent
    Reclaiming, Inc.
    (Morristown Plant)

Ottawa - Ottawa Radiation Areas
Pembroke - Cross Brothers Pail Recycling
Quincy - Adams County Quincy Landfills 2 & 3
Rockford - Interstate Pollution Control Inc.
    Pagel's Pit
    Southeast Rockford Ground Water
    Contamination
Rockton - Beloit Corp.
Savanna - Savanna Army
    Depot
South Elgin - Tri-
    County Landfill
    Co./Waste Management of
    Illinois, Inc.
Taylorville - Central Illinois
    Public Service Co.
Warrenville - DuPage County
    Landfill/Blackwell Forest Preserve
Wauconda - Wauconda Sand & Gravel
Waukegan - Johns-Manville Corp.
Outboard Marine Corp.
Yeoman Creek Landfill
Woodstock - Woodstock Municipal Landfill

ILLINOIS CHRONICLE

By virtue of its sheer number of people, events that happen in Illinois make national news promptly. By virtue of its location, it serves as a middle ground between North and South, East and West. By virtue of having served as the home of Abe Lincoln, it plays a prominent role in the historical legends of America and new legends are being made every day.

- The Indians
- When Illinois was French
- The Black Hawk War
- Adventuresome Settlers
- The Slavery Issue
- The Lincoln Saga
- Torn Between North and South
- Illinois on the National Scene
- Firsts for Minorities
- The Status of Women
- The Presidents
- Random History
- The World at War — I
- The World at War — II
- The Nazi Episodes
- Korea and Vietnam

THE INDIANS

The earliest signs

⭐ The earliest traces of humans in Illinois are found in the remains of a camp site at Modoc Rock Shelter in Randolph County, where many generations of nomadic Indians camped until perhaps 4,000 years ago. The site was explored by archeology students from the University of Chicago in 1952.

Temple Builders of Cahokia

⭐ A thriving Indian culture—now called the Temple Mound Builders or the Mississippian Culture—lived at Cahokia between A.D. 900 and 1300. Though there were once more of them, 85 mounds, built between 450 and 750 years ago, have been found along the Illinois River covering 2,000 acres. The largest, called Monk's Mound because early French missionaries used it for an orchard, covers about 17 acres. At 100 feet in height, it is the largest prehistoric earthwork in North America. The temple building that would have been on top has long since disappeared because it was made of wood instead of stone. The pits where the soil to build the mound came from are still visible.

The town around the mounds was probably peopled by at least 30,000 Indians. Temple Builders were dedicated farmers who resided in a complex and rigid caste system that concentrated on preparation for death. The remains of circles into which poles were placed in the ground indicate that the people either used poles as planting calendars or perhaps had Sacred Circles in which the priests carried on rituals. Some archeologists have called these circles "Woodhenges." There is no real evidence as to why these Indians died out or moved away. The name Cahokia was actually the name of a later tribe in the area.

Except for the mounds themselves, all traces of the Mound Builders had disappeared by the time white explorers reached the area. The site has been named a World Heritage site by UNESCO.

⭐ Dickson Mounds is the area where Indian mounds containing, in layers, the skeletons of 237 Indians were dug up, along with a village that was occupied from about A.D. 950 to 1200. The skeletons have been displayed in the positions in which they were found. However, in recent years many Native Americans have regarded such exposure of skeletons as sacrilege, and protests grew over a period of years. In 1992 Dickson Mounds was closed to the public.

Opening a burial site

⭐ Major Indian tribes present in Illinois when Europeans began to explore the area were all Woodland Indians from the Algonquian group. The Sac, Fox, and Kickapoo tribes were in the north; the Ojibwa (Chippewa), Ottawa, and Potawatomi near Lake Michigan; Tamaroa and Cahokia in the south; Kaskaskia, Peoria, and Illinois in the central prairie area. There is evidence that the Miami once lived in Chicago.

When the white men came

KEY

BOLD – pre 1700
ITALIC – after 1700

* = band of Illinois Indians
† = band of Miami Indians

WINNEBAGO
HURON
SAUK & FOX
POTAWATOMI
ASSEGUN
MIAMI
MASCOUTIN
KICKAPOO
TIONONTATI
ILLINOIS
ILLINOIS
*PEORIA**
*KASKASKIA**
KICKAPOO
KICKAPOO
KICKAPOO
WEA†
*KASKASKIA**
PIANKASHAW†
*CAHOKIA**
*TAMAROA**
KICKAPOO
DELAWARE
ILLINOIS
*KASKASKIA**
OSAGE

Pontiac and the myth of Starved Rock

After the British took over the territory, their treatment of the Indians caused Pontiac, an Ottawa leader, to try to harness the discontent and unify the Indians of the Ohio Valley and Great Lakes against the white men. But in the long run he failed. In 1769, Pontiac was in the Peoria region when one lone warrior, perhaps drunk, killed him.

What happened next may not even be true, but it has entered the legends of Illinois. Tradition says that Ottawa Indians, joined by the Potawatomi, sought revenge for Pontiac's death. They attacked some Illinois Indians, and forced them out onto a huge rock that loomed high over the Illinois River. Trapped, unable to escape, the Illini starved to death . . . except for a few who lived to tell the tale. The site of this event—if indeed it did happen—is now called Starved Rock. The 140-foot-tall promontory and some acreage around it make up the oldest Illinois state park.

The Piasa Bird and Great Manitou

The Illinois Indians believed that a great creature called the Piasa Bird lived in a cave in the bluffs along the Great River (near Alton). When an Illiniwek was seen on the river, it would emerge from its cave and carry off the Indian. An Illinois chief pleaded with the Great Manitou for a way to free his people from this threat. Following the god's orders, Quatonga stood out on the bluff, with his warriors hidden in the bushes behind him. When the mighty and fearsome Piasa Bird swooped down on Quatonga, the warriors shot it. The monster fell, dying, into the river. The painting was made to commemorate the conquest.

When Marquette and Jolliet traveled down the Mississippi in 1673, they saw the huge paintings of the Piasa Bird and other monsters on the bluffs. The rock paintings were destroyed by blasting operations in 1847. However, one Alton artist's attempt to recreate them is now visible on the stones. The Boy Scouts of America keep it in good shape.

WHEN ILLINOIS WAS FRENCH

What the French were doing in Illinois

⭐ While the French were developing New France (North America) in the mid-1600s, the central part that would become the U.S. was still unexplored. As fur traders ventured southward and became friendly with the Indians, they heard tales of a mighty river. The French hoped that such a river, if they could find it, would lead them to the Pacific Ocean. Ignoring the fact that many different groups of Indians already possessed the land, the French held a dramatic but—to the Indians—incomprehensible ceremony at an Indian village near the future site of Sault Ste. Marie, Michigan. In it, the French claimed title to all land in the interior of the continent. Louis Jolliet was put in charge of exploring the new territory.

With Jolliet and Marquette in Illinois

⭐ An Algonquian-speaking priest, Père Jacques Marquette, accompanied Jesuit French explorer Louis Jolliet as he ventured through the Great Lakes, hunting for the mighty river that the Indians had described. They located the Fox River and followed it into the Wisconsin and thus to the Mississippi in 1673. They turned back northward when they realized that the river went to the Gulf of Mexico and that the lands farther south were in the control of the Spanish.

Returning up the Illinois River, they explored along the river's edge. Impressed by what they saw, they

have seen nothing like this river for the fertility of the land, its prairies, woods, wild cattle, stag, deer, ducks, parrots, and even beaver." When the Illinois River ended in the Des Plaines River, they portaged, moving their canoes and supplies six miles to the Chicago River, finally coming out into Lake Michigan. Lingering for a day in the area where Chicago would someday be built, they noted how important a canal connecting the rivers might be. Marquette promised the Indians that he would return, and the explorers paddled off northward.

★ After wintering near Green Bay in 1674, Père Marquette and two Indian friends traveled south again on Lake Michigan, coming ashore at a natural harbor which came to be called Grosse Point, later Evanston. They drew their canoes up on the sand. Marquette was hoping to go inland and establish a mission to the Indians. However, as autumn was setting in, he paddled on down the lakeshore to where the Chicago River joined the great lake. There, at what would become Chicago, he built a mission, thus becoming the first resident of Chicago.

The founding of future Chicago

★ A Frenchman by birth, Robert Cavelier, Sieur de La Salle, went to Canada in his brother's footsteps and quickly became an avid explorer of the great new territory. Frontenac, the governor of Canada, an equally avid hater of Jesuits, gave La Salle the rights to develop the territory claimed by France, including Illinois, to avoid giving them to Jolliet, who was a Jesuit. La Salle and his one-handed Italian sidekick, Henri de Tonti, built Fort Creve Coeur (Broken Heart) near present-day Peoria at a wide spot in the Illinois River in 1680.

Shutting out Jolliet

★ When Sieur de La Salle returned to the Illinois River after a trip home to Canada, he found that the Iroquois Indians, altogether a tougher breed of Indian then the local ones, were killing off the Illinois tribes with ease. In 1681, he built a new fort atop Starved Rock, overlooking the river. Watch could be kept over a huge area into which moved bands of Illinois, Miami, Shawnee, Wea, and Piankashaw. Altogether, perhaps 18,000 Indians lived within the protective gaze of Fort St. Louis, which quickly became a trading center. But a new governor of Canada, wanting to appease the Iroquois, took away La Salle's authority. The French explorer was later killed by his own men when he was unable to locate the mouth of the Mississippi River from the sea. However, Tonti returned to Illinois and continued La Salle's work of trying to settle French people into the area. He moved Fort St. Louis to Peoria and changed its name to Fort Pimitoui. Illinois remained French until they lost control in the French and Indian War.

City of Indians

★ The British owned Illinois for only a brief time after they won the French and Indian War and before they lost the American Revolution. During that time, their seat of government in Illinois was at Fort de Chartres, which they renamed Fort Cavendish. The fort, an elegant stone structure, was built by the French in 1720. It was once at least 490 feet long and was surrounded by a moat. However, all the British did was upset the Indians with their strictness. The Indians were used to the more lenient French approach.

When Illinois was British

George Rogers Clark, messenger of Virginia

⭐ The original grant of Virginia included all land extending westward from the Atlantic, so the area that became Illinois was part of Virginia from the early 1600s. But then the French claimed it from the North, on the basis of their exploration of the Mississippi Valley via Canada. The British received it from the French as part of the Treaty of Paris, ending the French and Indian War in 1763.

During the American Revolution, control of America north and west of the Ohio River was taken from the British by George Rogers Clark, at the request of Virginia governor Patrick Henry. Clark began his mission on May 15, 1778, when he and his men, called "Long Knives," marched from Fort Massac. Appropriately enough, on July 4 —a date that would later be more famous than it was then—his men captured the Illinois settlements of Kaskaskia amd Cahokia.

The bell that was rung in celebration of the victory now hangs in the Kaskaskia Memorial Building. Older than the Liberty Bell in Philadelphia, it was donated by the French king. Called "The Liberty Bell of the West," it is now located in a church on Kaskaskia Island.

The land that Clark gained was annexed by Patrick Henry as Illinois County of Virginia on December 9, 1778. But because the Virginians couldn't control it, they let the law that created Illinois County lapse in 1782, leaving no government in charge until after the new United States claimed it.

THE BLACK HAWK WAR

⭐ In 1804, five Sauk and Fox chiefs happened to be in St. Louis when devious white men got them drunk, and conned them into signing an agreement. In return for a payment of $1,000 a year and the right to live and hunt in the area as long as it belonged to the U.S. federal government, the chiefs ceded their lands in Illinois—about 50 million acres of it! The agreement was renewed in 1816, 1822, and 1825, but the government failed to keep its part of the bargain (so what else is new?). More and more settlers moved into Indian lands.

Some Indians, seeing the handwriting on the wall, peacefully crossed the Mississippi to live. But others backed the rebellious chief, Black Hawk, also called Black Sparrow Hawk, to protest the lopsided deal. In 1831, Black Hawk and his followers abandoned their village and crossed the Mississippi just ahead of the advancing Illinois militia.

In the spring of 1832, Black Hawk and 400 braves and their families returned to Illinois, planning to plant corn where the Quad Cities now stand. The nervous whites misunderstood their intentions, and troops were sent out. Black Hawk's attempt at negotiating ended in gunfire. By July, Black Hawk's forces, never able to plant, were weak from hunger. He won only a few small skirmishes.

Agonizing, Black Hawk decided to surrender. But the officials wouldn't listen. Instead, the troops drove his warriors into Wisconsin, where, at the fiercely one-sided Battle of Bad Axe, they were savagely slaughtered. Survivors who tried to cross the Mississippi were fired on by gunboats. The few who got away were attacked by the Sioux Indians on the other side. Black Hawk himself was captured a few days later. Black Hawk "can do no more," he said. "He is near his end. His Sun is setting, and he will rise no more."

A 48-foot-tall statue of an Indian by Loredo Taft that is popularly supposed to be Black Hawk (but it looks too serene) stands along the Rock River near the Mississippi. It was cast in a gigantic mold in position, on a 30-foot-deep foundation.

"Stillman's Run" Defined as a rapid and chaotic retreat, named for Major Isaiah Stillman, whose 275 panicked soldiers fled up to 25 miles from an ambush by about 40 of Black Hawk's warriors.

A soldier named Elizabeth

A fort on the Apple River was attacked by more than 200 Indians on June 24, 1832, during the Black Hawk War. The settlers rushed to the fort, where their defense was led by a woman, Elizabeth Armstrong, because the men were away. They succeeded in driving away the Indians, with a loss of only about 50 horses. The town that was later built on the site of the fort was called Elizabeth in her honor.

AWESOME

★ Chief Shabbona (or Shabonee) was an Ottawa Indian who married a Potawatomi. He lived in Illinois near her people and became the chief when her father died. Refusing to join Black Hawk, he and his son left a war council and rode over 200 miles, from Princeton to the Chicago area, to warn the settlers. Most settlers heeded the warning, but Indian Creek settlement ignored it and was attacked on May 20, 1832. Fifteen men, women, and children were killed, while two girls were taken captive and held for ransom. Shabbona was later granted treaty lands but was forced across the Mississippi. When he returned to claim the lands, they had been sold. Friendly settlers bought him land near Morris, where he lived out his days.

The chief who took care of the settlers

★ During the winter of 1838-39, American soldiers forced Cherokee Indians from their homes in Georgia, Alabama, North Carolina, and Tennessee to a reservation in Oklahoma. Their march along what came to be called the "Trail of Tears" took them through southern Illinois, from Golconda to Jonesboro. They were stranded in Illinois for weeks by bad weather, during which many of them died. The Trail of Tears Campsite at Jonesboro has been preserved.

The Trail of Tears

ADVENTURESOME SETTLERS

The Mississippi Bubble

⭐ Scottish adventurer John Law convinced the French government that its economy could be rehabilitated by letting him sell rights to outsiders to trade and settle in the Mississippi Valley, which was French territory. On January 1, 1718, trading began in the Company of the West, and speculation that would continue for more than two years began. But then most investors went bankrupt—the bubble had burst. The picture that Law presented to investors and what was actually happening in the distant wilderness (virtually nothing) were two different things. Law died, destitute, in Venice, even before his company's charter was revoked in 1731.

The first known black in Illinois

⭐ About 1779 Jean Baptiste Point Du Sable, a black from Haiti, was released by the British, who had imprisoned him when the Revolution started. Du Sable settled on the north bank of the Chicago River near Lake Michigan and opened a trading post, becoming the first permanent settler at what would become Chicago. In 1800, he and his Potawatomi wife moved to Peoria.

The family with the feet

The members of the Eaton family of early Palestine were known far and wide for their extra-large feet. When the family decided to build their own fort because Fort LaMotte was too crowded, the new fort became known as Fort Foot.

Donners for dinner

⭐ You know the Donner Party was no party. It was a group of about 80 pioneers who sought a new land and who got caught by the worst winter snows the Sierra Nevada of northern California had seen in decades. Many of those who survived did so only because they ate the corpses of their fellow travelers.

What you might not know is that the Donner Party started from Illinois. George and Jacob Donner put together a group of hardy souls from Kentucky and southern Illinois and arranged to depart from the grounds of the capital building in Springfield on April 16, 1846. Unfortunately, the Donner men took advice from the wrong people and poorly timed their journey through the distant mountains. The place where so many died is now called Donner Pass, and it's a major eight-lane highway.

The road to Illinois

⭐ The National Road, also called the Cumberland Road, was the first federal highway in the United States. It started at Cumberland, Maryland, and ended at Vandalia, Illinois, in 1837, though it was originally intended to carry on to Jefferson City, Missouri. (US Route 40 follows the original National Road to Vandalia from the Indiana line.) Land sold along the road paid for its construction. Sales of land in Illinois from 1819 to 1837 amounted to $10.5 million, and settlers, mainly from Kentucky and Tennesee, began pouring in. The new settlers were described as people "clad in buckskin and coonskin caps

[who] handled long rifles with ease. . . They liked the taste of wild meat. . . ."

We complain today when we have potholes or the ride isn't too smooth. One traveler on the National Road described what it was like a few miles east of Vandalia. It wasn't paved or filled with gravel. Some farmers "blocked the pike with fences, not caring that such antics forced travelers to detour through wet . . . fields."

At the Vandalia end of the road is an 18-foot-tall statue, *The Madonna of the Trail*, one of a series constructed by the Daughters of the American Revolution in 1928 to commemorate the role of women in settling the interior of the nation.

Starting out cultured

Englishmen Morris Birkbeck and George Flower promoted the settlement of Illinois with the books they wrote about the territory. Flower's own collection of books became the first library in the state, located in the town they founded in 1818 with 200 settlers, Albion.

Nine novels depicting life among the settlers in Illinois

American Years by Harold Sinclair, 1938 - pre-Civil War Illinois (first in a trilogy based on Bloomington's history)

Beyond the Bedroom Wall: A Family Album by Larry Woiwode, 1975 - saga of a German family near Pekin

Children of the Market Place by Edgar Lee Masters, 1922 - English immigrants in Illinois

The Graysons by Edward Eggleston, 1887 - life in the settlements of early Illinois

Land of Strangers by Lillian Budd, 1953 - story of Swedish immigrants in Chicago, and its sequel, *April Harvest*, 1959

The Murphy Stories by Mark Costello, 1973 - life in early Decatur

Shaman by Noah Gordon, 1992 - life of a physician on the Rock River

The Valley of the Shadows by Francis Grierson, 1909 - frontier life in the early 1800s

Giving a leg up

Sergeant John Gill led a squad from Pekin that fought in the Mexican War in 1847. When his soldiers came upon a disabled coach with no horse, they explored it and acquired some unique booty—a bag of gold, a roasted chicken, and a wooden leg. Later they found out the leg belonged to the infamous Mexican commander, General Santa Ana, who had left the coach in a hurry after it broke down. Gill brought the leg home as a souvenir. It was later presented to the State of Illinois and is in the State Historical Society museum.

THE SLAVERY ISSUE

Illinois might have been a slave state

⭐ From the time Illinois became a state, its people were torn on the issue of slavery. The original constitution, approved in 1818, called for the gradual abolition of slaves and indentured servants. But those who favored slavery tried to hold a constitutional convention to reconsider legalizing slavery. Voters were against it. After eighteen months of heavy promotion, both for and against, the voters voted down a constitutional convention.

Abolition prevailed in the Constitution of 1848—slavery was abolished and it became illegal to bring new slaves into the state. But even then the matter was not settled. An act passed by the legislature in 1853 stated that free Negroes entering Illinois could be sold as slaves. Then, even during the Civil War, the constitutional convention of 1862 voted overwhelmingly to prohibit the migration of blacks into Illinois and the right of blacks to vote.

The dreaded Dred Scott decision

⭐ Dr. John Emerson came to Illinois from St. Louis in 1834 to serve as a physician at an army post. Along with him came his personal slave, Dred Scott. In 1836, Emerson took Scott to Fort Snelling in Wisconsin Territory (later Minnesota). After Emerson died, the slave became the property of Emerson's widow. She returned to Missouri with him. Dred Scott sued for his freedom on the basis that both Illinois and Wisconsin were free territory. Loath to lose her property, Mrs. Emerson fought in court and won—her ownership was confirmed. However, encouraged by abolitionists, Dred Scott's backers took the case to the U.S. Supreme Court. The court, under Chief Justice Taney, ruled in 1857 against Dred Scott. He died the following year, not seeing that the case was another nail driven into the coffin that separated the North and South.

"I have sworn eternal opposition to slavery"

⭐ Elijah P. Lovejoy, an abolition-minded minister-turned-editor, moved to Alton from the slave state of Missouri in 1836 and obtained a printing press from his friends. Upon its arrival, the press was destroyed by a slavery-minded mob and dumped into the river. Lovejoy's friends purchased another press and in a public meeting he defied the proslavery mob by stating, ". . . as long as I am an American citizen, and as long as American blood runs in these veins, I shall hold myself at liberty to speak, to write, and to publish whatever I please on any subject, being amenable to the laws of my country for the same."

Lovejoy became increasingly vehement in his anti-slavery editorials. His second press was destroyed—and a third. On November 7, 1837, a fourth press arrived in Alton protected by armed guards. But the protection failed Lovejoy. An angry mob set upon the warehouse and murdered him. The perpetrators were arrested, tried, and acquitted, but Lovejoy's name became a rallying point for the anti-slavery movement in Illinois. A memorial to Lovejoy in Alton says:

I have sworn eternal opposition to slavery
and by the blessings of God I will never turn my face.

⭐ The Old Slave House, located on a hill a few miles from Shawneetown, is a Southern Colonial structure originally called Hickory Hill mansion. It was probably used to house escaped slaves that had been kidnapped and brought back to the area until they could be sold into the South again. The house, owned by the Crenshaw family, showed a public face of well-to-do society on the main floor, but under the eaves were tiny chambers with chains sunk into the walls.

The terrible facade

⭐ Famous lawyer, politician, and senator, Stephen A. Douglas came to Illinois from Vermont in 1833 to build a career. He quickly became involved in the Democratic political machine, and in 1847 moved to Chicago and was elected U.S. Senator. When Abraham Lincoln decided to run for the Senate in 1858, he and Douglas held the famous Lincoln-Douglas Debates. Public opinion decreed that Douglas beat Lincoln, but his popularity was dwindling. The election of 1860 was the first time in U.S. history that two presidential candidates came from the same state. After losing the election, Douglas became a staunch supporter of Lincoln.

The much-maligned "Little Giant"

Though Douglas is often regarded as the "black hat" who ran against "good guy" Lincoln, he was the Illinois senator who introduced into Congress the Kansas-Nebraska Bill, which repealed the slave-state law called the Missouri Compromise. The bill allowed inhabitants of a new territory to choose whether they would allow slavery or not. It seemed like a good idea at the time, but the new law opened the floodgates of abolitionist sentiment, and the War between the States drew closer.

Some say that Douglas worked so hard to reconcile the North and the South that he ruined his health, dying of typhoid fever in Chicago on June 3, 1861. A stunning memorial to the "Little Giant" is located on the site of the home that Douglas built on the South Side of Chicago. Douglas County was named for him in 1859, two years before he died.

Lincoln in brief

Born: February 12, 1809
Died: April 15, 1865
Parents: Thomas and Nancy
   Hanks Lincoln
Moved to Illinois:1831-37
Married: Mary Todd in 1842-4
   children

THE LAND

FREEPORT – The second Lincoln-Douglas Debate was held at Freeport on August 27, 1858. Historians credit Stephen Douglas's "Freeport Doctrine" speech as helping Lincoln win the presidency and moving the Union step closer to Civil War. The Freeport Doctrine, which Douglas stated in his second debate with Lincoln, called for the elimination of slavery by individual areas refusing to protect slavery, thus making such areas unattractive to slave owners. This idea was his way of getting around the Dred Scott Decision. Lincoln's response was, "This government cannot endure permanently half slave and half free."

NEW SALEM — New Salem was the village where Abraham Lincoln lived from 1831-37. He owned a store there but suc-ceeded only in compiling debt. He spent many years paying off the debts, thus acquiring the reputation of "Honest Abe." New Salem was the size of Chicago then—12 families. After Lincoln moved on to Springfield, the town was abandoned, as residents moved to nearby Petersburg. The village has been pain-stakingly restored to look as it would have in the 1830s. Interest in the restoration project was started by William Randolph Hearst in 1906. Hearst purchased the land and gave it to the state in 1918 and reconstruction began in 1932.

QUINCY — The sixth Lincoln-Douglas debate took place at Quincy on October 13. A monument in the town by famed sculptor Laredo Taft shows the two senatorial candidates and an emotional audience.

ALTON — Lincoln summed up his position in the last debate, held at Alton on October 15: "the issue. . .is the eternal struggle between two principles—right and wrong—through-out the world. . .The one is the common right of humanity, the other is the divine right of kings. It is the same principle in whatever shape it develops itself. It is the same spirit that says, 'You toil and work and earn bread, and I'll eat it.'"

JONESBORO — Jonesboro was a Democratic stronghold that had little interest in Lincoln. When Lincoln arrived in town for the third debate on September 15, the Jonesboro band was in Cairo welcom-ing Douglas. The train that brought Douglas to Jonesboro was dec-orated with flags, and a brass cannon fired salutes. When the Jonesboro band marched up the road to the debate site, the band leader observed a tall, solitary figure walking along and asked him who he was—it was Lincoln. The people of the county hated aboli-tionists and Douglas had already intimated that Lincoln was one. They stayed away in droves.

OTTAWA — The first of the planned debates to take place between senatorial candidates Abraham Lincoln and Stephen A. Douglas occurred at Ottawa on August 21, 1858. The debate lasted three hours and was heard by almost 10,000 people.

DANVILLE — Lincoln often stayed at the McCor-mick Hotel in Danville with fellow attorneys on the Eighth Circuit. Here his colleagues once tried him in "kangaroo" court on a count of charging his clients too little. He was found guilty and paid his fine with a gallon of whiskey.

SPRINGFIELD — Abraham Lincoln married Mary Todd at Springfield on November 4, 1842. Mary came from a high-class family, and some people felt that she was marrying beneath her. She had previously been courted by Stephen Douglas. In Robert Sherwood's play Abe Lincoln in Illinois, Abe says, "They (the Todds) spell their name with two D's. Which is mighty impressive, considering one was enough for God."

CHARLESTON — Before a crowd of 12,000 people at Charleston on September 18, Lincoln had to answer Douglas' false charges that he advocated intermarriage with Negroes and that he had voted against sending supplies to the servicemen in the Mexican War. Dirty politics is nothing new!

Freeport

Dixon

Chicago

Ottawa

Galesburg

Peoria

Tremont

Bloomington

Lincoln

Clinton

Danville

New Salem

Bement

Quincy

Springfield

Decatur

Charleston

Vandalia

Alton

Jonesboro

OF LINCOLN

NEW SALEM — In 1833, Abraham Lincoln resided in New Salem at the Rutledge tavern when he was hired to survey the site of the new town of Petersburg. The innkeeper's daughter, Ann Rutledge, quickly became a major figure in his life. Unfortunately, their romance ended suddenly by her death in 1835. Originally buried in concord cemetery, she was exhumed in 1890 and reburied in Petersburg, where the epitaph on her grave, written by poet Edgar Lee Masters (see p. 99), reads:

I am Ann Rutledge who sleep beneath these weeds

Beloved in life of Abraham Lincoln,

Wedding to him not through union,

But through separation.

The possible-but-not-necessarily-so romance was revealed to the public by William Herndon, Lincoln's law partner, long after both participants' deaths in a lecture on November 16, 1866 at Springfield. Because of their friendship, Lincoln's name stayed on the Herndon law-offices sign until after the president's assassination.

GALESBURG — The fifth Lincoln-Douglas debate was held in Galesburg on October 7. It drew the largest crowd of any of the series—20,000. Special chartered trains brought people from Iowa and Chicago. The Galesburg site is the only one that still exists. The debate was held on the steps of Old Main on the campus of Knox College.

CLINTON — On July 27, 1858, Stephen A. Douglas falsely stated that Mr. Lincoln supported political equality for Negroes. During Lincoln's rebuttal speech he said his famous "You can fool all of the people some of the time; and some of the people all of the time; but you can't fool all the people all the time." Some historians believe that Lincoln never authored the remarks. Noted Lincoln scholar, Paul Angle, thinks that Lincoln may have said them but he's confused. "It's so good, if he said it once, why didn't he keep repeating it?" Ralph Newman, also a Lincoln scholar, agrees with Angle. Like all good politicians, Newman says Lincoln repeated his best lines. A statue of Lincoln on the DeWitt County Courthouse lawn commemorates this famous speech.

BLOOMINGTON — The speech that Lincoln made at Bloomington at the first Republican State Convention held on May 29, 1856, is called his "Lost Speech." He rose to denounce the Kansas-Nebraska Act, which allowed each new state to decide for itself whether to be slave or free and which had been sponsored by Stephen A. Douglas. Lincoln's impromptu speech so gripped his audience that no one recorded what he said, except for one phrase which appears on a memorial plaque in Bloomington: "We say to our southern brethren, 'We won't go out of the Union, and you shan't!'"

CHICAGO — The new Republican Party met in Chicago in May 1860 to nominate its candidate for the presidency. The favorite going into the convention was William H. Seward, who would later became lastingly known for having purchasing Alaska, "Seward's Folly." However, Seward was avidly antislavery, and the Republican Party was not yet ready to be so blatant. On the third ballot, they nominated Illinois's Abraham Lincoln, who was recognized as a moderate on the issue of slavery, though he would go down in history as the man who freed the slaves.

LINCOLN / DOUGLAS DEBATES — Abraham Lincoln and Stephen A. Douglas met at Frances Bryant's cottage (a friend of Douglas and cousin of poet William Cullen Bryant) and agreed to a series of debates to be held in seven congressional districts —Ottawa, Freeport, Jonesboro, Charleston, Galesburg, Quincy, and Alton— from August 21 to October 15, 1858. The cottage is now a state memorial.

TREMONT — The town of Tremont knew of Abraham Lincoln as early as 1842 because of the Lincoln-Shields duel. Mary Todd, to whom Lincoln was engaged, had made fun of the Illinois State Auditor of Accounts, James Shields, in the local newspaper. Always a gentleman, Lincoln told the angry Shields that he was responsible for the article and accepted his challenge to a duel.

On the day of the duel, many curious people accompanied Shields and Lincoln to the dueling site on the bank of the Mississippi. Lincoln, always a storyteller and crowd-pleaser, practiced swinging his sword while entertaining the crowd with his stories. The duel never took place. Shields finally accepted Lincoln's written apology in which Lincoln stated that he "did not think . . . that said article could produce such an effect;" he hadn't intended "injuring the personal or private character or standing of Mr. Shields." Lincoln saved the strong-willed Mary Todd from many scrapes and indiscretions throughout their married life.

DECATUR — Shortly after turning 21, Lincoln and his family left Indiana and settled in Macon County. The route they took is approximately the path now taken by Lincoln National Memorial Highway, from the Wabash to the Sangamon near Decatur. They built a cabin eight miles from Decatur on the Sangamon River in an area now set aside as Lincoln Trail Homestead State Park. Lincoln left Macon County for Coles County in 1831, but he often returned while traveling the towns of the Eighth Circuit. The slogan "Honest Abe the Railsplitter" was coined at a convention held in Decatur. Lincoln also gave his first political speech in Decatur.

THE LINCOLN SAGA

Seven novels that tell the Lincoln story

⭐ *For Us the Living* by Bruce Lancaster, 1940
Hoffman's Row by Walter Carnahan, 1963 - courtship of Lincoln and Mary Todd
Love is Eternal by Irving Stone, 1954
Mr. Lincoln's Wife by Anne Colver, 1943
The Senator's Lady by Shirley Seifert, 1967 - story of Stephen A. Douglas, his wife, and the Lincoln-Douglas debates
The Soul of Ann Rutledge by Bernie Babcock, 1919
Steamboat on the River by Darwin Teilhet, 1952 - life on the Sangamon River, with Lincoln as a steamboat pilot

Another Lincoln tale

⭐ The very short Stephen A. Douglas always tried to raise his stature during the debates by demeaning Lincoln. He told a crowd that when he first met Lincoln he was a poor shopkeeper who sold cigars and whiskey. "Mr Lincoln was a very good bartender!" But Lincoln was never outdone. He calmly replied, "What Mr. Douglas has said is true enough. I did keep a grocery, and I did sell cotton, candles, and cigars, and sometimes whiskey. I remember in those days that Mr. Douglas was one of my best customers. Many a time have I stood on one side of the counter and sold whiskey to Mr. Douglas on the other side, but the difference between us now is this: I have left my side of the counter, but Mr. Douglas still sticks to his as tenaciously as ever."

When Douglass came to tea

After Frederick Douglass had tea at the White House with Lincoln, the renowned black abolitionist leader told a friend, "Lincoln is the first white man I ever spent an hour with who did not remind me that I am a Negro."

The electable Mr. Lincoln

⭐ Abraham Lincoln was nominated on the third ballot by the new Republican Party as its 1860 presidential candidate at a convention meeting in a Chicago building called the Wigwam. Lincoln's running mate was Maine senator Hannibal Hamlin.

At the election in November, Lincoln received 1,865,593 popular votes and 180 electoral votes. Northern Democrat Stephen A. Douglas received 12 electoral votes—1,382,713 popular votes. The Southern Democrats' candidate, John C. Breckinridge, received 72 electoral votes, and Constitutional Union party candidate John Bell received 39 electoral votes.

TORN BETWEEN NORTH AND SOUTH

The New Egypt

⭐ When the Civil War began in 1861, there was considerable talk in Williamson County of parting from southern Illinois and forming a separate confederate state, to be called Egypt. Senator Stephen A. Douglas rushed back from Washington to stop the movement. Douglas was firmly for the Union and said in one speech, "Every man must be for the United States or against it. There can be no neutrals in this war, only patriots and traitors." Southern sympathies did not end, however. In fact, guerrilla bands in Williamson County and other places in southern Illinois, stayed in touch with Confederate officials and did what they could to encourage Union soldiers to desert. One Illinois regiment stationed in Mississippi had to be put under guard because of the numbers of men deserting.

★ Almost 260,000 Illinoisans—about 15 percent of the population of the state—actively fought in the Civil War, making it the second-highest percentage of citizens going to war of any state. Only Kansas had a higher proportion of soldiers to population. More than 35,000 of the Illinois soldiers died. Illinois produced 177 generals.

Illinois's role in the Civil War

★ Col. Elmer Ellsworth, head of a squad of New York firefighters called the "Fire Zouaves" in Washington, D.C., was killed by an innkeeper while taking down a Confederate flag outside a building in Alexandria, Virginia, on May 14, 1861. The 24-year-old soldier from Illinois became the North's first "martyr." He had worked at Abraham Lincoln's law office in Springfield during 1858.

First Illinoisan killed in the Civil War

★ Citizens of Illinois who were sympathetic to the Confederate cause were known as Copperheads. The name "Copperhead" was originally given derisively to Ohio Peace Democrats by a New York newspaper that thought these people were snake-like, striking without warning.

Copperheads and Southern Illinois

Extremely militant Copperheads formed a secret society called the Knights of the Golden Circle in 1862. The following year it changed its name to Order of the American Knights and then to the Sons of Liberty.

The 54th Illinois regiment was returning to the front when they were attacked by a Copperhead mob, headed by Sheriff John H. O'Hair, in Mattoon on March 28, 1864. The result was six Union soldiers killed, four wounded, and two Copperheads killed, five wounded.

★ Alton State Prison, the first state prison in Illinois, was abandoned in 1860 because it was on low-lying, miasmic ground. But during the Civil War the site became a Confederate prison. In 1863, the overcrowded prison was hit by a smallpox epidemic, with up to ten prisoners dying each day. Union authorities moved the prisoners to an island in the Mississippi, but none returned to the mainland alive. The Confederate Cemetery in Alton contains 1,354 Confederate graves.

Prisoners of war

Grierson's Raiders

Before Benjamin Grierson entered the Army in 1861, he was a quiet bandmaster and music teacher in Jacksonville. But he became a folk hero after his 16-day raid through Confederate Mississippi, April 17 to May 2, 1863. Grierson's Raiders traveled 600 miles, captured 1,000 horses and mules, destroyed 60 miles of railway and telegraph lines, captured or killed 600 rebels, and burned or destroyed cotton warehouses and other supply warehouses.

The lady with a mission

⭐ Mary Ann (Ball) Bickerdyke of Galesburg, widowed at 42, supported her family by practicing herbal medicine. But the Civil War soon put her in the limelight. A tireless volunteer, she was at the site of 19 battles, tending to the wounded, distributing supplies, and improving sanitary conditions. She spent seven months alone caring for the injured following the Battle of Shiloh, earning the honorary title of "Mother" Bickerdyke. The only woman at the battles of Lookout Mountain and Missionary Ridge, one of her major innovations was establishing military laundry facilities to avoid burning bedding and clothing. Mother Bickerdyke died at age 84 in 1901, and was buried in the Lindwood Cemetery in Galesburg, where a statue stands in her honor.

Grant and the Seneca

⭐ Ely S. Parker, a Seneca chief who was educated in civil engineering and law, arrived in Galena in 1858 to supervise the construction of the U.S. Custom House. The Indian, whose native name was Deioninhogawen, or "He Holds the Door Open," was recruited by Ulysses S. Grant for his staff and was one of the officers at the McLean House in Appomattox where Lee surrendered. In fact, Parker, because of his beautiful penmanship, was asked to write out the terms of the surrender. In 1868, the new President Grant appointed Parker his Commissioner of Indian Affairs.

The generals from Galena

⭐ Ulysses S. Grant, his wife and four children, moved to Galena in the spring of 1860. Grant was employed at his father's leather-goods store. When the call for Union troops was issued, Grant was made a brigadier general in August of 1861 and took charge of a post at Cairo, Illinois. Grant filled the ranks of the Union army with people he had known in Galena—eight Union generals were from Galena: John A.  Rawlins, who later became Secretary of War, William Rowley, Augustus L. Chetlain, John Eugene Smith, John C. Smith (which must have been confusing), John Duer, Ely S. Parker, and, finally, Jasper Maltby, inventor of the telescopic rifle sight.

Was she or wasn't he?

Jennie Hodgers of Belvidere enlisted in the Union Army as a man, Albert D. J. Cashier, in 1862. She served as a handyman with the 95th Illinois Volunteer Infantry. When she broke her/his leg, her secret was revealed. She is buried in Livingston County under the name Albert.

Thanks to her for Decoration Day

⭐ The wife of senator John Logan suggested, soon after the war ended, that flowers be placed on the graves in Woodlawn Cemetery in Carbondale. She had her husband introduce a bill into Congress that a day be set aside to place flowers on the graves of people killed in the war (though the bill mentioned only Union soldiers' graves).

ILLINOIS ON THE NATIONAL SCENE

⭐ General James Shields of Illinois, who first made his name serving in the Mexican and Civil Wars, later made it into national politics from four different areas! He served as governor of Oregon territory, and then as a senator first from Illinois (1849-55), then from Minnesota (1858-59), and many years later, perhaps having suffered painful withdrawal symptoms, he was elected to the Senate from Missouri in 1879.

One state just wasn't enough

Just couldn't let go

When the town of Danville elected Joseph Gurney Cannon, a lawyer from Tuscola, to Congress in 1873, no one could have forecast that the North Carolina native would still be representing the Illinois constituency fifty years later. Cannon served almost continuously that whole time, gaining considerable seniority. He served as Speaker of the House from 1903 to 1911 and became known as one of the most domineering (and arbitrary) speakers that the House has ever seen. He once sponsored a bill that navy bean soup be served in the House cafeteria every day as a tribute to the Michigan bean. The bill passed and navy bean soup is still served today. The Cannon Office Building in Washington, D.C., is named for "Uncle Joe."

⭐ Several people from Illinois have been named to serve on the U.S. Supreme Court:

Illinoisans on the Supreme Court

Abe Lincoln appointed **David Davis** in 1861. Davis was one of the few justices ever to resign to do something else. After serving on the court for 15 years, he resigned to serve as a senator from Illinois.

Melville W. Fuller, a Chicago lawyer, was named to head the court by Grover Cleveland in 1888 He served until 1910.

With a name like John Marshall (probably the greatest-ever Chief Justice of the U.S. Supreme Court) and a granddad who was on the Supreme Court, what else could **John Marshall Harlan** become? Well, he didn't make it to Chief Justice, but the Chicago-born federal judge was named to the Supreme Court in 1955 by President Eisenhower. His main occupation for 16 years was to try to keep Chief Justice Earl Warren from poking the court's nose into affairs where Harlan felt it didn't belong.

Like Davis, Chicagoan **Arthur Goldberg** resigned from the court. The son of a peddlar, he had been a powerful labor lawyer and was appointed as Secretary of Labor in 1961 by President Kennedy, who elevated him to the Supreme Court the following year. His service on the high court ended in 1965 when he accepted an appointment as ambassador to the United Nations.

Nashville (Illinois, that is)-born **Harry Blackmun** was named to the court in 1970 by President Nixon (after his first two choices were rejected by the Senate).

Chicagoan **John Paul Stevens**, an antitrust attorney, was named to the court in 1975 by President Ford. He filled the position held for so many years by William O. Douglas.

FIRSTS FOR MINORITIES

Firsts in Illinois for African-Americans

⭐ **First elected to the state legislature in Illinois** - J.W.B. Thomas, elected to the Illinois Assembly by the 2nd Legislative District in 1877.

First appointed to a high state position in Illinois - Joseph J. Bibb, appointed Director of Public Safety by Governor Stratton in 1953.

Firsts in the nation for African-Americans

⭐ **First female judge** - Edith Sampson was elected to a municipal judgeship in Chicago in 1962.

First to be named chief justice of a federal court - James B. Parsons, in 1975, at the U.S. District Court in Chicago. (See page 50)

First black congressman elected from a Northern state

⭐ Republican Oscar DePriest, a real estate broker in Chicago who was born in Alabama, was elected to the U.S. House of Representatives in 1929. After helping to organize the vote among blacks in Chicago, he got elected himself and gradually moved up onto the City Council and then into Congress. His vote against FDR's New Deal lost him his re-election in 1934 to Democrat Arthur Mitchell.

First black Democratic congressman in modern times

⭐ Democrat Arthur W. Mitchell of Chicago, also an Alabama-born lawyer and real estate broker, was elected to Congress in 1934, the first African-American Democrat to be elected in modern times. Three years later Mitchell gained additional prominence in an even more resounding way. He had been traveling by train, first class, to Hot Springs, Arkansas. He was asked to leave his first-class seat and sit in a car for blacks, the "Jim Crow" car, after the slang term for such practices. Mitchell brought suit against the Chicago and Rock Island Railroad and argued the case all the way to the U.S. Supreme Court. In 1941, he won a decision which declared such Jim Crow practices illegal on interstate transportation.

First Hispanic sent to Congress from the Midwest

⭐ Luis Gutierrez, born in Puerto Rico, was elected by Chicagoans in 1992 to be the first Hispanic sent to Congress from the Midwest. His first experience with government was delivering newspapers to Mayor Richard J. Daley's office. Gutierrez has said, "If you asked anyone back then: How far would this Puerto Rican boy go, this son of a cabdriver and a factory worker, they'd laugh if you said City Hall. And they'd never believe you if you said U.S. Congress." As an adult, Gutierrez became a revolutionary and was even known as a "bomb-thrower." He turned moderate working in Chicago politics under Mayor Harold Washington.

THE STATUS OF WOMEN

First American woman appointed to political office

⭐ Contrary to people's expectations, the first woman in America appointed to a government post had nothing to do with children or home economics. Instead, Florence Kelley, appointed by Governor Altgeld, became Illinois's Chief of the State Factory Inspection Department in 1893. Primarily through her efforts, the Illinois legislature passed laws prohibiting child labor, limiting women's working hours, and giving the state the right to control sweatshops.

Women get the right to vote — step by step

1870 - A new constitution was ratified giving the right to vote to blacks but not to women. One convention delegate opposed to female suffrage stated that proponents of voting rights for women were "long-haired men and short-haired women."

1891 - Illinois women were granted by the General Assembly their first right to vote, though only in school board elections.

1913 - The General Assembly expanded women's right to vote by allowing their participation in any political election not covered by the state constitution. That left them more say in local events.

1919 - On June 10, along with Wisconsin and Michigan, Illinois was the first state to ratify the 19th Amendment, giving women the right to vote in national elections.

A native of Rockford and a friend of Jane Addams, (see page 80), Julia Lathrop became an expert in the care of children and young people by public systems, working at Governor Altgeld's request. She told him of the injustices and urged that management of welfare institutions be made nonpolitical. President Taft appointed her in 1912 to be the first head of the U.S. Children's Bureau, which led the way in juvenile and maternal care nationwide. She held the position until 1921.

First woman to head a federal agency

What she did was more important than her license

After passing law courses with flying colors, Chicagoan Myra Bradwell, the editor of the *Chicago Legal News* and wife of a lawyer, applied to be admitted to the bar. She was denied admission, strictly because she was a woman. She took the matter all the way to the U.S. Supreme Court, which ruled in 1873 that "The natural and proper timidity which belongs to the female sex evidently unfits it for many of the occupations of civil life . . . . The paramount destiny and mission of woman are to fulfill the noble and benign offices of wife and mother." Fortunately, by the time that decision was handed down, Illinois had outlawed gender limitations to all occupations. Bradwell, up to her ears in her publishing business, didn't bother to reapply for admission.

In 1992, when Mary Ann G. McMorrow was sworn in as the first female justice of the Illinois Supreme Court, she said, in reference to Bradwell, that the ceremony was "an act of contrition for a sin committed by the Supreme Court many years ago."

First woman elected to serve in the Illinois Assembly - Lottie Holman O'Neill, elected in 1922; she served 38 years in the legislature.

First woman elected to serve in the Illinois Senate - Florence Fifer Bohrer, of Bloomington. She served from 1925 to 1933.

First woman elected by the entire state - Mrs. Earle B. Searcy, who was appointed clerk of the Illinois Supreme Court after her husband's death, ran in the statewide election November 1956, and won.

More state government firsts

**First women elected to
Congress from Illinois**

⭐ Winnifred Mason Huck of Chicago, the daughter of Illinois's at-large U.S. Representative, decided to run for the remainder of her father's term and the next term when he died in 1921. She won the election for the remainder of the term but lost her bid for the next one. She served from November 7, 1922, to March 3, 1923. Later, as an investigative journalist, she went undercover in an Ohio prison in order to write about the failure of the criminal justice system.

Six years after Huck, Ruth H. McCormick, daughter of Senator Marcus Hanna, and widow of Medill McCormick, was elected as an at-large representative from Illinois for one term. She later became chief political advisor to presidential candidate Thomas E. Dewey.

First African-American woman in the Senate

1992 was called the "year of the woman," and it was the year that the first black woman was elected to serve in the Senate—Carol Moseley Braun from Illinois. Braun, a native Chicagoan who had been in the General Assembly for ten years, was serving as the Cook County recorder of deeds, a position to which she was elected in 1988, when she became riled at the image on TV of white male senators questioning black woman Anita Hill in the hearings to confirm black male Clarence Thomas as a justice of the Supreme Court. Her forthright anger won her enough votes in the primary to beat long-time Senator Alan Dixon, who had voted in favor of Thomas. By winning the election, Braun also became Illinois's first black senator and first woman senator.

They did it on her own

⭐ The first congresswoman from Illinois to be elected without her husband first having been the representative or the candidate was Jessie Sumner in 1938 (although she first came to public attention by replacing her late uncle as the judge of Iroquois County). Sumner was an attorney born in Milford. She remained in Congress for four terms and was one of the few voices of isolationism during World War II.

Illinois's first African-American woman elected to congress was Cardiss Collins of Chicago, elected in 1973. She has served longer in the U.S. House of Representatives than any other black woman.

**First woman minister
to a foreign country**

⭐ Presidential candidate and great orator William Jennings Bryan's daughter Ruth was born in Jacksonville in 1885 before Bryan went to Congress. She herself was elected to Congress from Florida in 1928. After losing the election of 1932 because of her stance on Prohibition (like her father, she continued to favor it), President Roosevelt appointed her minister to Denmark, the first American woman to be named minister to a foreign country, a position she held until she married a Dane named Rohde in 1936, thus disqualifying herself.

⭐ The first African-American woman ambassador was Patricia Roberts Harris, who was born in Mattoon in 1924. A Washington, D.C., lawyer and an influential Democrat, she became involved nationally in civil rights under President Kennedy. Lyndon Johnson named her ambassador to Luxembourg in 1965. She was named Secretary of Housing and Urban Development in 1976 by President Carter—the first black woman to be named to the cabinet. In her confirmation hearings, she pointed out, "I am a black woman, the daughter of a dining car waiter. I am a black woman who even eight years ago could not buy a house in some parts of the District of Columbia."

Double firsts for a woman from Mattoon

⭐ The Equal Rights Amendment, giving full rights to women, was approved by Congress on March 22, 1972. The legislature of Hawaii became the first state to ratify it. Ten years later Illinois was still the only Northern state other than Utah that had not ratified the amendment, and so the amendment proposed more than a 100 years before died. In the final days, proponents borrowed tactics from the old English right-to-vote struggle and 7 women engaged in a 37-day hunger strike, while 17 others chained themselves to the statehouse railings.

Illinois's failure to ratify the ERA

THE PRESIDENTS

The death of a president

President Lincoln was shot by actor John Wilkes Booth, while attending a play called *An American Cousin,* at Ford's Theater in Washington, D.C., on April 14, 1865. He died the following day. The popular president's body was returned to Illinois, traveling on a slowly moving

train, which drew millions of mourners to the trackside as it passed. On reaching Chicago, his body lay in state at the City Hall. When the funeral train reached Springfield on May 3, Lincoln's body was moved to the House of Representatives, where it lay in state for an additional two days. After the funeral, the president's body was placed in a temporary vault while a memorial was built. The monument and tomb in Oak Ridge Cemetery were completed in 1874 at a cost of $180,000. In 1901, it was reconstructed and remodeled. When the reconstruction was finished, the casket was opened to make certain that the body was that of Abraham Lincoln. The familiar features were still recognizable to the official witnesses (photo).

Cleanliness is next to presidency

⭐ The Nachusa Hotel in Dixon has become an important landmark since it hosted five different U.S. presidents: local-boy-made-good Ronald Reagan, William Howard Taft, Theodore Roosevelt, Ulysses S. Grant, and Abraham Lincoln. However, its other claim to fame may be even more important: it is said to have had the first hotel bathtub in Illinois.

Always a bridesmaid, never . . .

⭐ Often called "The Great Commoner," politician William Jennings Bryan was born in Salem in 1860. He grew up in Jacksonville and practiced law in Illinois until 1887 when he moved to Nebraska. Famed for his sympathy to the common people, he was nominated for the presidency in 1896, 1900, and 1908, but lost each time. At the 1896 Democratic nominating convention in Chicago, Bryan made one of the most famous speeches in American history, called the "Cross of Gold" speech, which called for the coining of silver money to ease the current economic depression. Bryan was also the prosecutor at the famous Scopes trial in 1925 when a Tennessee high school biology teacher was charged with teaching Darwinian evolution instead of the Bible, in opposition to state law. Bryan won over Clarence Darrow's defense, but the effort killed him. Scopes's conviction was later overturned.

Silver screen to soap box

⭐ Ronald Wilson Reagan was the only Illinois-born president. Born in Tampico on February 6, 1911, he went to school in Dixon. Reagan wanted to be an actor from earliest childhood but turned to sports announcing because he wore glasses and thought that would bar him from the stage. He started acting while attending Eureka College, but it was sportscasting that took him to Hollywood. He was seen by a talent scout while covering a Chicago Cubs training camp on Catalina Island.

Reagan learned his political skills as president of the Screen Actors Guild from 1947-52 and 1959-60, gradually becoming an arch-conservative. In 1966, he won the first of two four-year terms as governor of California. One Hollywood writer observed of Ronald Reagan that "soap boxes were made with him in mind rather than soap."

Young Ronald Reagan and his mother

Vice presidents from Illinois

⭐ Illinois has produced only two U.S. vice presidents:
Adlai E. Stevenson, born in Bloomington - served 1893-97
Charles G. Dawes, who lived in Evanston - served 1925-29

Never anticipate

In one of the most famous newspaper headlines ever, the *Chicago Tribune* came out a bit too early in 1948 with an issue declaring in large type: "Dewey Defeats Truman!" Truman was photographed holding up the erroneous front page and laughing his head off.

ALL THE PRESIDENT'S MEN AND WOMEN

Cabinet members from Illinois:

Secretary of State
Elihu B. Washburne under Grant, 1869
Walter Q. Gresham under Cleveland, 1893
William Jennings Bryan under Wilson, 1913
Edward Stettinius, Jr., under FDR, 1944

Secretary of the Treasury
Lyman J. Gage under McKinley, 1897
Franklin MacVeagh under Taft, 1909
David M. Kennedy under Nixon, 1969
George P. Shultz under Nixon, 1972

Secretary of Defense
Donald H. Rumsfeld under Ford, 1975
Secretary of War

John M. Schofield under Andrew Johnson, 1868
John A. Rawlins under Grant, 1869
Robert T. Lincoln under Garfield and Arthur, 1881
James W. Good under Hoover, 1929

Secretary of the Navy
Paul Morton under Teddy Roosevelt, 1904
Frank Knox under FDR, 1940

Attorney General
Homer S. Cummings under FDR, 1933
N. de B. Katzenbach under Lyndon Johnson, 1964
Edward H. Levi under Ford, 1975

Secretary of the Interior
Orville H. Browning under Andrew Johnson, 1866
Walter L. Fisher under Taft, 1911
John B. Payne under Wilson, 1920
Roy O. West under Coolidge, 1929
Harold L. Ickes under FDR, 1933 and Truman, 1945

Secretary of Agriculture
John R. Block under Reagan, 1981

Secretary of Labor
Martin P. Durkin under Eisenhower, 1953
Arthur J. Goldberg under Kennedy, 1961
W. Willard Wirtz under Kennedy, 1962
George P. Shultz under Nixon, 1969
Lynn Martin under Bush, 1990

Secretary of Commerce
Robert P. Lamont under Hoover, 1929
Peter G. Peterson under Nixon, 1972
Philip L. Klutznick under Carter, 1979

Secretary of Transportation
Samuel K. Skinner under Bush, 1989

Secretary of Veterans Affairs
Edward J. Derwinski under Bush, 1989
    (Derwinski was the first person appointed to this position after the department was created by Ronald Reagan.)

RANDOM HISTORY

⭐ Nineteenth-century women knew how to take things that needed doing into their own hands. In 1856, a group of women in Farmington fought the "whiskey war" after trying to prohibit the sale of liquor. When they failed at doing it legally, they took the law into their own hands, marched on saloons, broke windows, smashed liquor barrels and bottles with axes, and threw it all out on the streets—years before Carry Nation became famous for her axe, and before Evanston became the headquarters of the Women's Christian Temperance Union.

The war against whiskey

Lawmen of the Old West

★ "Wild Bill Hickok"—the very name rings of the Old West (as well as a bit of television). Wild Bill was born James B. Hickok in Troy Grove, a village he abandoned as a teenager, seeking adventure in the West. Working in any job he could find, including guerrilla fighter in the Civil War, "Wild Bill" ended up in the Abilene, Kansas, area, where he served as sheriff in 1871. Renowned as a marksman, Hickok was shot in the back and killed on August 2, 1876, at Carl Mann's Saloon in Deadwood City, Dakota Territory, by Jack McCall. According to some versions of the story, many years earlier Hickok had killed McCall's younger brother by hitting him over the head with a hoe. Other reports insist that McCall had no more reason than that he wanted to be known for besting a famous gunman. McCall was hanged.

Bat Masterson, who was born William Barclay Masterson, was probably born in Iroquois County, Illinois, though some sources insist he was a Canadian. But though he grew up in Illinois, the frontier drew him to Kansas. Always stylishly and elegantly dressed, Masterson turned buffalo hunter and finally lawman. He had no intention of becoming a lawman, but when the Kansas City marshal, Larry Deger, bested him in a fight and jailed him, Bat ran against him in the election of 1877. Apparently he did a reasonably good job, but the townfolk didn't re-elect him after two years. He moved on to Tombstone, Arizona, and then to New York City where he changed occupations entirely, becoming a sports writer for the *Morning Telegraph*.

Floating into a riot

★ When Eugene Williams, an African-American swimming in Lake Michigan, accidentally floated into a "whites only" swimming area in Chicago, he was stoned to death. When police took no action, the black population gathered in the streets, and a riot broke out on July 17, 1919. After six days, the rioting was stopped by the National Guard, but not until 38 people (both black and white) had died, more than 500 had been injured, and thousands of others were left homeless by the resulting fires.

The Chicago 7 —or is it 8?

★ At the Democratic National Convention held in Chicago in 1968, anti-Vietnam War demonstrators filled the streets of the downtown area and Lincoln Park. Chicago police overreacted, using tear gas and bludgeons to impose order, and injuring more than 100 participants (and being injured by them). All told, 650 people were arrested while the party was nominating Hubert Humphrey to be president. Eventually seven young men, who came to be called the Chicago 7, were tried for conspiracy to violate the 1968 Civil Rights Act.

The trial, which turned into a three-ring circus, filled the front pages all over the country for weeks, while Judge Julius Hoffman made his own headlines with off-the-wall rulings. (An eighth defendant, Black Panther Bobby Seales, was even bound and gagged before being tried separately.) David Dellinger, Rennie Davis, Tom Hayden, Abbie Hoffman, and Jerry Rubin were convicted of crossing state lines to incite a riot. Two others were acquitted. Even the lawyers were cited with contempt of court by Judge Hoffman. The conviction of the five was overturned in November 1972 when the federal appeals court found "gross irregularities" in the judge's handling of the case.

THE WORLD AT WAR - I

⭐ Illinois was one of three states to furnish a complete National Guard Division for service in World War I. Officially known as the 33rd, the Illinois division was nicknamed the Prairie Division. It saw action at St. Mihiel, Verdun, Chateau Thierry, and Meuse-Argonne. Approximately 5,000 men were killed in action.

The Prairie Division

⭐ The Medal of Honor is the highest award given by the United States for bravery in combat. Truman said, "I'd rather have this medal than be president." Criteria for receiving it are: clear risk of life, voluntary act beyond duty, and two eyewitnesses.

"For conspicuous gallantry"

   Pilot Harold E. Goettler of Chicago won a Medal of Honor, posthumously, after trying to fly supplies to a unit cut off in the Argonne Forest on October 6, 1918. Although under continuous fire from the ground during a first flight, Goettler was unhappy with the inaccuracy of his drops. On a second flight, still ignoring the gunfire, he tried to fly lower over the cut-off battalion so that the supplies would not be wasted. Machine-gun fire killed him instantly as his plane was struck.

   Among other World War I Medal of Honor winners from Illinois:

John J. Kelly of Chicago	Thomas A. Pope of Chicago
Weedon E. Osborne of Chicago	Fred E. Smith of Rockford

THE WORLD AT WAR - II

⭐ Illinoisans answered the call to service in World War II in large numbers. From 1941 to 1945, 900,000 men and 19,000 women reported for duty. They totaled 11.5 percent of Illinois's population.

The willing people of Illinois

⭐ Walter E. Truemper of Aurora didn't make it through flight school—he was washed out in 1943 and was trained as a navigator instead. As part of a B-17 crew assigned to attack Leipzig, First Lt. Truemper was able to take control of a plane that was hit by enemy fire—pilot unconscious and co-pilot killed. He and the turret gunner leveled the craft and headed for a lower altitude where the crippled plane could get away from Nazi gunners. Treumper and two nonpilots took turns piloting the plane back to England. As they neared a field in England, Truemper told all conscious members of the crew to bail out, but Truemper and one crewman decided to attempt a landing. The tower thought differently—Truemper was told to head for open water and bail out. He said, "Sir, if that's a direct order, okay, but we'd rather try to bring her in." The colonel on the radio agreed when he heard that the pilot was still alive. Treumper's landing was not successful— the wings lost lift, the plane stalled, and crashed nose-first. But his willingness to try won him and his crewman Medals of Honor.

A pilot, nonetheless

More Medal of Honor winners

⭐ Illinois winners of the Medal of Honor in World War II (and where the heroic deed was performed; * indicates awarded posthumously):

Kenneth D. Bailey of Danville, at Guadalcanal*
Addison E. Baker, born Chicago, flying over Ploesti*
Stanley Bender of Chicago, in France
Vito Bertoldo, born Decatur, in France
Elmer C. Bigelow, born Hebron, at Corregidor*
Clyde L. Choate, born West Frankfurt, in France
John P. Cromwell, born Henry, near the Marshall Islands*
Russell E. Dunham, born East Carondelet, in France
Robert H. Dunlap, born Abingdon, at Iwo Jima
John P. Fardy, born Chicago, on Okinawa*
Eugene Fluckey, off the coast of China
Harold A. Garman, born Fairfield, in France
Robert Gerstung, born Chicago, on the Siegfried Line in Germany

Eric Gibson of Chicago, in Italy*
Richard E. Kraus, born Chicago, on Peleliu, Palau Islands*
Anthony Krotiak, born Chicago, on Luzon, Philippine Islands*
John Leims, born Chicago, on Iwo Jima
Fred F. Lester, born Downers Grove, on Okin-awa*
Joseph J. McCarthy, born Chicago, on Iwo Jima
Edward S. Michael, born Chicago, over Germany
Edward Moskala, born Chicago, on Okinawa*
Carlos Ogden, born Paris, in France
Joseph Ozbourne, born Herrin, on Tinian*
Robert Lee Wilson, born Centralia, on Tinian*
Frank Witek, on Guam*

Kenney the Conscientious

⭐ The little town of Kenney was recognized in World War II as being the first town in the nation where every household was contributing a husband, son, or effort to America's fight in the war. At that time, the town had a population of 483.

Profile in courage

John F. Kennedy saved the life of Wyanet native Patrick Henry McMahon when they served on the patrol boat Kennedy skippered during World War II. In 1943, while the boat was patrolling Blackett Strait in the Solomon Islands, a huge Japanese destroyer appeared from nowhere and sliced the patrol boat in half. Kennedy rescued McMahon, who was badly burned, by putting him across his back and holding him there as he swam by clenching McMahon's life-jacket strap in his teeth. Kennedy always kept in touch with McMahon, even when he became president.

THE NAZI EPISODES

A "sister" town

⭐ In the small town of Crest Hill is a monument to Lidice, Czechoslovakia, that recalls the terrible Nazi massacre that occurred there and the strong anti-Nazi feeling that existed in this country. Often called the "Czech Holocaust," the massacre was a retaliatory act against the Czech underground's killing of a Nazi leader, Reynard Heydrich, known as "The Hangman." Hitler, having lost one of his favorites, ordered the total annihilation of Lidice. Men were dragged out of their beds and executed. Women were sent to concentration camps, and children were sent to "educational" centers. The town was burned to the ground and the ground leveled by bulldozers. The world was outraged—even the small town of Crest Hill reacted by changing the name of a portion of the town known as Stern Park to Lidice. Within a month, a monument to Lidice was erected in Crest Hill.

★ People didn't laugh very hard when George Lincoln Rockwell, son of a comedian and founder of the American Nazi Party in 1958, claimed that he was going to be president of the United States. Born in Bloomington in 1918, he somehow acquired a great hatred for anyone who was different from his white, middle-America image, and a great love for the "principles" of Adolf Hitler, long after Hitlerism was dead. Rockwell was murdered by a sniper on August 25, 1967, in Arlington, Virginia, where the headquarters of his party were located. John Patler, a former assistant, was indicted for the murder.

Too late for Hitler

★ Frank Collin, head of his own neo-Nazi organization, the National Socialist Party of America, got his kicks out of setting up parades that he knew offended people. When, in 1977, the Chicago Park District established regulations that made it impossible for him to march, he applied to the neighboring, strongly Jewish suburb of Skokie for a permit. What followed was a year's worth of headlines, support of Collin by the American Civil Liberties Union, rulings negating the First Amendment by the Illinois Supreme Court, and considerable anger on everyone's part. Fascist techniques were being used to object to a fascist-minded man's activities. Finally, the U.S. Supreme Court ruled that Collin's parade could not be prohibited, and they called for quick action to repair the damage. However, it was June 1978 before Collin was finally free to parade—and then virtually no one came.
    The entire painful and unnecessary saga of the year-long event was fictionalized in the TV movie *Skokie*, which starred Danny Kaye as a vocal survivor of Nazi death camps.

Another neo-Nazi

KOREA AND VIETNAM

★ Captain James B. Stockdale, a native of Abingdon, had been the senior naval officer in a prisoner-of-war camp in North Vietnam for three years by 1968. Continually harassed and tortured by his captors, he knew that the prisoners would continue to suffer unless the North Vietnamese were made to accept the fact that he would sooner die than allow himself or the others to be used for propaganda purposes. On September 4, he deliberately mutilated his body and was close to death when the guards found him and revived him. Impressed with his determination, his captors left him and his men mostly alone. Stockdale wasn't released for almost another five years. He was awarded the Congressional Medal of Honor and eventually became a rear admiral. In 1992, he was chosen by independent presidential candidate Ross Perot as his running mate.

The POW who became a vice presidential candidate

More Medals of Honor ★ Illinoians awarded Medals of Honor in Korea (* means posthumous):

William F. Dean, born Carlyle, at Taejon, Korea

John E. Kilmer, born Highland Park, at Korea*

Edward C. Krzyzowski, born Chicago, near Tondul, Korea*

James I. Poynter, born Bloomington, near Sudong, Korea*

Richard G. Wilson, born Marion, at Opari, Korea*

William G. Windrich, born Chicago, vicinity of Yudam-ni, Korea*

Medals of Honor from Vietnam ★ Twelve Illinois natives in addition to Stockdale (see previous page) were awarded Congressional Medals of Honor for action in Vietnam (* means posthumous):

Robert C. Burke, born Monticello, in Quang Nam Province*

Harold A. Fritz, born Chicago, in Binh Long Province

Kenneth Michael Kays, born Mount Vernon, in Thua Thien Province

Leonard B. Keller, born Rockford, at Ap Bac Zone

Allen J. Lynch, born Chicago, at Binh Dinh Province

James H. Monroe, born Aurora, at Hoai Nhon Province *

Milton L. Olive III, born Chicago, at Phu Cuong*

James W. Robinson, Jr., born Hinsdale, at unknown location*

Lester W. Weber, born Aurora, in Quang Nam Province*

Jerry Wayne Wickam, born Rockford, near Loc Ninh*

Alfred M. Wilson, born Olney, at Quang Tri Province *

Gerald O. Young, born Chicago, at Khesanh

Some more historical novels of life in Illinois

The American by Howard Fast, 1946 - story of Governor Altgeld and the Haymarket Riots

Early Summer by Elizabeth Corbett, 1942 - farm life after the Civil War

The Eighth Day by Thornton Wilder, 1967 - life in a small Illinois town

The Father by Katharine Brown, 1928 - an abolitionist in Illinois

Faye's Folly by Elizabeth Corbett, 1941 - Civil War and romance

The Garnered Sheaves by Elizabeth Emerson, 1948 - life among Illinois Quaker farmers

The Head of Apollo by Elizabeth Corbett, 1956 - 1890s romance

Horse Shoe Bottoms by Thomas Tippett, 1935 - Illinois mining and labor saga

Measure of a Man by Dora Aydelotte, 1942 - life and business in a small town

Michael Beam by Richard Hallet, 1939 - the Black Hawk War

Noah by J. F. Burke, 1968 - radical politics and love in Illinois of early 1900s

The Shining Trail by Iola Fuller, 1943 - life among the Sauk Indians

Years of Growth by Harold Sinclair, 1940 - life in the late 1800s

CITIES AND TOWNS

Aptakisic, Cahokia, Chicago, Chillicothe, Dakota, Kankakee, Moweaqua, Niantic, Oneida, Shabbona, Watseka, Waubansee, Winnebago— Names that reflect the Indian heritage of the state. (No, Itasca is not an Indian name. It was created by H. R. Schoolcraft from the Latin words for "truth" and "head" when he discovered the source of the Mississippi River.) Names of other Illinois towns show the ego of the men who laid out the railways and dropped villages along the way, named for themselves, their daughters, or wives.

Of course, a name does not tell all there is to know about a town. Illinois cities and villages are the products of people's work, heritage, romance, and even quarrels. And Chicago has it all—but Chicago doesn't have all that much of this book because it will have its own AWESOME ALMANAC soon.

In the meantime, take a look at:
- A Hard Time A-Growin'
- Chicago
- The Great Chicago Fire
- Mayors are Special People
- A Random Glance at Some Towns

By their nicknames they shall be known

Illinois cities have been called lots of things, not all flattering. Here are a few (be sure to see p. 154, too):

Alton – City on Seven Hills
Auburn – Redwood City
Bloomington – Prairie City
Cairo – Egypt
Centralia – Population Center U.S.A., Gateway to Little Egypt
Champaign-Urbana – Twin Cities
Chicago – Big Potato (is that an insult?); City of Big Shoulders (from Carl Sandburg); City that Works (phrase of Mayor Richard J. Daley's not heard much anymore); Pigopolis; Second City; Windy City

Galena – Crescent City of the Northwest, City That Time Forgot
Lombard – Lilac Town
Nauvoo – The City Beautiful
Northbrook – Speed Skating Capital of the World (from 1972 Olympic skaters Diane Holum and Anne Henning)
Pana – City of Roses
Peoria – Progressive City
Quincy – Model City, Gem City
Rockford – Forest City, City of Beautiful Homes
Springfield – Flower City, City of Churches
Vandalia – Wilderness Capital

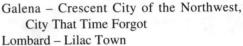

Hero Street U.S.A.
During the early part of this century, the town of Silvis near the Quad Cities drew a number of Mexican refugees from the Mexican War to work in the repair shop for the Rock Island Railroad. Gradually the group of immigrants began to thrive and 22 families bought land together on the edge of town, along Second Street. During World War II, 57 men went to war from Second Street; 8 of them died. Then, a few years later, 4 more went to fight in the Korean conflict and 2 of them died. When these veterans tried to join the Veterans of Foreign Wars, they were refused admittance and told to start their own post. They did. They also worked to get one of their own people on the city council. The councilman proposed that the name of Second Street be changed to Hero Street. The rest of the town laughed . . . until the Department of Defense confirmed that nowhere else in the United States had so many men volunteered from such a small defined area. On May 31, 1971, the name of Second Street was officially changed to Hero Street U.S.A. (Four years later the street was finally paved.)

10 cities in Illinois
In 1850 there were only 10 incorporated towns in Illinois. They were: Chicago, Alton, Springfield, Beardstown, Pekin, Quincy, Peoria, Bloomington, Galena, and Rock Island. One of the biggest issues of the day for these towns was what to do about the hog nuisance—the public streets and parks were virtual hog pens.

According to the 1990 census, only one Illinois city, Chicago, is among the 50 largest cities in the United States.

A HARD TIME A-GROWIN'

English author Charles Dickens was one famous speculator who invested in the Cairo City and Canal Company. But the company failed and many investors lost their money. Maybe that's why Dickens called the community a "detestable morass" and portrayed the town as the despicable "Eden" in *Martin Chuzzlewit*. Others said babies born in Cairo had fins or were web-footed. Dickens's impression of Illinois couldn't have been totally bad, because his brother, August Noel Dickens, came to the U.S. some years later. He landed in the small Lee County town of Amboy, where he started a newspaper in 1854.

A Dickens of a time

The Cahokia courthouse was probably built in 1737, nearly 40 years after Cahokia itself was settled by French missionaries. The courthouse remained in place for almost two centuries. Then, in 1904, it was moved to St. Louis for the Louisiana Purchase Exposition of "Meet Me at the Fair" fame. The Chicago Historical Society bought the building after the fair and set up part of it in Jackson Park in Chicago. Then, in the 1930s, as part of the Works Progress Administration, it was returned to Cahokia where it was reconstructed as a state memorial.

The wandering courthouse

Charles Reed first settled the Joliet area in 1831, naming the area after Shakespeare's Juliet because Romeo was a town slightly to the north. But when the town was officially incorporated in 1857, the name was mistakenly changed to Joliet in honor of an explorer, Jolliet, who accompanied Father Marquette to the Chicago Portage in 1673. However, the name is pronounced JO-lee-ett instead of ZHO-li-ay.

So much for Juliet

The courthouse for Macoupin County in Carlinville, called the "White Elephant," was one of the most expensive rural courthouses built in Illinois. The original estimated cost for the building was $150,000 in 1867, but the final cost, three years later, was $1.3 million. In July 1910, county residents had a massive festival to celebrate retiring the debt.

The million-dollar courthouse

The 10 largest cities in Illinois

Chicago - 2,783,726
Rockford - 139,426
Peoria - 113,504
Springfield - 105,227
Aurora - 99,581
Naperville - 85,351

Decatur - 83,885
Elgin - 77,010
Joliet - 76,836
Arlington Heights Village - 75,460

Follow that preacher!

🏠 The town of St. Anne was founded by a priest who was thrown out of his pastorate in Bourbonnais when part of the congregation rejected him. Those parishioners who sided with him joined him in founding a new town, called St. Anne because it was chosen on St. Anne's Day, July 26. Because the church contains a fragment of bone that many believe was part of St. Anne, mother of Mary, pilgrims come each year on St. Anne's Day.

Champaign-Urbana or Champaign vs. Urbana

🏠 The duel between the towns of Champaign and Urbana, now separated only by Wright Street, began in the early 1800s. Urbana was settled in 1822 by Willard Tompkins and is thirty years older than Champaign. In the early 1850s, the Illinois Central Railway had surveyed three possible routes. When the route that went two miles west of Urbana was chosen, the duel of the cities began. Urbana decided to stay put, but a new town, West Urbana, grew around the new railway station. The farmers called Urbana "Old Town," and they called West Urbana "Depot." In 1855, Urbana tried to incorporate West Urbana through a sneaky clause in an incorporation bill. Outraged Depot residents got wind of the plot and defeated the bill in 1860, incorporated "Depot," and renamed it Champaign. Trying to get even, Champaign tried to get the county seat out of Urbana. Urbana hastily realized that the courthouse was its only real asset and fought off the challenge.

None of that pioneering stuff for Galesburg

🏠 George Washington Gale, a Presbyterian minister from Oneida in upstate New York, wanted to establish a fundamentalist community focused around a manual labor college for training ministers. Families invested $20,000, and 20 square miles of land was purchased. In 1836-37, settlers built nice homes because no "crude" log cabins were allowed. Rev. Gale believed that a settlement built by hardworking farmers would raise the land values and produce a fund to endow the minister's college. Because of its New England roots, Galesburg was a strong anti-slavery town in a pro-slavery area.

Where two great rivers meet

Little Egypt

Pierre Francois Xavier de Charlevoix, a French missionary, wrote in 1721 that the point at which the Ohio and Mississippi rivers meet would be a good location for a fort and settlement. The community of Cairo began there more than a century later. A merchant from St. Louis, John Comega, thought the town site was probably similar to the site of Cairo, Egypt. His ventures in Cairo failed but the name survived. Residents of southern Illinois have often called the area around Cairo, where there's more water than land, "Egypt" or "Little Egypt."

CHICAGO

Reporter A.J. Liebling first called Chicago "the Second City," probably giving Chicagoans an inferiority complex ever after, though Los Angeles—when its population finally surpassed Chicago's in the 1990 census—proudly tried to take the title away.

The Second (Boo! Hiss!) City

Robert A. Kinzie went into the United States Land Office in the town of Palestine in southern Illlinois in 1831 and purchased 102 acres for the price of $127.68. The land was located on the shore of Lake Michigan, where there were few settlers. However, within three years the area was incorporated as the new village of Chicago.

Buying the land

A view of Chicago from outer space

In 1949, a huge, little-used airfield northwest of Chicago was named Chicago-O'Hare International Airport, though it did not begin commercial service until six years later. It was named in honor of Lieutenant Commander Edward H. "Butch" O'Hare, a U.S. Navy flyer and Medal of Honor recipient. In 1942, O'Hare attacked nine enemy bombers in the Pacific and managed to knock out six.

Chicago by air

On the same day that O'Hare officially opened, Chicago's other airports received new names. Chicago Municipal became Chicago Midway, and Northerly Island became Merrill C. Meigs Field. O'Hare had previously been called Orchard Place Airport, which kind of explains the ORD abbreviation on luggage tags.

**Chicago, trains,
and money**

🏠 The founders of the Chicago & South Side Rapid Transit Railroad company formulated a plan to ease congestion by constructing trains elevated above the streets. Steel framing for skycrapers, developed by Chicago's architects in the 1880s, was applied to the rail system. Thousands watched in amazement at the inaugural run of steam-driven trains on the raised tracks, affectionately called the "El," on June 6, 1892. Electric trains came on line six years later, and its electricity has moved masses of commuters since then. (Many people think Chicago's Loop was named after the elevated train system since it loops around the downtown, but that actually started in the 1880s when the cable-car tracks looped through the business district.)

Chicago's second El, opened in 1893, was built by Charles Yerkes whose philosphy of rapid transit was "Buy up old junk, fix it up a little, and unload it upon other fellows." Union Loop, which brought citizens downtown, was also his contribution.

The next Chicago transit mogul, Samuel Insull, apparently took Yerkes's advice to heart. In 1932, he left the city in a hurry for Greece to escape indictments on fraud and embezzlement! There were numerous scandals connected with the finances of the early El and in 1902 voters approved a measure that would let the city run it. However, that didn't finally happen until 1947 when the CTA was formed.

The El has been a major character in a number of movies, usually involving cops and robbers. Try *Running Scared, Code of Silence,* and *Bullitt* for some good chase and fight scenes.

THE GREAT CHICAGO FIRE

**The day that made
"Before" and "After"**

🏠 In 1869, Chicago was connected to San Francisco by railroad. This link promised Chicago great growth in years to come. Unfortunately, in 1871 this growth was stunted by, as legend would have it, a cow.

The Chicago Fire of 1871 was one of the worst disasters in the nation's history. Only five inches of rain fell between July and October 1871. Chicago's wooden sidewalks, wooden streets, and wooden buildings were vulnerable. The story goes that Mrs. O'Leary's cow kicked a lantern over behind her home on DeKoven Street. Because the fire department had fought a big fire the previous day, the exhausted firemen had to use untrained volunteers. The fire watchman gave wrong directions, and valuable time was wasted while firefighters tried to find the fire. A strong wind came up and the fire raged out of control, destroying 65 acres each hour. It is said that the fire was so hot its heat could be felt 100 miles away. Luck was with the city: a rare rainstorm began at midnight, putting out the flames.

The fire killed several hundred people, destroyed 17,000 buildings, and left almost 100,000 Chicagoans homeless for many weeks. Much of the rubble from the fire was dumped into Lake Michigan and is now under Grant Park. Help for Chicago came from as far away as Europe and from all over the United States.

The Chicago Fire of 1871 did not destroy what was truly vital to the business of Chicago. In fact, 75% of the grain elevators, 80% of the lumberyards, 600 factories, rolling mills, machine shops, the Union Stock Yards, 20 miles of Lake Michigan dockage and rail connections to 18 major railway lines were all saved. But homes of one-third of the population, 1,600 stores, 60 manufacturing businesses and other public and government buildings were destroyed. Chicago had a chance to rebuild itself in a more orderly fashion than it had developed in the previous forty years.

When the first election for the position of mayor was held after the Great Fire, *Tribune* publisher Joseph Medill was elected on the Fire-proof ticket.

The survivors

The only two buildings in the downtown area to survive were the Old Water Tower, now a Chicago landmark in the middle of the city's "magnificent mile," and the pumping station across the street, which now serves as a visitor information center for the city.

While the men went off to fight the Civil War, Illinois women worked hard to make things to sell at fairs where money was collected to support the war effort. At one of those fairs in 1865, the original draft of Abraham Lincoln's Emancipation Proclamation was auctioned, purchased for $3,000, and then presented to the seven-year-old Chicago Historical Society. Unfortunately, that important piece of paper was one of many that burned in the Great Chicago Fire.

A touch of Lincoln

Sinatra Street

🏠 No, Frank Sinatra didn't write "Chicago, That Toddling Town," but he might as well have because it is so associated with him. However, it was written by immigrant Fred Fisher who came to Chicago from Germany as a young man. Many years ago, the street signs of downtown State Street were changed to read "That Great Street," words taken from the song.

No Pied Piper needed

🏠 Chicago's own ratman, Frank Stemberk, found the solution in 1977 to the West Side's rat problem. He offered $1 for every rat brought to him. Because he was an alderman, he could finance the hunt from local businessmen and from local ward funds. When the rat fund ran out in a week due to zealous rat hunters (some families caught 20 each night), Stemberk turned to the federal government for "rat" aid—and got it.

MAYORS ARE SPECIAL PEOPLE

Took a while . . .

🏠 No one was happy when the results of the 1893 election for Aurora's mayor came in. Charges of fraud flew right and left. The results were so close a recount was demanded. It took four months and a decision from the State Supreme Court before the city had a governing official.

The power to indulge in absurdities

Big Bill Thompson, mayor of Chicago in the 1920s, was embarrassingly anti-British. In an effort to drive all signs of "old King George" out of Chicago, Thompson ordered all books that could be construed as pro-British out of the public libraries, and insisted that teachers never speak in favor of the British. At his urging, the Illinois State Legislature passed a bill in 1935 declaring, "The official language of the State of Illinois shall be known hereafter as the American language." Speaking English was expressly forbidden by Illinois law!

Assassination - 1

🏠 Visitors to the Columbian Exposition saw the enthusiastic mayor, Carter H. Harrison, bustling around, being important. He had been mayor of Chicago from 1879 to 1887, and was elected again in 1893, just in time to be the city's official greeter for the Columbian Exposition. The day the fair ended, Patrick E. Prendergast, a man whom some called a disappointed office seeker and others an anarchist, killed Harrison at his home on Ashland Avenue.

Assassination - 2

🏠 Anton J. Cermak, born in Bohemia, was brought to the town of Braidwood as a tiny infant and was raised there. As he became old enough, he worked in area coal mines, politics was more interesting. Cermak moved to Chicago at age 17 to begin making his way both in business and in Democratic Party politics. By 1931 he hit the top—mayor of Chicago. Cermak was riding in President-elect Franklin D. Roosevelt's open touring car by Bay Front Park in Miami on February 15, 1933, when Giuseppe Zangara tried to shoot Roosevelt. An alert watcher, a Mrs. W. Cross, hit Zangara's arm, deflecting the bullet, which hit Mayor Cermak instead. He died 3 weeks later of his injuries.

A short speech from a tall mayor

Colorful mayoral candidate "Long John" Wentworth made the shortest campaign speech in Illinois history in 1860. The 6-foot-6-inch (some sources say 7 feet) candidate for Chicago's mayor declared: "You damn fools—you can either vote for me for mayor or you can go to hell." A founder of the Republican party in Chicago, and the person who named Sandwich after his Massachusetts birthplace, Major Wentworth is now buried in Rosehill Cemetery.

Jane Byrne was elected Chicago's first female mayor in April 1979, obtaining almost 80 percent of the vote over Michael Bilandic, whom people blamed for the city's poor handling of a major winter storm in January. She was the first mayor in almost 50 years who was not part of the Democratic machine, though she was a Democrat who got her start in politics working for John F. Kennedy. In 1983, she and Richard M. Daley (Da Boss's son) split the white vote, allowing Harold Washington to be elected the first black mayor of Chicago.

Chicago's first woman mayor

Harold Washington for mayor!

A former U.S. Representative from Chicago, Harold Washington was the first African-American elected mayor of Chicago, in 1983. He received 52% of the vote in a city that is only 39% black. More whites voted for Washington than blacks voted for his opponent, Bernard Epton. Washington was re-elected with 54% of the vote in 1987, but he died of a heart attack the following November.

The new central Chicago Public Library is named for the late Mayor Harold Washington

Twenty-one years in office (the longest time for a Chicago mayor)—twenty-one years during which the character of Chicago changed totally—can't be described in a paragraph, or even a book. Richard J. Daley, Da Boss, also known as Hizzoner, ran what he called "the City that Works" from 1955 until his death in 1976. It was only afterward that we found out that Chicago wasn't working as well as he had always claimed. Chicago-born Daley, known as the "last of the big city bosses," suffered only one political defeat in his lifetime, losing the Cook County sheriff's race in 1946. He held numerous political offices before becoming mayor, including state representative, senator, state revenue director, Cook County clerk, and powerful chairman of the Cook County Democratic party. On a national level, any Democrat who wanted to make it to the presidency needed Daley on his side.

And where's Da Boss?

A RANDOM GLANCE AT SOME TOWNS

Mines and generals

🏠 Galena, now an interesting historic town, was the focus of pre-Civil War wealth in Illinois when 80 percent of the world's lead supply was mined there. It was the major port north of St. Louis on the Mississippi, though now the river has been revamped and the town isn't even on the Father of Waters. The lead ran out, but the town had a new claim to fame. One of their residents rescued the North from the possibility of defeat in the Civil War. Galena officials presented a beautiful house to Ulysses S. Grant in grateful thanks.

Galena, which bills itself as "the town that time forgot," is featured in several novels. You can try:
Bright Land by Janet Ayer Fairbank, 1932
Captain Grant by Shirley Seifert, 1946 (about Ulysses S. Grant)
Trail-Makers of the Middle Border by Hamlin Garland, 1926 (a Civil War story)

Royalty in Illinois

St. Peter's Danish Evangelical Lutheran Church attracted the attention of the people in Denmark when the church was being restored. The Danish Bicentennial Committee provided funds for restoring the church, which had been built by Danish immigrants to Sheffield in 1880. **Prince Henry of Denmark and Queen Margrethe II** came to the church in 1976 for a reconsecration program during the U.S. Bicentennial.

In 1860, **Edward, Prince of Wales**, Queen Victoria's son and heir, spent two days hunting near Breese. He was 19 years old at the time and beginning a long life jaunting around that would keep him occupied until he finally became king more than 40 years later.

Cleng Peerson started a permanent Illinois settlement, called Norway, in 1834 with 14 families of Norwegian immigrants. His Majesty King Olav V of Norway dedicated a memorial to Cleng Peerson at Norway in 1975.

Scrabbling for a name

🏠 Many towns can proudly point to public figures after whom they were named. Aledo has no such luck. It won its name in a kind of Scrabble game. Land speculators had to name the area they were trying to promote, but they couldn't agree on one. Finally they decided to

draw letters out of a hat, and **A L E D O** was the result.

From salt to coal to malls

🏠 The City of Danville was originally called Salt Works, because it was the site of a number of salt springs, from which saline water was taken and evaporated for salt. The supply of salt ran out early in the 1800s, but the business was replaced with coal mining.

Danville was the first town in Illinois to turn its randomly built downtown into an organized, unified mall, by planting trees and adding other elements that pulled it into a planned unit.

Commemorating East St. Lou

🏠 Jazz great Duke Ellington wrote the instrumental composition "East St. Louis Toodle-Oo" in the 1920s, working with Bubber Miles. Ellington, called "Duke" for the fine way he dressed, had nothing to do with East St. Louis—he wasn't even born in Illinois—but the memorable jazz melody heralded his radio show throughout the 1930s.

Evanston is the international headquarters of the Women's Christian Temperance Union, the main force behind America's experiment with prohibition, because its founder, Frances Willard, lived there. Trained as a teacher, she taught in both Harlem (Illinois) and Kankakee before restricting herself to Methodist Church-related schools. She later became the dean of women at Northwestern University but resigned because the president, her ex-fiancé, made life as difficult as possible for her. When she became involved in temperance organizations—first statewide and then nationally—she continued to do the work out of her home. Because of Northwestern's ban on alcohol within four miles of the university, Evanston became an acceptable, logical site for the headquarters of her new national organization, the Women's Christian Temperance Union. In the late 1800s, this organization made Evanston famous worldwide. In 1970, Evanston finally changed its laws and allowed alcohol to be served in bars in hotels, but the WCTU remains in the city. One particularly fascinating item in the headquarters is a bell that was cast from the opium pipes of a thousand smokers. Frances Willard represents Illinois in the U.S. Capitol's Statuary Hall. (see pg. 14).

NOTE: Evanston is also the national headquarters of the United Methodist Church and the world headquarters of Rotary International.

Superman and Illinois

Mary and John Kent of Smallville (Illinois) adopted a sweet little boy they found along the roadside in 1926. As he grew, he developed strange powers that gradually turned him into Superman. He hid those powers under the guise of mild-mannered newspaper reporter Clark Kent, who lived and worked in Metropolis.

Smallville isn't real, but Metropolis is . . . maybe. Proud of its superhero, the town has installed a phone booth from which a visitor can call and talk to Superman, and the *Planet* newspaper office issues copies of the fictional newspaper for which Clark Kent works. They placed a statue of the Man of Steel in the town square. Admittedly, it wasn't a very good statue—a bit like Elvis, in fact—but it is the focus of an annual Superman Celebration held the second week in June each year. The drama that is enacted is shown in the photo.

"They shouldn't kill off our heroes," said one woman after DC Comics, the owner of the Superman identity, had Superman killed by Doomsday, an escaped lunatic. Perhaps it won't matter. Superman is being supplanted in the hearts and minds of Metropolitans by the gambling riverboat anchored at Metropolis on the Ohio River. Slot machines are more fun than a dead hero. Besides, he is going to be brought back to life in some guise or another.

Lincoln never amounted to much

In 1853, lots were sold in a new town by three partners (Robert B. Latham, Virgil Hickox, John Gillett) for whom Lincoln had drawn up legal documents. While meeting in his Springfield office, the men suggested that the new town be called Lincoln. Lincoln replied that they could go ahead. . ."but I think you are making a mistake. I never knew anything named Lincoln that amounted to much."

Moose and children

Known as the "City of Children," Mooseheart is owned and operated by the Loyal Order of Moose, a fraternity founded in 1913. Here orphaned children of deceased members as well as other dependent children receive educational, citizenship, and religious training. The community covers about 1,200 acres, of which the campus occupies 313 acres. The remainder of the land is devoted to a dairy farm.

Turning a cardinal into a town

After Archbishop George Mundelein was elevated to cardinal in 1924, he was so popular that the northern Illinois town of Area renamed itself Mundelein. The town had previously had at least five names, starting with Mechanics Grove. But it was incorporated in 1909 as Area, which was said to be an acronym for Ability, Reliability, Endurance, and Action.

Nauvoo, the state's biggest city

When 12,000 Mormons were driven by angry citizens from Missouri in the middle of the winter of 1839, they crossed the Mississippi River and settled around the tiny, already existing community called Commerce City. Joseph Smith, the leader of the Mormons (officially known as the Church of Jesus Christ of Latter-Day Saints), changed the village's name to Nauvoo, from a Hebrew word meaning

"beautiful place." They quickly began work on the focal point of the city, the temple, shown in the very early photo at left.

Nauvoo quickly became the largest town in Illinois, with a population of almost 20,000. With such a strong, economically united community, Mormons began to involve themselves in partisan politics. Out-siders resented their solidarity. Also, Smith had a revelation that he and his followers should begin to take more than one wife, so that there should be no single women in the community. Neighbors, who had often harassed the Mormons, became violent, and Joseph Smith and his brother, Hyrum, were murdered in the Carthage jail in June of 1844. Eventually five men were tried for the crime and acquitted.

Thomas Ford, the governor of Illinois from 1842 to 1846, ordered the Mormons to leave Illinois "in the interests of peace." A new leader, Brigham Young, set about preparing the people to head for Utah, where they hoped to establish new communities.

Two novels that tell the story of Nauvoo are *The Corinthians* by Nicholas Wyckoff and *The Devil's Rainbow* by Joseph C. Furnas.

🏠 Some people stayed behind in Nauvoo because they did not accept Brigham Young as their leader, especially his very vocal support of polygamy. They eventually formed the Reorganized Church of Jesus Christ of Latter-Day Saints, with Joseph Smith III as their leader. They prefer not to be called Mormons because of that term's association with polygamy. Their headquarters are now in Independence, Missouri. However, they retained ownership of Joseph Smith's house and some other buildings in Nauvoo. In recent years, the Utah church has acquired many of the ruins of the town and rebuilt them as they would have been in the 1840s. The work has turned Nauvoo into a beautifully reconstructed town often compared with Williamsburg, Virginia.

Those who stayed behind

🏠 Étienne Cabet was a French political theorist who believed that the only good way to run society was communistically, with all property held in common for all. He and about 330 followers moved from Texas into the abandoned buildings in Nauvoo in 1849. As with many communes, this one fell apart within ten years as the communists argued over Cabet's leadership. However, in the few short years of their existence they contributed vineyards and wine- and cheese-making (Roquefort) skills to Illinois life. Many of their old wine cellars are still in use. Each year at Nauvoo State Park, a traditional French ceremony called the Wedding of Wine and Cheese is celebrated. The one-time major city now has fewer than 1,200 residents.

The second time around

Renewing New Salem

New Salem, the rough, log village Abraham Lincoln lived in from 1831-37, though it looms large in Lincoln legend, never amounted to much as a town. It was the same size as Chicago then—12 families. After Lincoln moved on to Springfield, the town died and was abandoned (not necessarily because Lincoln left). Wind and weather gradually deteriorated the remains until newspaper publisher William Randolph Hearst called attention to the place in 1906. Hearst purchased the land, gave it to the state of Illinois in 1918, and reconstruction began in 1932. New Salem has been painstakingly restored to look as it would have in the 1830s. Shown here is the Rutledge Tavern.

🏠 Paul Butler, who at one time owned 95 companies, took as much, if not more, interest in the founding of a town, Oak Brook, which is now the fastest-growing deluxe suburb of Chicago. *Celebrity Register* once described Butler and Oak Brook: "Laird of 'Oak Brook,' an estatus quo of the Old School which includes 14 polo fields (in each polo field you can put nine football fields), three golf courses, two entire villages, a $200 million suburb, a game preserve and the largest archery center in the world." The wide-open spaces of sport are not so wide-open these days, but the luxury is still there.

Butler of Oak Brook

**Tan-colored shoes
were outlawed**

John Alexander Dowie was a Scottish fundamentalist who attracted a large group of followers and bought land in Lake County to build the city of God, Zion. He planned to have the "rule of God in every department of the government." The church owned all industrial and business establishments. No drug stores, pharmacies, or theaters were allowed. Physicians or surgeons were not allowed to practice or live in Zion.

Clergyman, bigot, and fundamentalist crackpot, Wilbur Glenn Voliva was Dowie's assistant around 1900. For Voliva it was only a short step to putting Dowie out to pasture and taking control of the town. He forbade alcohol, tobacco, humming, oysters, cosmetics, high heels, or any tan-colored shoe. He believed that the world was flat and that it was going to end, though the Earth failed to live up to Voliva's expectations. His colony didn't last after he declared himself to be Elijah. The community went bankrupt and "regular" people moved in.

**Scraps in the
Illinois scrapbook**

In the 1860s, bands of young hoodlums were reponsible for getting **Odin** labeled "the hell-hole of the Illinois Central." The young thieves would hide along the railway embankments, then rush on board and steal passengers' luggage when the train stopped.

In 1678, French explorer John (Jean) LaMotte, a member of the party traveling with LaSalle, saw an area that reminded him of the Biblical land of milk and honey and called it **Palestine.**

From 1816 to 1836 Fort Armstrong was located on the limestone island in the Mississippi called **Rock Island**. In 1829, Congress decreed that the island would always be kept for a military purpose. Developed as an arsenal during the Civil War, it remains one today.

Mary Todd Lincoln, widow of the assassinated president, was a patient at Fox Hill Home in **Batavia** for several months in 1875, after a jury judged her insane from grief over the death of her son, Tad. Later, she was allowed to go live with her sister, Elizabeth, in Springfield.

September 10, 1890. As **Cairo** residents went about their normal business, there suddenly fell from the sky a shower of fish.

Peoria-native Scott Heimdall was kidnapped in northern Ecuador on April 28, 1990, while working for a mining company. The people of **Peoria** collected $60,000 from piggy banks, bake sales, and children's lemonade stands to pay the ransom demanded by his guerrilla captors.

In 1939 the leaders of Chatham and Harrisburg met to combine their separate towns, with the name of the town to be decided by a flip of a coin. Chatham West chose "Sterling" as the town's new name and Harrisburg chose "Pipississiway" (a local flower). Thank goodness **Sterling** won.

There is a town of Summit, Illinois. It even has about 10,000 people. What it didn't have for a long time was its own name on its post office. The post office at **Summit** was called Argo because Argo Corn Starch received most of the mail.

Abraham Lincoln's house in Springfield

LIVING AND LEARNING

The first "Education President" was Abraham Lincoln. As early as 1832, when he was running for State Assembly, he said, "I desire to see the time when education, and by its means, morality, sobriety, enterprise, and industry, shall become much more general than at present," and "I view [education] as the most important subject which we as a people may be engaged in."

But not all education happens in a classroom. There are settlement houses, where people like Jane Addams tackled the education of whole communities. There are world's fairs—not many, of course, but always fascinating. Illinois had the first one in the whole world. And there are organizations with a purpose—usually education, or broadening the mind or spirit. Here is a collection of interesting tidbits about life and scholarship.

- World's Fairs
- Gee-Whiz Museums
- The Top of the Learning Ladder
- Women in the Classroom
- People Taking Action
- The Life of the Spirit
- Studying People
- Searching the Heavens
- Extraterrestrials
- Into Space
- Into the Nucleus of the Atom
- More Illinois Scientists
- Not Shy about Nobel Prizes

WORLD'S FAIRS

So long at the fair

♦ Chicago was chosen over New York, St. Louis, and Washington, D.C., as the site for the celebration of the 400th anniversary of Christopher Columbus's arrival in the New World. In 1893 (a year late) the World's Columbian Fair and Exposition, the first world's fair, opened, one year later than originally planned. The site, today is Jackson Park, basically contained the "wonders of the world," including the first Ferris wheel, Linotype, and Pullman cars. The 150 buildings were mostly all white and brightly lit, so the area of the fair became known as White City. The Exposition used more electricity than the entire city of Chicago.

The newfangled Ferris Wheel at the Columbian Exposition curved 264 feet into the sky and had 36 cars, each of which held 40 or more people for the 20 minute ride. The huge wheel was the centerpiece of the great midway.

The fair was officially opened on May 1, 1893, by President Grover Cleveland. During the long summer, more than 27 million people came to the fair, some of them many times. It closed on October 30, having been, all agreed, a huge success. Built of a puny plaster material, most buildings were destroyed as soon as the fair ended. However, the building called the Palace of Art became the Museum of Science and Industry. Starting in 1926, the plaster building was reproduced in stone.

Women and the world's fair

♦ When the news went out that a world's fair was to be held in Chicago in 1893, society leader Bertha Honoré Palmer, wife of Potter Palmer, set about making darn sure that women weren't slighted. She knew enough people in positions of power to get a Woman's Building added to the plans for what would become the Columbian Exposition. The building was even designed by a woman, famed San Francisco architect Julia Morgan. By calling on all her acquaintances throughout the world, Mrs. Palmer got 47 nations to send exhibits, showing both women's achievements and the forces contending against them. As Chairman of the Board of Lady Managers, Mrs. Palmer vied with only one attraction that kept her from getting all the attention at the fair: Little Egypt, the exotic dancer whose apparel scandalized at the time but would now not attract a second glance, even on the street. One statue in the Woman's Building, a figure of a woman welcoming the world to Illinois, now stands in the main entry of the capitol in Springfield.

Women had a world's fair all to themselves in 1925. Also held in Chicago, it may well be the only world's fair ever to have been paid for before the first visitor arrived. The week-long fair, opened by Mrs. Calvin Coolidge, featured women's progress in 70 industries.

♦ The Century of Progress Exposition in Chicago was held in 1933 to celebrate the one hundred years of growth since Chicago officially began to exist. It was constructed on 91 acres of landfill out in the lake, an area that is now Meigs Field. Italian Air Minister Italo Balbo led 24 seaplanes to a safe landing near Navy Pier on Lake Michigan for the grand opening on May 27, 1933. The exposition, which concentrated heavily on science and technology, was open for two summers, during which more than 38 million visitors enjoyed the exhibits and special demonstrations. One such special demonstration featured fan dancer Sally Rand, who was just as popular—and even more revealing— than Little Egypt had been. She never said whether or not she wore anything under the fans, and they moved so fast that the audience couldn't tell.

100 years of Chicago

GEE-WHIZ MUSEUMS

Some of Illinois's more intriguing museums

• The John Shedd Aquarium in Chicago was endowed by an executive of Marshall Field & Company in 1924.

• Not to be outdone, Max Adler, a Sears executive, donated Chicago's Adler Planetarium, the first planetarium in the world, which opened in 1930. A planetarium is not a building but a complex optical instrument made by Zeiss, a German company, that projects stars on a domed ceiling.

• The only known cookie-jar museum in the world is located in Lemont. It houses over 2,000 of Lucille Bromberek's cookie jars collected from all over the world. Some are more than 100 years old.

• The Bradford Museum of Collector's Plates in Niles is home to the largest collection of limited edition collector's plates.

• Hardin County Fluorspar Museum in Rosiclare boasts the only museum in the world dedicated to the common mineral that is Illinois's state mineral, its mining, processing, uses and history.

• The Time Museum in Rockford has the most complete collection of time-keeping devices in the world, from the era of Stonehenge to the atomic clock.

• The Lizzardo Museum of Lapidary Art in Elmhurst includes one of the best collections of jadeite and nephrite carvings in the world. It features many historically important artifacts from the Imperial Palace in Beijing, China.

• The Frasca Air Museum at Urbana has World War II airplanes that were used in the movies *Midway* and *1941*.

• The Svoboda Nickelodeon Museum, located in Chicago Heights, contains one of the world's largest collections of music boxes.

• The major display in the Lake County Museum is the Curt Teich Postcard Collection, numbering 1.5 million postcards. Teich was a printer in Chicago from 1898 to 1974, who kept a sample of everything.

The Raven Totem Pole

♦ The Raven clan of the Tlingit Indians on Tongas Island built a 50-foot totem pole in 1867 with Abraham Lincoln, complete with stovepipe hat, perched on top. These Indians, who had practiced slavery for years, were informed that year by a passing American ship of the Emancipation Proclamation of 1863 and the 13th Amendment. The Raven clan built the totem to honor Lincoln and the emancipation and to shame the slave-taking Tlingit Eagle clan, which was forced to give up the practice when Alaska became a U.S. territory. The story of Lincoln freeing the slaves became a permanent legend told at all festivals. Three Lincoln totems now exist—the original one is in Juneau, Alaska, in a museum; a copy is in Saxman, Alaska; and the third is in the Illinois State Museum in Springfield.

A bit of the Nazi navy

The United States Navy captured only one German submarine, or U-boat, during World War II, and it's in Chicago, hundreds of miles from the sea. Just two days before D-Day, on June 4, 1944, a task force captained by Chicagoan D.V. Gallery captured *U-505* when the German crew failed to scuttle their submarine. Gallery towed the submarine to a base in the Caribbean, and eventually got it donated to the Museum of Science and Industry. At left, Captain Gallery is shown aboard *U-505* after the capture.

A visit to the macabre

What does an undertaker do when he comes across a piece of obsolete embalming equipment in his cupboards? He sends it to the National Foundation of Funeral Services in Evanston. There, the nation's funeral directors have, inadvertently, established a Museum of Funeral Service Artifacts. "Inadvertently" because the exhibits started arriving out of the blue when undertakers found choice items and didn't know what else to do with them. One prize exhibit is a 200-year-old cast-iron, mummy-shaped coffin found (with body) in the sewers of Belleville.

THE TOP OF THE LEARNING LADDER

Illinois's first college

♦ John Peck, a minister, established Rock Springs Seminary in 1827 at O'Fallon, to train ministers and teachers. Church officials moved the seminary to Upper Alton 5 years later, changing its name to Alton Seminary. The college and theological divisions split, and in 1936 a Bostonian, Dr. Benjamin Shurtleff, endowed the college. Shurtleff College, named after him, closed in 1957, and the buildings and property were purchased by Southern Illinois University. The college's original building, the oldest college building in the state, is still standing.

♦ Progressive Knox College in Galesburg was the first in the state to support higher education for women although women were required to study six years for a degree and men only four! It was also the first Illinois college to establish a Phi Beta Kappa chapter. Knox graduate Barnabas Root was the first African-American to graduate from a college in the state, and Hiram Revels, senator from Mississippi and a Knox alumnus, was the first black U.S. senator after the Civil War.

The college, founded in 1838, wasn't always quite so progressive. Jonathan Blanchard, a stiff, religious New Englander of a college president in 1854, was offended by the railroad running on Sundays. After being riled to breaking point, he stood on the tracks and stopped the train. He ordered the engineer to refrain from running his train on Sundays, but the man replied, "You can go to hell and mind your own business!" Blanchard blustered, and the train continued to run.

A school ahead of the others, kind of

♦ In 1851, several Methodist leaders in Chicago decided to establish "a university of the highest order and excellence." They obtained a state charter for North Western University (it later became one word). The man they hired to head the university advised them to buy a farm, keep part for the university, and sell or lease the rest as lots. A lakeshore farm north of the city was purchased for $25,000. The town was platted and named Evanston in honor of Dr. John Evans, one of the leaders. The university opened in 1855 with ten students. The first trustees amended the charter to prohibit the sale of alcohol within four miles of campus. Evanston remained dry for 116 years!

The university that started a city

♦ Jesse Fell was a land speculator in Bloomington in the 1850s when the state voted to establish a normal school (for teaching teachers). Everyone assumed that Peoria was going to get it, but Fell persuaded businessmen of Bloomington and McLean County to support the school to the tune of $150,000. Illinois State Normal opened in 1857 with three teachers and nineteen pupils. Its building was ready by 1861 out in the country north of Bloomington, around which the town of Normal developed. The school went on to become Illinois State University, while Jesse Fell went on to become the main force behind the Lincoln-Douglas Debates and the nomination of Abraham Lincoln for president.

Bloomington's Jesse Fell

♦ Urbana lost out when the route for a railroad was being chosen, but it retained its status as county seat and instead landed, in 1867, Illinois Industrial College, which turned into the University of Illinois. The town beat out Chicago, Bloomington, Lincoln, and Jacksonville for the college by offering 970 acres, county bonds, a building, landscaping, and $50,000 free freight on the railway. When the doors opened on March 2, 1868, there were three teachers and fifty students. The students were expected to put in two hours each day building sidewalks, fences to keep out livestock, furniture for classrooms, and roads.

The University of Illinois

It might have been . . .

♦ Woodrow Wilson, a professor at Princeton, was offered the presidency of the University of Illinois in April 1892. The offer included a salary of $6,000, an expense account, a secretary, and a business manager. But Wilson thought the college was still too agriculturally oriented (a polite way of saying it was a cow college). Because it didn't have an endowment, he would have had to spend a lot of time, like present-day university administrators, begging the legislature for funds. That was distasteful to him, as was the fact that girls were part of the student body. He said to his wife, "I am not at all in sympathy with coeducation."

University of Chicago started as it has continued

♦ A major university was formed in 1891 with contributions of $400,000 from the American Baptist Education Society, $600,000 from John D. Rockefeller, and land from Marshall Field. Rockefeller refused to have his name on the school, so instead of being called Rockefeller University it was called the University of Chicago. Its original purpose of training Baptist missionaries faded away quickly. William Rainey Harper, age only 36, became the university's first president. Harper, determined to make it an outstanding university from the start, paid high salaries, built the best laboratories, and bought library collections.

When the university opened for classes on October 1, 1892, there were 594 students and 103 faculty members. That same day, Amos Alonzo Stagg organized a football team to play high school and YMCA teams. The U. of C. is often called the "teacher of teachers" because almost 90 percent of its graduates go on to graduate study. Many Nobel Prize winners have been associated in some way with the university.

Good-bye "Monsters of the Midway"

♦ Robert Hutchins became president of the University of Chicago in 1929 when he was 30 years old (he had been Dean of Yale Law School at 29), the youngest president of a major university. And he "turned the educational world upside down" during his 22-year tenure. An opponent of over-specialization, pragmatism, and task-oriented education, he thought there was undue emphasis on athletic pursuits in colleges. Hutchins successfully led the fight to abolish intercollegiate sports at the university in 1939, shutting down the famed "Monsters of the Midway." (The varsity football team was reinstated in 1969.) There weren't too many objections because by that time the university had made a proud tradition of losing all its games. Hutchins was chairman of *Encyclopaedia Britannica* from 1943 until 1974 and editor-in-chief of the 52-volume *Great Books of the Western World*, which he developed with Mortimer Adler.

WOMEN IN THE CLASSROOM

Recycling a superintendent of schools

♦ The first woman in the United States to head a major metropolitan school system was Ella Flagg Young, who became Superintendent of Schools in Chicago in 1909. She had been appointed assistant superintendent in 1887 but gave up the position to complete work on her doctorate at the University of Chicago. Returning to the public school system as superintendent, she faced, in common with many superintendents of big city school systems, very vocal opposition to her policies, primarily making decisions without constantly running to the school board for approval. Because of that trait, her six years in office were marked by cycles in which the board would vote "no confidence" in her; she would resign; and they would then rehire her. She finally quit that cycle in 1915. In the meantime, however, in 1910, Young became the first woman president of the National Education Association.

◆ The Jacksonville Female Seminary opened in 1833, the first institution of higher learning for women in Illinois. That same year, the Ladies Education Society was started in Jacksonville. It has been called the oldest women's club in America. Always education-minded, the state's first free public high school was organized in town in 1851.

Jacksonville believes in education

◆ The nation's first female surgeon was Dr. Mary Harris Thompson of Chicago, who began her career in 1865. Avoiding those few cities where women physicians were already established, Dr. Thompson headed for Chicago after her graduation in 1863 from New England Female Medical College. Within two years she founded the Chicago Hospital for Women and Children. As chief physician and surgeon, she performed major surgery herself. The male surgeons of the city reluctantly had to admit that women, at least that woman, were capable of performing surgery.

First female surgeon

◆ The first woman in the United States to graduate from a law school was Ada H. Kepley, who graduated from Union College of Law in Chicago on June 30, 1870. This was a year before Phoebe Couzins, the first woman to graduate from a university law school, won her diploma from St. Louis University.

First female law school graduate

PEOPLE TAKING ACTION

Dr. Leslie E. Keeley, a Dwight physician who had served in the Civil War, started the Keeley Institute in 1880 for the treatment of alcoholics and drug addicts, of which there were many after the war. Joseph Medill, editor of the *Chicago Tribune,* sent six alcoholics to Dr. Keeley on a bet. When the six returned, Medill conceded that "they went away sots, and returned gentlemen." The doctor's "Keeley Cure" became famous throughout the Midwest.

The man with the cure

◆ The first person to organize Jewish women in America was Hannah Greenebaum Solomon. A native Chicagoan, she became a confirmed clubwoman, and she used the occasion of the World's Columbian Exposition to gather as many outstanding Jewish women as she could into a congress, meeting under the auspices of the Parliament of Religions. That meeting became the National Council of Jewish Women. Inez Haynes Irwin says that Hannah Solomon formed the group "to prove to the world that Israel's women, like the women of other faiths, are interested in all that tends to bring men together in every movement affecting the welfare of mankind."

Organizer of Jewish women

From Hull House to the world

◆ Born in Cedarville, Jane Addams lived to make her ideas felt around the world. Determined to do something that would benefit the urban poor, she and her friend, Ellen Starr, bought a rundown mansion on South Halsted in Chicago's slums and turned it into a settlement house called Hull House. She gathered about her women who were determined to make the world a better place for everyone. She said, "If it is natural to feed the hungry and care for the sick, it is certainly natural to give pleasure to the young, comfort to the aged, and to minister to the deep-seated craving for social intercourse that all men feel." She and the women who joined her at Hull House fed people, found them jobs, taught children, and organized clubs of many different kinds. They worked just as hard to get legislation passed that would improve the lot of women, children, and the poor everywhere. The most frustrating task was the perpetual need to raise donations to pay for the work.

A fighter for women's suffrage and a pacifist who fought passionately for world peace, she helped found the American Civil Liberties Union. Once regarded as a gadfly, Jane Addams became honored the world over, and in 1931 became the first American woman to win the Nobel Peace Prize.

First American Boy Scouts

◆ Chicago publisher William D. Boyce of Ottawa founded the Boy Scouts of America in the United States after a visit to England in 1909. Apparently he was assisted on a dark and foggy night in London by a British Boy Scout. He learned about Lord Baden-Powell's efforts and brought back to the U.S. the idea of establishing Scouts. He incorporated the organization in Chicago on February 8, 1910, and from there it spread throughout the nation.

Baking up a winner for Pillsbury

The first woman to win the national biannual Pillsbury Bake-Off Contest was Mrs. Ralph E. Smafield of Rockford, in 1948. She entered the contest with her memorable Water-Rising Twists.

Other Illinois winners include: Mrs. Peter Harlib of Chicago in 1952, with Snappy Turtle Cookies, and Mrs. James S. Castle of River Forest in 1974, who made Savory Crescent Chicken Squares.

Founder of modern feminism

◆ Betty Friedan, born Betty Naomi Goldstein in Peoria, was one of the first of the modern activists to get people to examine women's roles in society, business, families, and even nations. Her book, *The Feminine Mystique,* published in 1963, pointed out that women were trained from birth to be unquestioning about the roles that society gave them. Three years later she founded the National Organization for Women (NOW), which continues to be active in national issues.

THE LIFE OF THE SPIRIT

Another Lincoln story

◆ Lincoln attended a sermon given by pious Rev. Peter Cartwright during his Congressional race in 1846. At the end of his sermon, Cartwright called on all those who were going to heaven to stand up. Lincoln didn't budge. The minister then called on all those going to hell to stand. Again, Mr. Lincoln remained in his seat. Whereupon Cartwright boomed, "I am surprised to see Abe Lincoln sitting back there unmoved by these appeals. If Mr. Lincoln does not want to go to heaven and does not plan to escape hell, perhaps he will tell us where he does want to go."

Lincoln finally stood up and confidently announced, "I am going to Congress."

♦ Swedish fundamentalist Erik Jansson founded Bishop Hill as a utopian settlement in 1846. He believed firmly that the Bible alone must rule life. The immigrants who followed him from Sweden spent their days working and eating in community, but they lived separately in families. The leader was murdered in 1850 by a man whose wife and children had run away to follow Jansson. Jansson's widow proved to be an inept administrator. By 1861 the colony, which had attracted 1,000 immigrants during its first 15 years, was in such disarray that it was dissolved. Many historians say the Swedish colony had a big influence on the later immigration of millions of Swedes and other Scandinavians to the United States. Descendants of early Janssonists started restoring Bishop Hill in the early 1970s, and it is now an important tourist site.

Utopia ends in murder

A spirited young girl, indeed

In 1878 a 13-year-old girl named Mary Lurancy Vennum of Milford, who had been visited by ghosts and spirits for the previous three years, became possessed by the spirit of Mary Roff, the daughter of a family friend who had died twelve years before. Everyone was so accepting of the fact of the possession that the young girl moved in with the Roff family. She knew everything the real Mary would have known, though Mary Vennum had been an infant when Mary Roff died. Several months later, Mary Vennum "awoke" to find herself living in the wrong house. She returned home and, except for brief visits by the spirit of Mary Roff, became her old self again.

♦ Augustine Tolton, born a slave in Missouri in 1854, went to school in Quincy. There he was encouraged to go to Rome to become a Catholic priest. Ordained in Rome in 1886, he returned to Quincy, where he was pastor of St. Joseph's Church. He later founded St. Monica's Church for Negroes in Chicago.

First African-American priest

♦ An Italian nun founded the Missionary Sisters of the Sacred Heart in 1880, but rather than stay home, Mother Frances Xavier Cabrini traveled to New York to minister to the poor Italian immigrants in America. In Chicago Mother Cabrini founded a parish school at the Church of the Assumption, and turned a hotel into Columbus Hospital, where she died in 1917, eight years after becoming an American citizen. Cardinal Mundelein requested in 1928 that the Vatican investigate her merits for sainthood, and she was canonized on July 7, 1946. Her main shrine is at a school she founded in New York City. Unfortunately, one of the worst public-housing projects in the United States, called Cabrini Green, is located in Chicago.

First American saint

Sunday's for the Lord

♦ Billy Sunday got out of Iowa when spotted by the Chicago White Stockings in 1883. He played pro ball for seven years, but somewhere in that time (he told several different stories), the Lord spoke to Billy and said he should be evangelizing in His name. Billy went to work for an evangelist, and learned the ropes, especially those of keeping the audience entertained and the collection plate moving. He incorporated vaudeville turns with prayer, quickly getting the attention (and dollars) of millions of people—long before radio or TV.

Starting on a small scale in tents and county fairs in Illinois, Billy Sunday worked up to full-scale productions in which he railed, frequently using baseball expressions, against every immorality he could find, from alcohol to modernism, to slang, to motion pictures. In the process he drew his audiences into an emotional frenzy that often left them ill—and convinced that Sunday had fought a battle with the Devil inside their souls. Within a period of about twenty years, Sunday spoke directly to more than 100 million people, and millions of them walked forward "claimed by God." But because his biggest enemy was alcohol, people began to lose interest in him when Prohibition started—it just wasn't as much fun hearing him. With a long career behind him, Billy Sunday returned to preaching at county fairs or, in fact, where anyone would listen. He died in Chicago in 1935.

Cross of Peace

♦ One of the highest points of southern Illinois is Bald Knob Mountain, near Alto Pass. In 1937, a postman and a minister spread the word that there would be a sunrise service on Easter Sunday on top of the "mountain," which is more of a hill. That year's moving service led to more and even bigger Easter sunrises, until in 1951, a foundation was created to buy the hilltop and construct the 110-foot-tall Bald Knob Cross of Peace on the site. During the remainder of each year, the U.S. Forest Service uses the top of the cross as a lookout point.

Primetime religion

♦ Probably the only Catholic priest to have had a long-running prime-time nationwide network TV program and to win an Emmy was Fulton J. Sheen, a native of El Paso (that's Illinois, not Texas). Originally named Peter John Sheen, he later took his mother's maiden name as his first name. Actually, Bishop Sheen had two TV programs: "Life is Worth Living" and "Mission to the World." His programs in the 1950s were an unusual combination of anti-Communism and evangelism. Probably one of his most famous converts was Clare Booth Luce, author, congresswoman, and wife of the founder of *Time* magazine. He acknowledged that his success was due to his four writers: "Matthew, Mark, Luke, and John." Long before he became a writer himself, he had served as a parish priest in Peoria.

She picked her spot for eternity

In 1978, Mrs. Lillian Kopp became the first human buried in Paw Print Cemetery, a pet cemetery outside Chicago. Before her death, she expressed her desire to be buried near her beloved dog, Rinty. Thereupon, her whole family decided to make Paw Print the final resting place for the entire Kopp family.

STUDYING PEOPLE

◆ Psychic investigator Manuel Eyre, working with a woman named Mrs. Seymour of Waukegan in 1869, saw her make writing gestures in the air with a finger of one hand. The word she wrote appeared on the skin of her other arm. The letters, raised on the surface of the skin, disappeared after twenty minutes or so. When the phenomenon was investigated by a committee of psychics, they observed that the skin writing seemed real but could come to no conclusions about how it happened.

The skin writer of Waukegan

The tallest known humans

Robert Wadlow was a normal 8 1/2-pound baby when he was born on February 22, 1918, in Alton, where his father was the mayor. But then he began to grow and didn't stop. He was the size of an adult when he started kindergarten. Finally diagnosed as uncontrollable pituitary-gland secretion, the problem sent Wadlow zooming to 8-feet-11- inches in height and 491 pounds, though he looked thin. In his final years, the gentle man traveled for the shoe company that began making his special shoes (size 37 AA) when he was twelve. It was because of his traveling job that Wadlow was in Michigan when his body's systems shut down, and he died at age 22. He was buried in Alton in a 10-foot coffin.

Don Koehler, a native of Denton, Missouri, was a resident of Chicago as an adult. At 8 feet 2 inches, he was, according to the *Guinness Book of World Records,* the fifth tallest person in the world. He also lived longer than any other 8-footer, living from 1925 to 1981.

◆ Naturopath Dr. Robert A. Wood believed that an enema, or colonic irrigation, would cure any disease from syphilis to cancer to mental illness. When he became president of the American Naturopathic Association, he vigorously promoted colonic irrigation as the "greatest fever reducer" and natural cure for disease. When coupled with the ingestion of raw cow's milk, distilled water, fruit and vegetable juices, and chlorophyl enemas could result in miraculous healing.

The "enema king"

SEARCHING THE HEAVENS

◆ Astronomer George E. Hale was responsible for some of the most famous astronomical observatories and telescopes in the U.S. Born in Chicago in 1868, he graduated from MIT in 1890 and shortly thereafter organized the Kenwood Observatory in Chicago. He convinced Chicago streetcar magnate Charles Tyson Yerkes to build a large observatory now known as the Yerkes Observatory in Williams Bay, Wisconsin. He planned and built (with the help of funds from Andrew Carnegie) a larger telescope on Mount Wilson near Pasadena, California, in 1908. Because of the urban growth of Los Angeles, Hale located another site for an observatory, Mount Palomar, and persuaded the Rockefeller Foundation to pay for a huge telescope. When Hale died in 1938 before its completion, the 200-inch reflecting telescope at Mount Palomar was named for him.

The man who loved telescopes

Perseverence, Percival, and Tombaugh

◆ Astronomer Clyde Tombaugh, whose family in Streator was too poor to send him to college, was the discoverer of the planet Pluto in 1930. He was able to get a job at Lowell Observatory in Flagstaff, Arizona, without a degree. There, he spent long hours, day after day, comparing hundreds of thousands of dots of light on photos of the heavens, looking for the Planet X that Percival Lowell had predicted must exist. On February 18, 1930, he found the moving dot of light and knew he had found the mysterious planet. Tombaugh still wanted academic credentials. After his discovery of the ninth planet in our solar system, he was awarded a scholarship to the University of Kansas and was able to get his degrees. Ultimately he became a full professor of astronomy at New Mexico State University.

Preparing for the space age

◆ Dutch-American astronomer Gerard Peter Kuiper, on the faculty of the University of Chicago, was instrumental in stirring up new interest in the solar system before the beginning of the "space age" of the 1950s. His main field of expertise was the satellites of planets and their atmospheres. He discovered several satellites of Neptune and Uranus; an atmosphere on Titan, the largest satellite of Saturn; and the fact that Pluto was smaller than most astronomers thought. In 1951, he theorized that planet satellites had formed as independent condensations of gas not connected to the mother planet. This theory ultimately replaced the idea that moons are broken-off pieces of the mother planet.

EXTRATERRESTRIALS

The backyard astronomer

◆ Now we take radio telescopes for granted (at least those who care about such things do), but it wasn't so long ago that the very first one was constructed in a Wheaton backyard. Born in 1911 in Wheaton, Grote Reber became completely fascinated with the discoveries of Karl Jansky, the man who found that there were radio waves coming from space. Reber started playing with the discovery and tried to bounce radio waves off the moon. Attracted by the idea of capturing some waves, he constructed an instrument in his backyard in 1937 that would collect and receive radio signals from space. Using his home-built device, he discovered "stars" that emit radio signals but cannot be seen.

The search for ET

Astronomer Frank Drake, born in Chicago, conducted the first organized search for extraterrestrial life. From April to June 1959, Drake kept the 85-foot radio telescope at the U.S. National Radio Astronomy Observatory near Greenbank, West Virginia, turned toward two stars about eleven light years from Earth. They had been chosen because they resemble our sun and might have planets in orbit around them. The project was called Ozma, because Oz is a "mythical land far away." Extraterrestrial life is still in the realm of myth.

◆ Astronomer J. Allen Hynek, born in Chicago, spent much of his working life treading a fine line between serious astronomy (he was made a professor of astronomy at Northwestern in 1960) and what some might call the "lunatic fringe." Hynek was teaching at Ohio State University when Air Force types from Wright-Patterson Air Force Base in Dayton invited him to participate in the air force's study of unidentified flying objects. They wanted him to "weed out" obvious astronomical phenomena. He remained fascinated and open minded. Of all the UFO sighting that have occurred, he said in his own book, "I can establish beyond reasonable doubt that they are not all misperceptions or hoaxes." That didn't mean he thought they were visitations by extraterrestrials—he was just willing to keep checking and see what happened. In 1973, Hynek established the Center for UFO Studies in Evanston.

The astronomer with the open mind

◆ Members of the Ancient Astronaut Society, based in Highland Park, are dedicated to the study of ancient astronauts, space travelers who supposedly visited Earth in ancient times, according to Erich von Däniken's book *Chariot of the Gods*. The members look for evidence to support their beliefs that it was these astronauts who produced such creations as the statues on Easter Island and the great pyramids. Some believers in ancient astronauts even suggest that these space travelers created the human race by mating with Earth animals. Others feel that the biblical story of Adam and Eve is actually an account of ancient astronauts attempting to create a perfect race. The society was formed in 1973 and holds a yearly conference in Chicago.

Ancient astronauts in Highland Park

The inside-outside world

Cyrus Teed, originally from Utica, New York, promoted the theory that we are actually living on the inside of the Earth and that he was a messianic messenger anointed to bring this truth to mankind. The followers who joined Teed called themselves the Koreshan Movement after his book, *Illumination of Koresh: Marvelous Experience of the Great Alchemist at Utica, New York*. He established a commune called Koreshan Unity in Chicago in 1886. He attracted, or perhaps mesmerized, many converts, 75 percent of them women. Several years later he founded the new world capital of his inside-out world, Estero, near Fort Myers, Florida. This "New Jerusalem" was to accommodate 8 million inhabitants, but by Teed's death in 1908 only 200 had settled there.

INTO SPACE

◆ James A. McDivitt was born in Chicago in 1929. He joined the air force, was a combat pilot in Korea, and had all the experience necessary when the National Aeronautics and Space Administration put out a call in 1962 for more astronauts after the first Mercury Seven astronauts survived the first few American spaceflights. McDivitt was the pilot of 1965's Gemini 4 flight, during which an American astronaut made the first walk in space. He was the commander in 1969 of the Apollo 9 flight that checked out the lunar module before the first flight to the moon.

First Illinoisan in space

And more

◊ Eugene Cernan, born in Chicago but raised in Maywood, piloted the Gemini 7 mission in 1966, Apollo 10's trip around the moon in 1969, and the final Apollo 17 mission in December 1972. He walked in space on both the Gemini and the last Apollo missions.

Chicagoan Thomas Mattingly II (born 1936) flew on Apollo 16, the fifth lunar-landing flight, in 1972. He also was a space shuttle pilot for two flights, one of which was a secret military mission.

Joseph P. Kerwin, born in Oak Park in 1932, participated in a month-long sojourn on Skylab 2, the orbiting research laboratory, during which he walked in space.

First African-American woman in space

On September 12, 1992, the space shuttle Endeavor was launched into orbit. Aboard it was Dr. Mae Jemison, a physician-astronaut who was born in Decatur, Alabama, but grew up in Chicago. A Stanford University graduate in chemical engineering, she went to Cornell University to earn her medical degree. Jemison then spent several years in the Peace Corps, working as a doctor in Sierra Leone and Liberia. She gave up her Los Angeles medical practice in 1987 to become an astronaut. During the flight she did a variety of medical experiments, including one on herself—she took no motion-sickness medicine and used mind over matter to fight the nausea that most astronauts experience.

Other Illinois-born space shuttle astronauts and mission specialists include:

Carl J. Meade, born Chanute Air Force Base, 1953
Steven R. Nagel, born Canton, 1946
Charles Lacy Veach, born Chicago, 1944

INTO THE NUCLEUS OF THE ATOM

Preparing for the Bomb

◊ A man ahead of his times, chemist William Harkins, a professor at the University of Chicago in 1912, predicted the existence of the neutron in the nucleus of an atom. Through his work in determining the structure of a nucleus, he was the first to deduce the process of nuclear fusion, which is the basis of the thermonuclear bomb. He was also among the first scientists to try to calculate the proportion of elements in the universe.

Physicist Arthur Dempster of the University of Chicago discovered in 1935 the isotope of uranium U-235, which played a role in the bomb.

When Hitler came to power, physicist Maurice Goldhaber left Germany and became a professor at the University of Illinois in 1938. Working on the possibility of splitting neutrons in atoms, he discovered that the element beryllium could slow down speeding neutrons and thus make it easier to fission uranium-235 by bombarding it with neutrons.

The start of the nuclear age

◊ "The Italian navigator has reached the New World" reported the University of Chicago's Dr. Arthur Compton to the head of the U.S. Office of Scientific Research and Development on December 2, 1942. With that cryptic message Compton was telling the government that

Italian-born scientist Dr. Enrico Fermi, working in a laboratory under the stands of the University of Chicago's Stagg football field, had successfully controlled a nuclear chain reaction for the first time. The message was in secret code because the ultimate goal of the research (and the Manhattan Project, of which it was part) was to develop an atomic weapon that might play a major role in the war.

Fermi had earlier discovered that he could make an atom of uranium give off radioactivity by blasting it with neutrons. For that work he had received a Nobel Prize. The ceremony to receive it in Sweden allowed Fermi and his Jewish wife to escape from fascist Italy. Very soon thereafter, however, Germany announced that Nazi scientists had split the atom. Albert Einstein, also an immigrant, warned the U.S. government that Germany could possibly put the new process, called nuclear fission, to work in a weapon. The government agreed to fund Fermi's research, which was later moved to the University of Chicago.

Fermi's accomplishment in creating a self-sustaining nuclear reaction meant that a new kind of bomb could be developed. Eventually the work led to the development of nuclear electric power. Fermi, who won a Congressional Medal of Merit in 1946, died in Chicago in 1954 at age 54. The Atomic Energy Commission's top prize, of which he was the first winner, is now called the Fermi Prize. In addition, chemical element number 100 was named fermium in Enrico Fermi's honor.

Nobel Prize-winning novelist Pearl Buck told the story of the people and events leading up to the first controlled nuclear chain reaction in her 1959 book *Command the Morning.*

More high-powered research

♦ Argonne National Laboratory was founded in 1946 west of Chicago in what is now the town of Argonne. It was established to carry out research into peaceful uses of nuclear energy after the worldwide shock of seeing its impact as a weapon on two cities in Japan. Operated by the University of Chicago and a group of about thirty other universities for the U.S. Department of Energy, the laboratory does research into environmental, life, and physical sciences; nuclear fusion and fission; conservation of fuels; and renewable and fossil fuels. It employs about five thousand people and covers close to four thousand acres. Argonne has a branch facility at Idaho Falls, Idaho.

This 180-ton superconducting magnet at Argonne National Laboratory is one of the world's largest. It is used for advanced energy research.

A dubious record

♦ Illinois has more nuclear power plants and greater nuclear-energy generating capacity than any other state. There are 13 plants, supplying more than 50 percent of the energy needs of the state. The first plant to open in Illinois was Dresden Nuclear Power Station, near Morris, which went on-line in 1958 and is still providing power to a major portion of northern Illinois.

Speeding protons at Batavia

Fermilab, or the Fermi National Accelerator Laboratory, located at Batavia, is a high-energy physics research facility. Its mission is to shatter protons to see what holds them together and what happens when they break apart. In one of the largest particle accelerators in the U.S., about one thousand electromagnets in a long, half-buried, helium-cooled tube, accelerate the 800 billion-electron-volt protons, until they travel at almost the speed of light.

MORE ILLINOIS SCIENTISTS

Opening a new world of exploration

♦ Geologist John Wesley Powell was a professor of geology first at Illinois Wesleyan in Bloomington and then at Illinois Normal College (later Illinois State University) at Normal. As a teacher at Normal, he put together an expedition to explore the Colorado River by boat. In 1869, he and his group became the first white men to face the rapids on the river that runs through the bottom of the Grand Canyon, during a three-month exploration of the canyon. It was his writings that made the world realize what a spectacular treasure the Grand Canyon is. One of the first scientists to investigate American Indian languages, Powell was the first director of the Smithsonian's Bureau of Ethnology and of the U.S. Geological Survey.

You've heard of illinium?

♦ Chemical element number 61 was historically pretty elusive. Two Italian scientists thought they discovered it in 1924 and proudly named it florentium, after their beloved city of Florence. Then chemist S. B. Hopkins of the University of Illinois located a mineral in an ore that he found to be different from florentium. Claiming it was actually element number 61, he named it illinium, after the state of Illinois. But finally that discovery, too, turned out to be a fluke. It was not until 1946 that physicists at Oak Ridge, Tennessee, isolated the true element 61 in the fission of uranium. They named it promethium.

A bevy of Illinois scientists

♦ • Jacksonville-born geneticist Alfred Sturtevant was one of the first scientists to warn about the health hazards of nuclear fallout.

• University of Illinois biochemist William Rose showed in 1930 that amino acids play an essential role in the body.

• Springfield-born astronomer Seth Barnes Nicholson discovered the ninth, tenth, and eleventh satellites of Jupiter.

• Russian defector Vladimir Ipatieff, working for Universal Oil Products Company in Chicago, developed high-octane gasoline from "poor" gasoline.

• African-American chemist Percy Julian synthesized physostigmine, a glaucoma drug, in 1935 and became the Glidden Corporation's director of research in Waukegan.

• LaSalle-born astronomer James Keeler proved that the rings of Saturn aren't solid but are made up of separate particles.

NOT SHY ABOUT NOBEL PRIZES

❖ University of Chicagoans won three Nobel Prizes for Economics in a row. 1990's prize went to Merton Miller, a business professor. 1991's went to law professor Ronald Coase, and then 1992's went to economics prof Gary Becker. The Economics prize, which was started in 1969, was won by three other U. of C. professors between 1969 and 1990.

A run of luck

❖ One of the more versatile of prominent Illinoisans was Charles Gates Dawes. An Ohio native, he moved to Evanston at age 30 and lived there the rest of his life—at least when he was home. As a reward for organizing President McKinley's campaign in Illinois, he was appointed to a banking position in Washington. Harding appointed him the first director of the budget. Later, his scheme to keep the economies of European countries from collapsing in the 1920s was called the Dawes Plan, for which he received the 1925 Nobel Peace Prize. By that time, he had been elected vice president of the United States, serving with Calvin Coolidge. And what is this illustrious man best known for today? An amateur musician, he composed a song in 1912 that he called "Melody in A Major." In 1958 it was recorded by Tommy Edwards under the name "It's All in the Game."

Illinois's first Peace Prize to a songster

❖ James Watson was known as a child prodigy and radio "quiz kid" around Chicago. He entered the U. of C. at age 15, graduating in 1947. The famous geneticist and biochemist shared the Nobel Prize for Medicine and Physiology in 1962 with Francis Crick and Maurice Wilkins, for their discovery of the now-famous spiral double-helix molecular structure of DNA, or deoxyribonucleic acid. Being able to visualize the structure has allowed scientists to understand how genes can duplicate themselves and form new chromosomes and thus how heredity happens. The discovery has been described as being as important to the future as Columbus's opening of the New World. Watson wrote his personal story of the discovery in *The Double Helix*. In the photo, Watson (left) and Crick stand in front of a huge model of the DNA structure.

The man who described DNA

The first American Nobel Prize scientist

♦ German-American physicist Albert Abraham Michelson was only four years old when he came to the United States with his parents. Although he graduated from the U.S. Naval Academy, his real love was science, not seamanship. In 1878 he began pursuing his life's mission, the accurate measurement of the speed of light. Later, he became the first head of the department of physics at the newly organized University of Chicago, where he worked from 1892 to 1929. He was rewarded for his optical studies with the Nobel Prize in Physics in 1907, becoming the first American to receive a Nobel Prize for science.

Illinois's first native-born Nobel Prize winner

♦ Physicist Robert Millikan, who was born in Morrison in 1868, was not planning a career in physics. After he graduated from Oberlin College with a degree in Greek, he taught at the school for several years because there wasn't a qualified teacher. He fell in love with physics and obtained the first Ph.D. in physics granted by Columbia University in 1895. He became a professor at the University of Chicago in 1910. Millikan is most famous for his oil-drop experiment through which he was able to determine the amount of the electrical charge on a single electron. He also proved Einstein's photoelectric equation. He received the Nobel Prize for Physics in 1923. When he died in 1953, Millikan was acknowledged not only for his scientific contributions but also as one of the few scientists who tried to reconcile science and religion.

Illinois's double Nobel Prize winner

♦ Physicist John Bardeen, born in Madison, Wisconsin, was a professor at the University of Illinois from 1951 to 1978. He was the first person in the world to twice be awarded the Nobel Prize for Physics. As one of the discoverers of the transistor, he shared the 1956 prize with William Shockley and Walter Brattain. In 1972, he again shared the Nobel Prize for his work in superconductivity. The initials of Bardeen and co-winners Leon Cooper and John Schrieffer are used in the term "BCS theory," which is the fundamental basis of superconductivity.

Discoverer of the quark

♦ Chicago-born and -educated physicist Jerome I. Friedman became involved at Stanford University with Henry Kendall and Canadian Richard Taylor. Using the Stanford Linear Accelerator Center, they were able to prove that protons, neutrons, and electrons in atoms are actually made up of something smaller, a unit called a quark. The three of them shared the 1990 Nobel Prize for Physics.

Other Nobel laureates born in Illinois

♦ Many Nobelists have done some or all of their work in Illinois, especially at the University of Chicago, but others were born in Illinois:
- Chemist Clinton Joseph Davisson, born Bloomington, 1881
- Biochemist Edward Doisy, born Hume, 1893
- Chemist Paul John Flory, born Sterling, 1910 (see pg. 98)
- Physicist Edward Purcell, born Taylorville, 1912
- Biochemist Stanford Moore, born Chicago, 1913
- Chemist Robert Holley, born Urbana, 1922
- Physicist Ben Mottelson, born Chicago, 1926
- Physicist John Robert Schrieffer, born Oak Park, 1931

THE ARTS

Where civilization builds, the realm of the arts grows, too—and Illinois has artists in full measure. Best-selling novelists such as Ernest Hemingway, Andrew Greeley, Sidney Sheldon, Scott Turow, Irving Wallace, and John Jakes were born in Illinois. Early Chicago was the center of the music publishing business; today the city can boast the fledgling talents of Quincy Jones and Lionel Richie. For those to whom art means painting, Illinois has two extremes—worldwide recognition of the animation art of Walt Disney and one of the greatest art museums in the world, Chicago's Art Institute. Poets and playwrights, both black and white, contribute mightily to the literary heritage of America.

Come and dabble. The arts are available to all.

- With Brush, Pen & Clay
- Skyscraper Capital
- Send Forth Cartoonists
- Whole Notes and Half
- Words Turn into Prizes
- Poetry in the Soul
- Stories to Tell
- A Swerve in the Mainstream
- Speaking to the Children

WITH BRUSH, PEN & CLAY

The world's longest piece of art

❦ John David Mooney's *Great River Project* is a plan for a piece of art that should be happening any day now, if Mooney succeeds. "Happening?" Yes. Like Christo's work, Champaign-native Mooney's art happens instead of just being. In 1990, he had several dozen arc lights dancing in the sky over the Chicago River in celebration of American Airlines' new terminal at O'Hare Airport. His "Lightscape '89" filled the entire IBM Building in Chicago with colored lights in different rooms, making a gigantic, three-dimensional canvas. But the *Great River Project* is intended to be a months-long work of art consisting of 15 barges moving from Chicago to the Gulf of Mexico. On the barges will be paintings, sculptures, musical pieces, dance and drama performances commissioned from around the world. Mooney's dream may happen—if he can find enough corporations to support the project.

Definitely not a purist

❦ In 1936, sculptor George Gray Barnard donated a group of classical statues to the town of Kankakee. The school principal, a bit of a prude, tried to get their classical anatomy covered with clothing. A long, public, and very acrimonious controversy ensued, which the principal ultimately lost. The Greek figures remained in their marble birthday suits.

The art of evil

The Carl Hammer Gallery in Chicago sells art by people who have been or are in prison. Joliet's Stateville Correctional Center, a tough maximum security prison, has a painting and ceramics program which serves as the gallery's "talent pool." While serving time for drug dealing and a shooting, inmate Hector Maisonet from Humboldt Park has made several thousand dodllars by selling his beautiful acrylics and figurines. Another inmate, Arkee Chaney, admitted that he probably wouldn't have become a criminal if he'd known he was artistically talented. His African masks and clay statuettes are unique.

Now-deceased murderer of eight nurses on the south side of Chicago, Richard Speck wasn't in the prison program but painted anyway. He sold his paintings with the distinctive "R. Speck" for as much as $500 to collectors fascinated by the criminal mind. All Speck wanted, however, was money for cigarettes.

Anthropology turns her into a sculptor

In perhaps the largest commission ever given to an artist in modern times, Malvina Hoffman was contracted in 1930 by the Field Museum of Natural History in Chicago to create more than 100 life-sized figures of various racial types. She spent two years traveling the world, studying people everywhere and making sketches. The former student of Auguste Rodin then spent three more years sculpting the figures and casting them in bronze. The bronze bust shown here is of a bedouin man from North Africa.

One of the great monument sculptors of the last century was Elmwood-born Lorado Taft. Son of a geology professor at the U. of I., Taft worked with stone, often using allegorical themes for his great works. He gained major public notice in 1893 with decorative groups sculpted for the Columbian Exposition. A teacher at the Art Institute, he had his studio on the University of Chicago campus, where the building is now a national monument. The artists' colony called Eagle's Nest that Taft and his friends founded at Oregon in 1898 is now part of Northern Illinois University. An Elmwood park contains his bronze work *Pioneers of the Prairies*. On its base are the words: "To the pioneers who bridged the streams, subdued the soil and founded a state." His 48-foot-tall *Black Hawk* stands on the Rock River (see page 36).

A monumental talent

SKYSCRAPER CAPITAL

Chicago shows the world how to build upward

New York may have more of them, but Chicago had the first and now it's got the biggest—skyscraper, that is. Architecturally, the skyscraper is Chicago's most important contribution to urban life. The first dictionary definition of "skyscaper" said, "A very tall building such as are now being built in Chicago." In 1883, construction started on the Home Insurance Company building, built by Chicago's William leBaron Jenney. The ten-story building was the first to use a metal framework to bear the weight of the exterior masonry and walls. The walls supported no weight.

German-American architect Ludwig Mies van der Rohe built the first glass-and-steel skyscraper. He eliminated all the outer facing and siding and kept just the essential steel frame and glass. Two apartment buildings on Lake Shore Drive built about 1951 introduced this concept to the world. After Mies van der Rohe built the Seagram Building in New York in 1956, the world embraced his concept.

The tallest building in the world, shown at the right, is the Sears Tower, built 1971-74. It rises 110 stories, or 1,454 feet. Its design has been described as "a clutch of nine squared cigarettes of varying lengths banded together." It includes a 1,700-seat cafeteria that fills two-thirds of an acre and 102 elevators.

Prairie style in the city

Famed architect Frank Lloyd Wright designed 25 of the 120 buildings that are in the Frank Lloyd Wright Prairie School of Architecture National Historic District in Oak Park. His home and studio, located at 951 Chicago Avenue, Oak Park, are included in the district as well. Both became a testing ground for the Wisconsin-born architect whose experiments with design meant the buildings were under continuous remodeling from the time they were constructed in 1889 through 1911.

The 1902 unveiling of the Willits House in Highland Park featured what would become Frank Loyd Wright's distinctive trademark style, that of long, low interiors. Today, that style is known as "Prairie Style" architecture.

In the 1950s, just before his death, Wright unveiled his plan for a mile-high skyscraper to be built in Chicago. He is shown here working on a sketch for the project. No one has attempted to build it yet.

SEND FORTH CARTOONISTS

The world of Walt Disney started in Chicago

Movie-maker extraordinary and amusement-park magnate, Walt Disney was born in Chicago. But perhaps it was only at his grandfather's farm in Missouri that he got a big enough surface to try out his cartooning ideas—he used the barn door. His older brother, Roy, persuaded Walt to move to California and start a business. The creation of "Steamboat Willie," who became Mickey Mouse in 1927, saved his young studio from ruin. (Disney wanted to name the animated character "Mortimer," but his wife's choice overrode his.)

During his lifetime Disney received 39 Oscars (the most ever) and 4 Emmys. The first full-length animated film, *Snow White and the Seven Dwarfs* (the plural was always "dwarves" until Disney decided otherwise), was presented a special Oscar, accompanied by seven miniature-sized Oscars, one each for dwarf! When Walt died in 1966, he was supervising the construction of DisneyWorld in Florida. There are very few places where Disney's characters are unknown.

Comic strips

1 Cartoonist Bud Fisher, a Chicago native, was the creator of the first true comic strip. On November 15, 1907, Fisher began the bizarre adventures of a rather loutish racetrack tout named "Mr. A. Mutt." The following year he met an equally simpleminded gentleman named Jeff—where else but in an insane asylum. The terms "Mutt and Jeff" now indicate two people of vastly different heights.

2 The comic strip that became a stage musical and then a movie was created by Kankakee-born cartoonist Harold Gray. Working originally as an assistant to "Andy Gump" creator Sidney Smith, Gray introduced "Little Orphan Annie" in 1924. The stories he created for her and her wealthy champion, Daddy Warbucks, were among the first comics that were deadly serious instead of whimsical or fantastic.

3 First there was "Thimble Theatre," a comic strip drawn by Chester resident Elzie Crisler "E.C." Segar, starting in 1919 for King Features. It featured a family made up of Olive Oyl, her parents, an idiot brother, and a fiancé named Ham Gravy. Olive had still not married in 1929 when the family journeyed to Africa by ship. On the journey, a bit player named Popeye the Sailor Man was introduced on January 17, 1929. Popeye was patterned after Chester fighter Frank "Rocky" Fiegel. Popeye's first appearance in an animated cartoon was released on July 14, 1933, as part of a "Betty Boop." The large statue (shown on the right) of the spinach-loving sailor is located in the Segar Memorial Park in Chester, overlooking the Mississippi River.

4 1924 was a bounty year for Illinois cartoonists. Chicagoan Chic Young (known to his mother as Murat Bernard) began to produce "Blondie," which, of course, also featured her husband, Dagwood. Young's boss at King Features thought he was "the greatest storyteller of his time since the immortal Charles Dickens." The story of Blondie and her man goes on—in 1992 Dagwood Bumstead quit the job he had held for 68 years to work for his wife.

5 Cartoonist Chester Gould's outrage at gangster Al Capone's activities spurred him to create, in 1931, what would become one of the best-known fictional detectives, "Dick Tracy." The comic strip, the first to present violence in such a medium, first appeared in the *Detroit Daily Mirror* on October 4, 1931. Gould, who retired in 1977, lived in Woodstock, Illinois, from 1935 until his death in 1985.

⚜ Helen Hokinson, a native of Mendota, appeared in *The New Yorker* magazine regularly for almost 25 years, starting with the first issue. The daughter of a farm equipment salesman, she drew often-captionless cartoons showing the trials and tribulations of naive, big-bosomed, suburban clubwomen. One of the first major female cartoonists, she died in a very strange airline crash. She was on her way to speak in Washington, D.C., on November 1, 1949, when an air force fighter just purchased by Bolivia crashed into her airliner. All 55 aboard were killed.

Observations at an afternoon tea

⚜ Political cartoonist Herblock was born in Chicago as Herbert Lawrence Block. He got his start at the *Chicago Daily News,* but spent most of his working life attached to the *Washington Post,* where he was close to the figures he portrayed in his trenchant political cartoons. Republicans were convinced that he was a dedicated Democrat, and Democrats knew that he was a closet Republican. Herblock coined the term "McCarthyism." He won Pulitzer Prizes in 1942, 1954, and 1979.

Drawing "some of the deepest blood in Washington"

WHOLE NOTES AND HALF

⚜ Black composer Florence Beatrice Smith Price, a Chicago resident, was the first black woman to have a work, *Symphony in E Minor,* performed by a major orchestra—the Chicago Symphony Orchestra. Marian Anderson made many of Price's compositions famous.

The big time

From Africa to East St. Louis

As a student in anthropology at the University of Chicago, Katherine Dunham was sent to the West Indies to study ritual dance, and there she discovered a whole new world of dance that stemmed from the life of the people rather than a formalized stage presentation. The African-American woman became a professional dancer in her own right, developing a troupe that traveled the world from 1938 to 1964, showing audiences everywhere her own special combination of ballet, modern dance, and native and tribal dances. She is credited with founding the famed Ballet Folklorico of Mexico. A Kennedy Center Honoree in 1983, Dunham doesn't separate dance from the rest of life. In 1992, at age 83, the dancer fasted for 47 days in protest against the U.S. policy of forcing Haitian refugees to return to their home island. She lives in East St. Louis, where the Katherine Dunham Museum displays instruments and other artifacts from nations around the world.

Creating a great orchestra—and dying of it

German-born Theodore Thomas founded the Chicago Symphony Orchestra in 1891, making it the third-oldest symphony orchestra in the nation. Eastern friends who saw the renowned violinist and conductor head for Chicago thought that was the end of a promising career. Through his influence with a group of 8,500 wealthy Chicago patrons, he was able to raise the money to build the Theodore Thomas Orchestra Hall, designed by Daniel Burnham. When the building opened in 1905, some say he was so upset over the acoustics that he died of a broken heart. He conducted only three concerts in the new building.

Chicago songwriters made the nation weep

Chicago songwriter and publisher Henry Clay Work wrote "Come Home, Father" in 1864. The sappy, yearning lyrics pleaded with a drunk father to come home from the saloons, and the song became a favorite with temperance workers the nation over. Less popular with half the nation was Work's other big hit, "Marching Through Georgia." His moving "Grandfather's Clock" is still played by would-be pianists.

Another major songwriter of the time also came to Chicago to work. George Frederick Root's hits were equally memorable: "Tramp, Tramp, Tramp" and "Just Before the Battle, Mother."

Carrie Jacobs Bond epitomizes the sweet little lady of the Victorian era though she lived until World War II. A Wisconsin woman who was widowed at an early age and left with a son to support, she moved to Chicago and opened a boardinghouse. When she couldn't quite make it on that income alone, she also handpainted china pieces to order. She still had time for social occasions, however, and at those her friends enjoyed hearing her sing her own sweet songs. Those same friends lent her the money to publish them. Her book, *Seven Songs as Unpretentious as a Wild Rose*, was published in 1901 and became an immediate hit. One song from that collection, "I Love You Truly," is still frequently sung at weddings.

🎝 A blackface comedian, "Honey Boy" Evans, a native of Streator, was head of the Cohan and Harris minstrel show that traveled America about 1900. He wrote the music to "In the Good Old Summertime."

An important person in Tin Pan Alley and early Hollywood, composer Richard Whiting was born in Peoria in 1891. One of his most popular songs is "Till We Meet Again." At least 50 of his songs appeared in movies, including Shirley Temple's "On the Good Ship Lollipop" and Jack Benny's theme song, "Hurray for Hollywood."

Classic popular music by Illinois natives

🎝 Born in England but raised in Chicago after age 7, young Julius Stein was a child protegy on the piano and even played with the Chicago Symphony. However, he turned to popular music and jazz after he discovered that his hands weren't going to grow enough to handle classical music with true ease. Changing his name to Jule Styne, he began playing nightclubs and composing in high school. Michael Todd. He played with Benny Goodman and Glenn Miller before being lured to Hollywood by Darryl F. Zanuck. Eventually turning to Broadway, Styne composed with such writers as Sammy Cahn, Frank Loesser, and Stephen Sondheim. His shows include *Gentlemen Prefer Blonds, Bells are Ringing, Peter Pan, Gypsy,* and *Funny Girl.*

It's only a step from Chicago to Broadway

🎝 Three Chicago-area popular musicians worked together to create one of the most successful songs ever written. Native Chicagoan Quincy Jones, Joliet resident (transplanted from Alabama) Lionel Richie, and Michael Jackson, originally from neighboring Gary, Indiana, combined their talents to write "We Are the World," which was the theme of the internationally broadcast 1985 LiveAid concert to benefit starving children in Africa.

"We Are the World"

🎝 Quincy Jones, a native of Chicago, has won more awards than any other musican of his time. A composer, conductor, arranger, and trumpeter, he produced *Thriller* by Michael Jackson. He's been nominated for 74 Grammys —the greatest number of times in history, and has won 26. He also wrote the score of *The Color Purple.* From earliest childhood when his mother was institutionalized, Jones has had to fight serious difficulties, including two brain surgeries. He allowed some of the problems of his life to be revealed in the film *Listen Up: The Lives of Quincy Jones.* In 1992, Jones was working with Time-Warner to create a new magazine for the rap and hip-hop generation, called *Vibe.* He was in charge of music for President Clinton's inauguration.

The talented Mr. Jones

WORDS TURN INTO PRIZES

🎝 Two very erudite brothers were born in Hope about a hundred years ago. Carl Van Doren, born 1885, became a biographer, winning a Pulitzer for his biography of Benjamin Franklin in 1938. His younger brother, Mark, born 1894, won the 1939 Pulitzer for poetry for his *Collected Poems.* Both men were fully involved in American literature, Carl serving as the editor of the classy *Cambridge History of American Literature* and Mark writing biographies of Thoreau and Hawthorne.

The brothers Van Doren

The macho man Nobel Prize- and Pulitzer Prize-winning novelist and short-story writer Ernest Hemingway was born in Oak Park in 1899. One of the rare writers whose life became fascinating to the public—especially his involvement with bullfighting and other "masculine" enterprises—he went to Europe in World War I (when he was turned down for military service because of a bad eye) as a driver of a Red Cross ambulance. Remaining in Europe after the war, he wrote *The Sun Also Rises. A Farewell to Arms* was a love story as well as a war epic. *For Whom the Bell Tolls* grew out of the Spanish Civil War. Always popular, Hemingway failed to win a Pulitzer Prize until 1952, when his short novel, *The Old Man and the Sea,* was published using background information he acquired while living in Cuba. Two years later he was awarded the Nobel Prize for Literature. In a state of depression, Hemingway committed suicide in 1961 in his cabin in Idaho, following in the steps of his physician father, who had shot himself in 1928.

A Sterling reputation

Be it in the water or in the air, there's definitely something suspicious (in a positive light) going on in Sterling. Author Jesse Lynch Williams was born there in 1871 and penned the first play to ever be awarded the Pulitzer Prize, for the 1917 production of *Why Marry?* The play was based on his 1914 novel *And So They Were Married.* Not to be outdone, Odell Shepard, who was also Sterling-born in 1884, won the 1937 biography Pulitzer for *Pedlar's Progress, The Life of Bronson Alcott.* In 1978, Sterling-born Don E. Fehrenbacher won a Pulitzer Prize for history for *The Dred Scott Case.* In 1910 chemist Paul Flory was born in Sterling (well, he wasn't a chemist when he was born). Together with Wallace Carrothers, he won the Nobel Prize in Chemistry for the development of synthetic rubber, neoprene, and nylon.

More Pulitzers for Illinoisans

- Alison Lurie of Chicago, won in 1985 for *Foreign Affairs.*
- Robert Lewis Taylor of Carbondale won for his 1958 novel, *The Travels of Jamie McPheeters.*
- Chicagoan Ernest Poole's novel, *His Family,* won in 1917.
- Novelist Margaret Ayer Barnes, born in Chicago, won in 1931 for *Years of Grace.*
- Chicagoan James Gould Cozzens won the 1949 prize for *Guard of Honor.*
- Chicagoan David Mamet's 1984 Pulitzer-winning drama, *Glengarry Glen Ross,* became a movie in 1992.
- Allan Nevins, born in Camp Point, won two Pulitzers for biographies of Grover Cleveland in 1932 and Hamilton Fish in 1937.
- Chicagoan Ernest Samuels got his Pulitzer for his 1964 biography of Henry Adams.
- Poet James Schuyler of Chicago, won in 1980 for *The Morning of the Poem.*
- Vernon Louis Parrington, born in Aurora, won a history Pulitzer for *Main Currents in American Thought* in 1927.
- Evanston-born drama critic Walter Kerr, who was as well known for his humorist wife, won a Pultizer for criticism.

And there's lots more in the pages that follow.

POETRY IN THE SOUL

❧ When John Greenleaf Whittier visited the Mark Curtis family of Sheffield in June of 1868, he got his inspiration for "The Barefoot Boy." A small, young, Danish farmhand wore oversized overalls with the pant legs rolled up and a straw hat. A good-natured worker, he whistled while he worked in his bare feet. Whittier, fascinated, asked to take his picture. While coming home from church one Sunday with Whittier, Mr. Curtis passed by the lad and was heard to say, "There goes the barefoot boy."

> Blessings on thee,
> little man,
> Barefoot boy, with
> cheek of tan!
> With turned-up
> pantaloons,
> And thy merry
> whistled tunes.

Lindsay walks at midnight

❧ Vachel (Nicholas) Lindsay wandered from his Springfield birthplace in the early 1900s to become a vagabond poet, traveling on foot

across the United States. Legend says that he sold his sketches and gave poetry readings in exchange for meals and lodging. He was the first American poet to be invited to attend Oxford, in 1920. Walking tours of the South taught him the "gospel of beauty," and gave birth to one collection, *Adventures While Preaching the Gospel of Beauty*. He wrote the well-known poem "Abraham Lincoln Walks at Midnight," as well as a favorite poem of children, "Johnny Appleseed." His heavily rhythmic poetry had become old hat and he was losing popularity when he committed suicide on December 5, 1931, in Springfield. His home is now a museum.

❧ One of America's most famous books of poetry is Edgar Lee Masters's *Spoon River Anthology*. Masters lived much of his life in Lewistown, and wrote a collection of poems telling of the lives of great and humble people and places in and around Lewistown. The poems are written as if the disillusioned spirits of the dead in Oak Hill Cemetery were speaking of their lives. When *Spoon River Anthology* was published in 1915, a number of citizens recognized themselves portrayed in an unfavorable light in Master's clever epitaphs. The book was banned in the local library for a while. The anthology is frequently produced by little theater groups as a drama, with ghosts of the people speaking from their graves.

The spirits of the dead spoke to him

Before publishing his bitter but memorable poems in 1915, Masters worked in Chicago as Clarence Darrow's law partner. His book *Lincoln the Man* was not well-received by critics. Masters, who died in 1950, is buried in Petersburg with Ann Rutledge and poet Vachel Lindsay.

Carl Sandburg

With a folk song along the way

Son of a Swedish-immigrant blacksmith in Galesburg, Carl Sandburg began working for his father at age 11. He didn't graduate from junior high or high school, yet he went to Lombard College for four years. Though he didn't graduate from college, he acquired several dozen honorary degrees over the years. After leaving home, Sandburg traveled the country as a hobo, listening to America, taking some time out to work on different newspapers and serving as secretary to the socialist mayor of Milwaukee, Wisconsin, for a few years. Although his poetry had been published since 1904, he didn't become well-known until his poem "Fog" appeared in Harriet Monroe's *Poetry* magazine in 1914. The following year, his *Chicago Poems* established him as a first-rank poet. In it, he gave Chicago its famous nickname: "Hog Butcher for the World." In 1918, he won the Pulitzer Prize for *Cornhuskers.*

Always listening for the sounds of America, Sandburg collected two books of folk songs, the *American Songbags.* He won another Pulitzer in 1940 for the last volume of his six-volume biography of Abraham Lincoln. His third Pulitzer was won in 1951 for his *Complete Poems.* Behind the Galesburg house where he was born is Remembrance Rock, his gravesite, named for Sandburg's only novel, which told the saga of American history.

Mother Monroe and the poets

Influential editor and writer Harriet Monroe was one of the leading forces in the development of modern poetry—an activity she took on out of necessity. The Chicago-born, unassuming woman of many talents was already in her fifties in 1912 when she gathered her courage and talked her friends into contributing funds to start a new magazine. *Poetry: A Magazine of Verse*, said one critic, "quickly became the leading poetry journal in the English-speaking world." Every important poet of the time was published in the journal, including Ezra Pound, Robert Frost, T. S. Eliot, and James Joyce. An inveterate traveler, Harriet Monroe died in the Inca ruins at Cuzco.

❦ Many people remember him only for such poems as "The End of the World," "Ars Poetica," and "You, Andrew Marvell," but Glencoe-born Archibald MacLeish was a virtual Renaissance man. A professor at Harvard, he also worked as a journalist, won three Pulitzer Prizes for poetry, served as Librarian of Congress (which is not just an honorary post), and was Assistant Secretary of State, during which time he actively supported the United Nations. His 1959 verse play, *J.B.,* the biblical story of Job in modern dress, was a sell-out on Broadway. MacLeish, who once played football, said, "From the beginning of my more or less adult life, I have been plagued by the fact that I seem to be able to do more or less well things which don't commonly go together."

Poet to a nation

❦ Always interested in poetry, Gwendolyn Brooks, who was born in Kansas but lived in Chicago from infancy, had her first poem published at age 13. Growing up in the black community gave Brooks ample material to compose poetic portraits of the African-American experience. In 1950, she became the first black woman to earn a Pulitzer Prize, for a collection of poems entitled *Annie Allen,* about a young girl growing up. Her novel *Maud Martha* also told of similar experiences. In 1969, Brooks was appointed Poet Laureate of Illinois.

Illinois's poet laureate

STORIES TO TELL

❦ Richard Wright is considered one of the most important black authors of our time, probably the first African-American protest writer. Born in Nachez, Mississippi, he was an errand boy who used his white employer's library card to obtain the works of Sinclair Lewis and Theodore Dreiser. Migrating to Chicago, he wrote for the Federal Writers' Project. His greatest book, *Native Son,* published in 1940, was the story of a Chicago black man who accidentally kills a white girl. It was dramatized for Broadway by Orson Welles. Wright's autobiography, *Black Boy,* was published in 1945, before he moved to Paris.

**Black protest
from a Chicagoan**

❦ To anyone who grew up in the '50s, the beach scene from the movie of Robinson-born James Jones's novel *From Here to Eternity* was infinitely sexier than all the virtually real sex scenes that appear in today's movies. The novelist, James Jones, joined the army right out of high school, and the huge, sexy, compelling novel was based on his experiences in the Pacific during World War II (the beach scene, too?). The film, which put Frank Sinatra on a comeback trail, won eight Academy Awards. Jones used his Illinois background in another long, long, good, good novel, *Some Came Running.* English teachers have often disliked Jones's novels because he had his characters use bad grammar when speaking to make them seem real.

**The writer who helped
change the movies**

Parish priest turned best-selling novelist

The writer who still insists that he's a simple priest, Andrew Greeley, was born in Oak Park in 1928. Ordained in 1954, he served in a parish only a short while before becoming a lecturer in sociology at the University of Chicago, from which he earned his doctorate. He began his writing with several books on the plight of teenagers in contemporary American culture. However, he scandalized many Catholics in 1981 when he published the first of his novels, *The Cardinal Sins.* In each of his almost annual best-selling novels he has tracked the story of one member of a vast, interrelated network of characters who live in Chicago, all within the same Irish-Catholic culture. Even his mysteries and fantasy novels tie into the same group of fictional characters that are influential in the political and Catholic life of the city. In 1991, the "simple priest" donated $2 million to the University of Chicago, though he has maintained an attachment to Loyola University.

History on a paperback shelf

Had Chicago-born author John Jakes continued to write advertising for Abbott Laboratories, which he did from 1954 to 1960, the action-packed "American Bicentennial Series" might never have been written. Luckily for his fans, Jakes followed his true calling and began writing fiction instead, giving us the series that includes *The Bastard, The Rebels, The Seekers, The Furies,* and *The Titans,* to name a few.

The man who does it all

Samuel Shepard Rogers is multitalented actor and writer, who was born at Fort Sheridan in 1943. He authored a variety of one-act plays beginning in 1964, one of which, "Rock Garden," was incorporated into the first all-naked Broadway hit, *Oh, Calcutta!* Rogers earned a Pulitzer Prize in 1979 for *Buried Child.* In the acting community he is better known as Sam Shepard. He appeared in *The Right Stuff,* for which he wrote the screenplay in 1983. He also co-starred in *Country* with his wife, actress Jessica Lange.

A SWERVE IN THE MAINSTREAM

Granddaddy detective

Philip Marlowe, the epitome of the hard-boiled detective—which was such a break from the mystery tradition of English noblemen and tea cozies—was invented by Chicagoan Raymond Chandler. All other such detectives since Chandler's time owe their existence to him. His two most popular Marlowe books, *The Big Sleep* and *The Lady in the Lake,* have been equally popular movies. Much of Humphrey Bogart's image came from his role as Marlowe in *The Big Sleep.* Chandler also wrote the screenplays for the Alfred Hitchcock classic *Strangers on a Train* and Billy Wilder's *Double Indemnity.* Though raised in England, Chandler returned to the U.S. to become an oil-company executive before he started publishing stories in the pulp magazine *Black Mask.*

Jungle fantasy on Mars?

Edgar Rice Burroughs, born in Chicago in 1875, was a would-be entrepreneur who tried his hand at many things but succeeded only at writing. His first novel, *A Princess of Mars,* was written as he waited for business to pick up in one of his failing enterprises. Never satisfied with dealing with normal life, he then tried his hand at a jungle story featuring an infant English nobleman who is abandoned in the jungle and grows up to be Tarzan. Although Burroughs lived in California (where a town is named Tarzana based on his ape-man) on and off, he owned homes both in Chicago and Oak Park. He was living in Oak Park when *Tarzan of the Apes* was published. At age 66 he served as the oldest newspaper correspondent in the Pacific during World War II.

At what temperature do books burn?

Ray Bradbury knew. He told us in the title of his great science fiction novel, *Fahrenheit 451*. Waukegan-born Ray Bradbury is also the author of the oft-filmed *Martian Chronicles*. Just as successful in another writing career, Bradbury earned an Oscar for his screenplay of *Moby Dick*. The author is in Waukegan's Walk of Fame.

One of the great ones

A Raisin in the Sun, published in 1959, is the first play by a black woman ever to appear on Broadway. Lorraine Hansberry's play was based on her own experiences growing up in Chicago. As her theme, she used the Langston Hughes poem about a "dream deferred" drying up "like a raisin in the sun." Her parents challenged the status quo in the 1930s by buying a house in a white neighborhood. They had to take the purchase all the way to the U.S. Supreme Court in order to get the sale completed, but the neighborhood had other ideas and often attacked the house and the family. Hansberry, who was only 29 when her play was published, died of cancer at the age of 35 before she could see major changes in the racial situation of the United States. The scene at the right is from a 25th-anniversary production of *A Raisin in the Sun* at Chicago's Goodman Theatre.

SPEAKING TO THE CHILDREN

St. Louis-born humorist, journalist, and poet Eugene Field worked primarily as a newspaper columnist in Chicago in the late 1800s. Hired as a special writer on the *Chicago Daily News Record* in 1883, he enjoyed poking fun at any of the barons of Chicago industry who, in Field's estimation, needing taking down a peg or two. Intended as satirical humor was a collection of poems that he published in 1889, *A Little Book of Western Verse.* Included in it were several poems which caught the attention of children, such as "Little Boy Blue" and "Wynken, Blynken, and Nod." To his perpetual dismay, this man of the biting wit was known ever after as a children's poet, and he came to regret that he had ever written those poems. Lincoln Park contains a monument to Eugene Field.

The man who hated Little Boy Blue

Every child needs one

When John Gruelle's beloved daughter, Marcella, died suddenly, he took an old rag doll she had found in the attic, drew a face, and pinned an "I Love You" heart on the doll's chest. That was the beginning of Raggedy Ann. Gruelle, born in Arcola in 1880, patented his Raggedy Ann doll and the entire family got into its production. In 1918, the Raggedy Ann stories and the doll were put on the market with instant success. Until he died in 1938, Johnny Gruelle put out one Raggedy Ann story each year. After Gruelle died, his wife, Myrtle, established the Johnny Gruelle company to continue the Raggedy Ann legacy. Today Arcola celebrates Johnny Gruelle through its Raggedy Ann Festival held each year in June.

A bit of the Old West

Before becoming a TV show, even before becoming a radio show, *Hopalong Cassidy* was a long and very popular series of novels by Streator-born author Clarence E. Mulford. Hoppy first appeared in 1907 in the novel *Bar-20.*

The poet who speaks to the funny bone

It's a far cry from being a cartoonist during the early years of *Playboy* magazine to one of the most popular children's poets ever, but that's the leap that Shel Silverstein has made. The versatile Chicagoan, whose real name is Shelby, created the parable *The Giving Tree* and two required-for-all-children books of illustrated poems, *A Light in the Attic* and *Where the Sidewalk Ends.* The man with the weird mind also wrote the song "A Boy Named Sue."

Top medal for children's authors

Marguerite Henry, who won the 1949 John Newbery Medal, spent most of her writing life in the rural town of Wayne. There she was able to keep the horses that she loved and which she wrote about in her books. Her medal-winning book was *King of the Wind.* Other favorites include *Brighty of Grand Canyon, Justin Morgan had a Horse,* and *Misty of Chincoteague.*

Some other Illinoians who were awarded Newbery Medals for their quality young adult books include:

Irene Hunt, born in Pontiac, who won in 1967 for *Up a Road Slowly.*

Cornelia Meigs, born in Rock Island, who won in 1934 for *Invincible Louisa.*

Elizabeth Enright, born in Oak Park, who won in 1939 for *Thimble Summer.*

THE ENTERTAINERS

The Blues Brothers were Jake and Elwood Blues, played by John Belushi and Dan Aykroyd. In the film of the same name, the brothers were raised in a West Side Chicago orphanage and learned how to sing the blues as teenagers. When they find out that the orphanage is facing tax problems, they decide to pull together their old band and put on concerts to raise the money. The plot takes wild twists and turns through various Chicago locations including Maxwell Street, Lower Wacker Drive, Lakeshore Drive, and the Daley Center.

Chicago means entertainment and entertainment means Chicago. The two have been synonymous for a hundred years or more. Illinois has long been the birthplace of fine actors, memorable comedians, and great ideas in film and television. They're all here—but be sure to also see "Illinois—Day by Day," starting on page 172 for information on Illinois's celebrities.

- Live, On Stage
- The Comedians
- The Dance
- Jazz
- The Pop Music Scene
- Legends of the Screen
- Oscar Comes to Illinois
- Illinois at the Movies
- Looking at Chicago in Films
- Center of the Radio Universe
- TV Time
- Television World in Illinois

LIVE, ON STAGE

They flew through the air

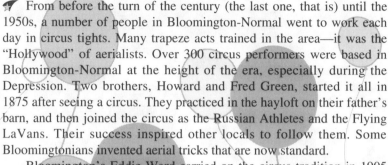

From before the turn of the century (the last one, that is) until the 1950s, a number of people in Bloomington-Normal went to work each day in circus tights. Many trapeze acts trained in the area—it was the "Hollywood" of aerialists. Over 300 circus performers were based in Bloomington-Normal at the height of the era, especially during the Depression. Two brothers, Howard and Fred Green, started it all in 1875 after seeing a circus. They practiced in the hayloft on their father's barn, and then joined the circus as the Russian Athletes and the Flying LaVans. Their success inspired other locals to follow them. Some Bloomingtonians invented aerial tricks that are now standard.

Bloomington's Eddie Ward carried on the circus tradition in 1905 when he and his sister, Jennie, built a practice barn in town, training and managing a whole generation of aerialists. Ward and his wife, Mayme (the first woman to do a double somersault), were noted for training women performers. One of their famous students, Mickey King, was known for spinning by one arm high above the crowd—her record was 276 spins. Her sister, Antoinette Concello, was almost ready to become a nun when she saw her sister perform in Detroit . . . and found a new goal. Ward trained Antoinette into becoming the greatest woman high flier and the first woman to do a triple somersault.

Girls, girls, girls

He didn't write songs, he couldn't sing, he didn't dance, but he certainly knew how to put on a show. Chicagoan Florenz Ziegfeld was the showman extraordinaire of Broadway for almost three decades. Starting with *The Follies of 1907*, he demonstrated that girls, and more girls, were always the answer to drawing an audience—along with as much public relations as the traffic would bare. He made Anna Held, a beautiful Frenchwoman, famous long before she appeared on his stage, and then married her. During twenty-five years of annual Follies productions in New York, the Great Ziegfeld introduced many other stars, including Billie Burke (whom he also later married), Eddie Cantor, Will Rogers, W.C. Fields, and Fannie Brice. The photo, from the film *Ziegfeld Follies,* featuring Fred Astaire, shows the grandiosity of Ziegfeld's stage visions.

☛ There have been three Miss Americas from Illinois:

1927 - Lois Delaner of Joliet was only 16 years old and a junior in high school.

1969 - Judith Anne Ford of Belvidere was the first blond Miss America in ten years, a fact to which some people objected—somehow they figured that it was more Miss American to be brunette. Frank Deford, writing in *There She Is*, noted that "To many Pageant conservatives it seemed that the judges had gone slumming" when the winner was someone who performed on the trampoline.

1991 - Marjorie Judith Vincent of Oak Park, the daughter of Haitian immigrants, was a law student at Duke who worked the summer before the big pageant at a Wall Street internship.

Here she comes!

THE COMEDIANS

☛ Anyone over the age of 39 will remember Waukegan's own special comedian, Jack Benny. From vaudeville to radio to Hollywood to television, the man born Benny Kubelsky spent well over 39 years making people laugh. Probably the first comedian to let the outside world know that writers wrote his great one-liners, he didn't have to give anyone else credit for his delivery or the famous "look." Waukegan first acknowledged its native son by naming a junior high school after him. The town has a Jack Benny Center for the Arts at 39 Jack Benny Drive, and in 1992, it put Benny in its Walk of Stars.

☛ Accountant-turned-comedian (what's funner than an accountant?) Bob Newhart made his name (and won a Grammy) with his 1960 album, *The Button-Down Mind of Bob Newhart.* Many of his routines portrayed a person talking on the telephone. Since his first TV show in 1961, the Chicago-born Newhart has always had his own name on the show. His first non-plot stand-up comedy show was "The Bob Newhart Show." It was followed in 1972 with another "The Bob Newhart Show." From 1982 to 1990, his sitcom was called "Newhart," and he started a fourth series, called "Bob" in 1992. The second and the fourth shows used Chicago as the setting.

It's the Bob Show!

☛ *Ebony* magazine said of African-American comedian and actor Richard Pryor's introduction of black humor to a wider audience that he "mirrors the black condition without exploiting it." Born in Peoria in 1940, he spent his early childhood in a brothel run by his grandmother. His biting street-corner humor became the stuff of nightclubs and TV —at least as long as he refrained from obscenities, which he wasn't always willing to do. The winner of Grammys for five comic albums, Pryor eventually fell victim to cocaine addiction, though not before he was in a number of movies. After disappearing from view for several years, Pryor began to appear again in 1992, playing in nightclubs again, despite being afflicted with multiple sclerosis.

Biting black humor

The famed Second City was a cabaret featuring improvisational comedy, established in 1959 in a second-hand Chinese laundry. Its early days of satire produced Elaine May and Mike Nichols. Later products of Second City introduced Dan Aykroyd, Chevy Chase, and Gilda Radner.

THE DANCE

**Even Lincoln danced,
well, kind of**

When Lincoln was courting Mary Todd he once asked her to dance by saying, "Miss Todd, I should like to dance with you in the worst way." He wasn't a good dancer—fairly clumsy and awkward—and as he returned Miss Todd to her group of giggling friends, they asked, "Well, Mary, did he dance with you in the worst way?" To which she replied, "Yes, the worst way!"

**Hoofer turned
animal protector**

After the death in 1918 of Vernon Castle, of the world-famous dancing pair of Irene and Vernon Castle, his widow and partner, Irene (Foote) Castle, gave up dancing and married a Chicago business-man. As she raised a family, she began the activity that was to interest her the rest of her life—rescuing animals. She founded Orphans of the Storm in Deerfield and regularly held dances and other fund-raiser activities to operate the shelter, which took in many animals that would have otherwise been put to death in municipal dog pounds. The story of her dancing life was told in the 1939 movie, *The Story of Vernon and Irene Castle,* with Ginger Rogers playing Irene and (surprise!) Fred Astaire playing Vernon. In 1958 she published her autobiography, *Castles in the Air.*

**Dance, draperies,
and adoration**

Best known for being the person under the voluminous skirts and floating draperies seen at the Folies-Bergère and other interesting spots around Europe and the United States, Loie (real name: Marie Louise) Fuller was born in Fullersburg (a burg later incorporated into Hinsdale) in 1862. Loie, a child prodigy on the stage, found adulthood hard to deal with until she discovered that she could be "different"—and thus draw crowds—by dancing in huge quantities of material under—or over—interesting lights. Even though she didn't remove her draperies, she was immensely popular in Paris, where she lived most of her later years. Fuller was a transitional dancer between classic dance and the sheer modernism of Isadora Duncan, who danced with the Illinoisan's troupe as a beginner.

**The woman who
danced as a fruit bowl**

Her childhood in East St. Louis did little to prepare Josephine Baker (originally Freda Josephine McDonald) for a life on the stage. But racial tensions in that city in the early part of the century encouraged her to run away from home. Making it to Broadway as a dancer and comedienne, she gained enough renown to take her to Paris. Her dark skin made her seem exotic to the French, who made her the toast of Paris for almost forty years. She often made her entrance in such clubs as the Folies-Bergère wearing rather limited costumes that were gradually shed as she sang and danced. One time she appeared clothed only in fruit. Although Josephine Baker never achieved the recognition in the United States that she wanted, she returned to America and was actively involved in the equal rights movement of the 1960s.

🎵 Geneva-native Gower Champion and his wife, Marge (born Marjorie Celeste Belcher in Hollywood, where her father was Gower's dance teacher), were the most popular dance team of the 1950s. They met in junior high in Los Angeles, and as adults were ready to make the move from nightclubs to television with bubbling ease. Though Gower once said "we are almost repulsively in accord," the pair were divorced in 1973. Gower Champion won Tonys for his choreography for *Lend an Ear* in 1948, *Bye, Bye, Birdie* in 1961, and *Hello Dolly* in 1964. He died of a rare blood disease in 1980, just hours before the Broadway opening of *42nd Street,* a production which also won a Tony.

The dancer from Geneva

🎵 Chicago-born dancer-turned-choreographer-turned-director-turned-producer Bob Fosse got his first job choreographing for Broadway by lying to producer George Abbot about his experience. His talent at lying got him the job on *Pajama Game,* for which Fosse won a Tony. He went on to win more of them for *Pippin, Dancin', Damn Yankees, Sweet Charity,* and *Redhead.* He also won an Academy Award in 1972 for directing the movie of *Cabaret.* He told much of his own life story, including alcoholism and a heart attack, in the film *All That Jazz.*

Lies and all that jazz

JAZZ

🎵 Mel Torme, nicknamed "The Velvet Fog," began singing at age 4. He organized the Mel Tones, wrote some songs ("The Christmas Song," "Lament to Love"), made several movies, and became somewhat successful. It wasn't until he found his niche in jazz that he became popular and, he says, "the world of music . . . opened up for me." Though he rarely appeared on the show, he was an ever-present spirit to Judge Harry Stone on "Night Court."

The Velvet Fog

🎵 After starting in New Orleans, all true jazz came out of the night clubs of Chicago's South Side. Almost all great jazz bandmen grew up or learned their trade in Chicago—Sidney Bechet, Benny and Harry Goodman, Louis Armstrong, Hoagy Carmichael, Freddie Keppard, Louis Panico, Eddie Condon, Jess Stacy, Rapolla and Teagarden, and Ben Pollack. From Chicago they spread to New York, Hollywood, and the world.

Chicago jazz

🎵 One of the best-selling jazz albums of all time was recorded live when Chicago clarinetist Benny Goodman took jazz to the stage at New York's Carnegie Hall in the 1930s. It was the heyday of the big bands, and Benny put together a group of musicians (including African-Americans, which was an innovative move) who were later recognized as among the finest in jazz history. The first part of his story was told in the movie *The Benny Goodman Story* (with Steve Allen as Goodman), for which he recorded the sound track. "The King of Swing" was the first jazz musician to play in the Soviet Union, where Khrushchev didn't like his sound but the young people did. Throughout the years, Goodman never left classical music entirely, frequently doing concerts of clarinet concertos and other nonjazz works.

The Goodman sound was a Chicago sound

The drumbeat of jazz

🎵 Though he didn't get together with Benny Goodman until they were both in New York, jazz drummer Gene Krupa was, like Goodman, a Chicagoan, born in 1909. He got sidetracked temporarily by the idea of being a priest, but then his drums took him to the nightclubs. After playing with Goodman for several years (including the famed Carnegie Hall concert), Krupa left to form his own band in 1938. Chicago song stylist (that's fancier than a singer) Anita O'Day joined Krupa's band, bringing her jazzy style with her, for some of the greatest jazz recordings of all time. Krupa was several times voted the nation's outstanding drummer.

Sexy made good music

🎵 It was the big band era. But only one of the great bands was made up of all female musicians conducted by a woman—Ina Ray Hutton's. The Chicago-born woman put together her band in the 1930s, but it wasn't terribly well-received. Gradually she added men, and by 1940 she stood before an all-male orchestra in a slinky, low-cut gown, making music that was great for dancing.

Singer June Christy was known for her "cool" jazz sound. She became popular in 1945 when singing for the Stan Kenton Orchestra. Born in Springfield as Shirley Luter, she began singing with a local group at age 13. She was discovered in Chicago singing in a small club by Anita O'Day. Christy's signature song was "Something Cool."

Evil genius of jazz

🎵 Jazzman Miles Davis, born in Alton in 1926, started out as a classical trumpeter, but he discovered jazz, not in Chicago, but at the Juilliard School of Music in New York. His talent was extraordinary, but his attitude toward the rest of the world, including his audiences, caused him to be called "the Evil Genius of Jazz." He had a knack for putting together the right artists to get just the right, new sound on his recordings, which always worked, and sold.

THE POP MUSIC SCENE

Elvis is definitely being seen

Clark Stafford of Seneca has gone from truckin' and tradin' to hustler (in more ways than one) of a 10-foot-tall concrete statue of Elvis. Created by Florida ironworker-turned-folk sculptor T. J. Neil, the statue caught Stafford's eye while he was vacationing in Florida in January 1992, and he knew right then that he had found his future. Stafford offers his cumbersome Elvis to parades, groupie parties, and any other event that might benefit from having concrete evidence of Elvis's continued existence. Stafford benefits to the tune of $400 per showing.

When harmonicas were big stuff

🎵 One of the more unusual musical groups was the Harmonicats, which, with an obviousness rarely found today in the names of musical groups, played the harmonicas. The members, all Chicagoans, were Jerry Murad, Al Fiore, and Bob Nes. They had a hit record with the old-time favorite, "Peg O' My Heart," in 1945.

No overnight success, Frankie Laine has observed, "Those of us who didn't hit quick with one record had time to survive a series of misfortunes and starvation. By the time we were lucky and made it, we were pros." The Chicagoan (born Frank Paul Lo Vecchio) had already been at it for ten years when he recorded "That's My Desire," and finally hit it big. His biggest hit was the 1948 novelty song, "Mule Train."

The mule train to fame

Sam Cooke, often called the "father of today's soul music," wrote and sang a 1957 #1 hit record, "You Send Me." Born in Chicago in 1935, Cooke started singing with a gospel group called the Soul Stirrers. He soon became a teen idol for black teenagers and then was able to introduce soul to a wider audience. However, before Cooke could top his own first hit record, he died in 1964 at a Los Angeles motel. He was bludgeoned to death by the owner of the motel after the owner's wife shot him, shouting accusations of rape.

Spreader of soul music

The jazz-rock group called Chicago began as Chicago Transit Authority at DePaul University, formed by Walt Perry, Dan Seraphine, Walt Parazaider, Lee Loughnane, Jim Pankow, and only one musician not from Chicago, Robert Lamm, who hailed from Brooklyn. Their first album had the same name as the group, which riled Da Boss, Mayor Richard J. Daley, because Chicago's subway and bus system is called the Chicago Transit Authority. Forced to change, they just shortened their name to Chicago. The group made it to #1 in 1976, just before the mayor died, with "If You Leave Me Now." They had another #1, "Look Away," in 1988.

Mass transit

♪ **Johnny Gilmer** of Johnny Gilmer and the Fireballs was born in Chicago but raised in Amarillo, Texas. He hit the #1 position on the pop music charts in 1963 with "Sugar Shack."

♪ **Kevin Cronin** was born in Evanston in 1951. He was the main songwriter and founder of the group REO Speedwagon, which had a #1 hit in 1981: "Keep on Loving You."

♪ **Gene Chandler**, who was born Eugene Dixon in Chicago in 1937, had a #1 hit in 1962 with "Duke of Earl."

And some more who made it to #1

FarmAid

At the LiveAid concert to benefit people in Africa, Willie Nelson suggested that the entertainers should contribute their time to benefiting farmers in America. The resulting FarmAid concert, organized by Nelson and John Mellenkamp, was held in Bloomington on September 22, 1985. It featured Bob Dylan, Billy Joel, Johnny Cash, B.B. King, and Roy Orbison.

LEGENDS OF THE SCREEN

From bad guy to dad

✍ One of the most consistent actors in Hollywood, with rarely a down time in work, Fred MacMurray, originally of Kankakee, started his career as a saxophone player in a jazz band. Though most frequently a heavy in his early movies in the '30s and '40s, MacMurray became best known as a comedy actor and, later, as the father on TV's "My Three Sons." He was married to actress June Haver for many years.

The manufacturing process

✍ Actress Kim Novak, starred with Jimmy Stewart in several romantic mysteries back in the 1950s, was a product of Hollywood, just like her movies. Born in Chicago in 1933, Marilyn Pauline Novak went to Hollywood as a model, just when Columbia producer Harry Cohn—ruthless in an era when the studios could dictate an actor's life—decided he would create a glamorous star to take the place of Rita Hayworth. In walked Novak, with classical beauty and a great figure. He changed her hair, her name, and her eyebrows and started the publicity machine rolling. Within three years she was the number-one box office favorite.

The first of the strong, but fake, names

✍ Romantic Hollywood lead Rock Hudson was born in Winnetka as Roy Scherer, Jr., whose name was later changed to Fitzgerald after his mother remarried. In California, driving a truck, young Fitzgerald was found by an ever-hopeful agent, whose hope worked for him . . . at least once the handsome truck driver learned to read a line. Audiences discovered Rock (a name he took from a particularly prominent and durable one called Gibraltar) could act in *Giant,* which won him his only Oscar nomination. But women preferred him with Doris Day in *Pillow Talk.* Hudson and Susan St. James had a TV series, "McMillan and Wife," (1971 to '77). He played a San Francisco police commissioner.

Hudson was the first big Hollywood actor to die of AIDS, on October 2, 1985. Homosexual, he had briefly married his agent's secretary to keep suspicions hushed, when such a suspicion could kill a career. After his death—the harbinger of many more to come—Hollywood became more active in the fight against AIDS.

The girl with one name

Swedish-born beauty Ann-Margret was raised in Fox Lake and Wilmette—part of the time living in a funeral parlor. After a decade of charming, fluffy comedy film roles, she proved to critics that she could act in *Carnal Knowledge.* Her husband, Roger Smith, has since managed her career.

The Blues Brothers

✍ Actors John Belushi and his younger brother Jim were born in Chicago, John in 1949, and Jim in 1954, and raised in Wheaton. John became famous on "Saturday Night Live" and starred in the classic film *The Blues Brothers* with Dan Aykroyd (see page 105). Jim also appears in movies and worked on the program in the years following John's death of an overdose of drugs on March 5, 1982. He is buried at Martha's Vineyard, Massachusetts. The story of his hectic life and tragic death is told in *Wired,* by Illinoisan Bob Woodward.

OSCAR COMES TO ILLINOIS

The town of Quincy has produced interesting things, including Lucile V. Langhanke. Huh? The actress better known as Mary Astor often teamed in silent films with John Barrymore. But even more widely known was her penchant for love affairs (including one with playwright George S. Kaufman), especially after her diary, which recorded some of her sexual doings, was widely quoted in 1936 when her husband was suing for divorce and custody of their child. The judge refused to admit the diary in to evidence because of its obscenity, but her husband's lawyers made certain that it was widely quoted in newspapers. Mary won the suit, however, because her husband's affairs, though not recorded in pornographic detail, were just as easily proved. Although scandal frequently killed careers at that time, Astor went on to win an Oscar for the *The Great Lie* in 1941, the same year she made *The Maltese Falcon* with Humphrey Bogart. Mary Astor finished her 50-year career in movies with *Youngblood Hawke* in 1964.

Talent won out over scandal

Carl Sandburg called Burl Ives "the mightiest ballad singer of any century," but his sheer bulk and acting ability brought Ives many roles, both on Broadway and in Hollywood. The Hunt Township-born singer started playing the banjo and listening to folk music as a child. He collected folk music and tales in his books *Wayfaring Stranger* and *Tales of America.* Though he was in many plays and movies and won a Best Supporting Actor Oscar for *The Big Country* in 1958, he is best remembered in the role of Big Daddy in *Cat on a Hot Tin Roof.*

Ballads and Big Daddy

Marlee Matlin, born in Morton Grove, was the first deaf person to win an Oscar for an acting role. In 1987, she won the Best Actress Oscar for *Children of a Lesser God,* her very first acting job. At the 1988 Oscar presentations, after intensive speech therapy, she spoke on camera for the first time without signing, depending on her speech alone. Born in Chicago with normal hearing, Matlin lost her hearing from measles when she was 18 months old. She was educated in criminal justice at Harper College, a background she uses to benefit in her role in the TV series "Reasonable Doubts." The first deaf person to lead in a major TV series, Matlin is adamant that she is not a deaf actress, but an actress who is deaf.

No handicap for Matlin

- Mercedes McCambridge, born Joliet, Best Supporting Actress for *All the King's Men* in 1949 (and the voice of Satan in *The Exorcist*).
- William Holden, born William Franklin Beedle, Jr., in O'Fallon, Best Actor for *Stalag 17* in 1953.
- Dorothy Malone, born Chicago, Best Supporting Actress for *Written on the Wind* in 1956.
- Charlton Heston, born Evanston, Best Actor for *Ben-Hur,* 1959.
- Jason Robards, Jr., born Chicago, Best Supporting Actor for *All the President's Men* in 1976 and for *Julia* in 1977.
- Elizabeth McGovern, born Evanston, Best Supporting Actress for *Ordinary People* in 1980.

More Oscar-winning actors from Illinois

ILLINOIS AT THE MOVIES

Thumbs up for Roger Ebert

🖘 Movie critic Roger Ebert (who, with his partner, Gene Siskel, started the "thumbs up" way of rating movies) was born and grew up in Urbana. In his annual volume of *Roger Ebert's Movie Home Companion,* he frequently makes reference to being an avid movie-goer on Saturday afternoons in Urbana. Ebert is the only film critic to have won a Pulitzer Prize for his work.

Chicago is its own satire

🖘 Satirist-in-charge-of-the-1940s, Preston Sturges, born Edmund Preston Biden in Chicago, got his start on Broadway in 1929, but he discovered quite quickly the greater versatility of Hollywood. His first Oscar came for a Chicago-related story, *The Great McGinty,* the tale of a man who manages to sell his vote many times over in one mayoral election, putting himself on the path to becoming governor. Hmmmm.

Zorro came from Ottawa?

🖘 Yup. Johnston McCulley, who would later write many novels and screenplays, was born in 1883 in Ottawa, where he let his imagination run wild. The result was numerous romantic adventures both in novels and on the screen. The longest lasting hero in movies and on TV was his do-gooder, Zorro, who first appeared in *The Mark of Zorro.*

LOOKING AT CHICAGO IN FILMS

A day off in Chicago, by a Chicagoan

🖘 Many of the familiar landmarks of Chicago—Sears Tower, Wrigley Field, the Art Institute, the Board of Trade—are showcased in the 1986 film *Ferris Bueller's Day Off,* starring Matthew Broderick. Ferris Bueller is a suburban high school student who skips a day of school to go to the Loop to try help to his friend gain some self-respect in spite of his father's suffocating materialism. The movie was written, directed, and produced by Chicago-born John Hughes.

Two years earlier, Hughes had been successful in getting Skokie authorities to open up the shuttered, unused high school, Niles East. It was temporarily cleaned up for the filming of his 1984 movie, *Sixteen Candles,* starring Molly Ringwald.

The other side

🖘 The 1990 movie *Flatliners* was shot in and around the neo-Gothic buildings of the University of Chicago. This setting helps create the science fiction mood as young medical students decide to learn what it's like on "the other side" by clinically dying and then being resuscitated. It stars Keifer Sutherland and Julia Roberts.

Affluent Chicagoland

🖘 Set in suburban Lake Forest, the novel *Ordinary People* by Judith Guest explores the communication problems in family relationships. In the movie version, the successful Chicago attorney is played by Donald Sutherland and his wife by Mary Tyler Moore. After the death of their oldest son in a boating accident, no one in the family adjusts to the loss, nor do they talk about their feelings. On the surface, love and family harmony in a beautiful, well-to-do suburb is taken for granted. The Oscar-winning film was actor Robert Redford's directorial debut.

Chicago—a great place for making films

Many more movies are now made in Illinois than used to be because Mayor Richard J. Daley (he's the original one) objected. Now it's a favorite place to film because the city cooperates and the scenes are not so overdone as New York. Look for the city in:

Adventures
  in Babysitting
The Apprentice
The Breakfast Club
Backdraft
Bad Boys
Big Shots
The Big Town
Bix Beiderbecke
Candyman
Chains
Child's Play
Club Paradise
Code of Silence
The Color of Money
Come Around
Continental Divide
Cooley High
Curly Sue
Damien — Omen II
Death in California
Dennis the Menace
Desire
Dutch
End of the Line
Endless Love
Escape from New York
Excessive Force
Field of Dreams
Flatliners

Folks
The Fury
Gladiator
Groundhog Day
Hambone and Hilly
Heartbreakers
Hero
Hidden Rage
Hoffa
Home Alone I & II
I Was a Mail Order
  Bride
A League of Their Own
Let's Get Harry
Light of Day
Looking for Mr.
  Goodbar
Lucas
Mad Dog and Glory
Major League
Manhunter
Men Don't Leave
Midnight Run
Mo' Money
Monkey Hustle
Music Box
My Bodyguard
The Naked Face
National Lampoon's
  Vacation
Native Son

Next of Kin
Night in the Life of
  Jimmy Reardon
No Mercy
Nothing in Common
On the Right Track
One Cup of Coffee
Only the Lonely
Opportunity Knocks
Overexposed
The Package
Pennies from Heaven
The Perfect Circle
Planes, Trains and
  Automobiles
Prelude to a Kiss
Promises in the Dark
Rapid Fire
Raw Deal
Red Heat
Rent-A-Cop
Risky Business
Rollercoaster
Rookie of the Year
Running Scared
She's Having a Baby
Silver Streak
Sleepless in Seattle
Somewhere in Time
Stony Island
Straight Talk

Streets of Fire
Switching Channels
Thief
Things are Tough All
  Over
Things Change
Torn Between Two
  Lovers
Touch and Go
Uncle Buck
The Untouchables
V.I. Warshawski
Vice Versa
A Wedding
Weeds
Weird Science
When Harry Met Sally
Where the Night Begins
Windy City
Your Life is Calling, Jo
  Jo Dancer
Zoning

Fright begins in Chicago

On October 30, 1938, listeners to "Mercury Theatre of the Air" were startled to hear the music of Ramon Raquello and his orchestra from New York City interrupted by a news bulletin announcing that "Professor Farrell of Mt. Jennings Observatory, Chicago" had discovered major explosions on Mars. Thus began the great Halloween hoax that young Illinois-educated movie genius Orson Welles pulled on the radio public. The terror of poisonous meteors and death-ray-equipped Martians landing in New Jersey was integrated so well into genuine-sounding news bulletins that hundreds of terrified people ran from their homes. There is no Mt. Jennings Observatory, let alone, as far as we know, a Professor Farrell, but there was very real terror in the hearts of many listeners.

CENTER OF THE RADIO UNIVERSE

Illinois firsts in radio and TV

WDZ, the first radio station in Illinois was started in Decatur in 1921. The first commercial TV station in Illinois went on line in 1940. It was WBBM-TV in Chicago. There was certainly no inkling at the time that Chicago would become a major television force.

The Lone Ranger lives on

"The Lone Ranger" was a peculiarly Illinois institution, though it was created by a Michigander. Brace Beemer, the first Lone Ranger on radio, was born in Mount Carmel. Starting on September 15, 1949, Chicago-born Clayton Moore began to play the perennially popular character in the TV version, on ABC. Moore played the part for so long (at least 220 episodes) that he went to court in the 1980s to get the right to continue appearing at shopping malls as the Lone Ranger after the Wrather Corporation obtained an injunction against him. The court agreed to let him.

Who's that man at the breakfast table?

"Don McNeill's Breakfast Club," broadcast across the United States from Chicago, was an early-morning variety show that was intended to appeal to "the solid citizens, the churchgoers, the 'squares,' the butcher, baker, and candlestick maker, the Eds and Ednas." It offered prayer, inspiration, a chance for kids to march around the breakfast table, songs to drink your coffee by, and occasionally very bad jokes. McNeill was born in Galena and was raised in Wisconsin before beginning in radio in California. A dearth of jobs brought him back to Chicago in time to audition for a casual early-morning chat show called "Pepper Pot" in 1933. He changed its name, added variety acts, and lots of comfortable humor that wouldn't alienate early risers. And soon he was commuting from Winnetka. The show ran for 35 years.

The old version of black humor

Freeman Gosden was a Virginia-born magician's assistant and Charles Correll of Peoria was a bricklayer. Together, starting in 1928, the two white men wrote the dialogue for and played the famous blacks, "Amos 'n' Andy," who worked for the Fresh Air Taxicab Company. When the popular comedy moved to TV in 1950, CBS bought the rights and the parts of Amos and Andy were played by real African-Americans. The show lasted only two years but continued in syndication until its stereotypecasting of blacks was condemned by the NAACP.

Bergen was no dummy

The ventriloquist who controlled the famed dummy Charlie McCarthy was originally a medical student. Edgar Bergen was born Edgar Berggren in Chicago. Charlie, created by a woodcarver named Charlie Mack, took Bergen along when he got his own radio show in 1937. Charlie himself said, "Radio is just what a lousy ventriloquist like Bergen needed. The big stiff moves his lips." And who should know better? Charlie was so popular for so long that many people thought he was real. He's now in the Smithsonian Institution—Charlie, that is, not Edgar. Edgar is better known now for being the father of Emmy-winning actress Candice Bergen.

☛ If the plot of your favorite soap opera seems unreal but you don't care, you can thank Chicagoan Irna Phillips for inventing your daytime staple. Trained as a teacher, she had the good luck to work summers at WGN radio in Chicago. In 1930, asked to create a family serial drama, she produced "Painted Dreams." It took place in Chicago and is considered the first radio soap. NBC came after Phillips and she invented for them another serial called "Today's Children." By 1937, she and Emmons Carlson had created "The Guiding Light," the longest running soap on radio and then television, to which it moved in June 1952. This series switched the soap opera focus from common, everyday people to the wealthy. In the 1940s, Phillips wrote and hatched plots for five different soaps running at once.

Queen of the soaps: a Chicago phenomenon

"The Guiding Light," however, was not the first TV soap. That was another of Irna Phillips' babies, "These Are My Children, " which started broadcasting from Chicago on January 31, 1949. Phillips left "The Guiding Light" in the mid-'50s to develop "As the World Turns." Agnes Nixon, also Chicago born, took over "The Guiding Light."

TV TIME

☛ The man who practically single-handedly invented the big-money TV game show was Chicagoan Louis Cowan. Starting with the very popular Chicago-based radio show "The Quiz Kids," on which children astonished adults with their knowledge, Cowan developed his own production company that eventually created the famed "$64,000 Question" and its spinoffs, as well as the long-running "Stop the Music." The man whom *Time* magazine called the "Quizzard of Quiz" became the president of CBS in 1958. But only months later, the scandalous news that not all contestants answered their difficult, high-money questions without help destroyed the quiz-show fad and forced Cowan, who was never accused of any wrongdoing, to resign.

The quizzard of quiz

☛ The young African-American phenomenon known as Oprah Winfrey moved from Baltimore to Chicago in 1984 to take over a dying talk show and quickly became the most popular local talk-show host — even more popular than Phil Donahue. Her own show went national in 1986, and she was gradually able to acquire ownership of it. Also an actress, Winfrey starred in the 1985 film, *The Color Purple.* She owns her own television production company, which is located in Chicago. It has contributed mightily to making her the wealthiest woman in television. The whole of America has also been fascinated by her private life—watching her lose weight and regain it, and gossiping about her long-standing romance with Stedman Graham, a man whom she finally decided in the fall of 1992 to marry.

She made Chicago the center of an industry again

Tonight began with a Chicagoan

✐ The first late-night TV talk show began in 1950, when Chicago-born comedian Morey Amsterdam got together with Jerry Lester and Dagmar to discuss show business on "Broadway Open House." Amsterdam, who began in vaudeville, described himself as "The only comedian who started at the top and worked his way down." He is best known for his role as a comedy writer on "The Dick Van Dyke Show."

Wayne's World

✐ Wayne Campbell and Garth Algar of "Wayne's World," on "Saturday Night Live" and then in the film, enjoy stars coming to their cable-access channel in Aurora, Illinois, where they broadcast from Garth's basement.

THE TELEVISION WORLD IN ILLINOIS

Illinois remained a location for many TV shows over the years—mysteries, sitcoms, and others. You may find one of your favorites in the following list:

"American Dream," Chicago family drama show of 1981
"Anything But Love," Chicago magazine sitcom of 1989-1992
"Arthur Godfrey," comedy and talent show of 1958-59
"Bob," sitcom featuring a cartoonist, from 1992
"The Bob Newhart Show," sitcom featuring a psychologist, from 1972-1978
"Crime Story," Chicago cop show of 1986-1988
"Ding Dong School," educational series of 1952-1956
"Family Matters," Chicago black family sitcom of 1989-present
"Father Dowling Mysteries," Chicago mystery series of 1989-91
"For Richer, For Poorer," Chicago situation comedy show of 1977-1978
"Generations," Chicago daytime serial of 1989-1991
"Good Times," Chicago family drama show of 1974-1979
"Hawkins Falls," Illinois family drama show of 1950-1955
"Jack and Mike," Chicago family comedy-drama of 1986-1987
"Life with Luigi," Chicago ethnic sitcom of 1952-1953
"M Squad," Chicago crime show of 1957-1960
"Out on the Farm," Illinois farm documentary series of 1954
"Kup's Show," Chicago talk show starring columnist Irv Kupcinet of 1962-1986
"Mr. Wizard," Chicago educational series of 1951-61; 1971-72; 1983-present
"Music from Chicago," Chicago-based music variety show of 1951
"The Oprah Winfrey Show," Chicago-based daytime talk show of 1986-present
"Perfect Strangers," Chicago "buddy" sitcom of 1986-92
"The Phil Donahue Show," daytime talk show which began in Dayton, Ohio, in 1970, moved to Chicago in 1977, and to New York in 1985, after he married Marlo Thomas.
"Punky Brewster," Chicago child sitcom of 1984-1988
"The Quiz Kids," Chicago-based quiz show featuring brilliant children of 1949-1956
"Roseanne," Illinois blue-collar family sitcom of 1988-present
"Siskel & Ebert," Chicago-based film critics show of 1986-present
"The Untouchables," Chicago crime show of 1959-1963
"Webster," Chicago family sitcom of 1983-1988
"Welcome Travelers," Chicago daytime show of 1952-1955

America watched Highland Park-born Fred Savage grow up on the TV sitcom "The Wonder Years."

THE ILLINOIS ATHLETE

Fans and participants in today's sporting events aren't quite as genteel as those who participated in an archery tournament at the White Stockings Park in Chicago in 1879. *Harper's Weekly* reported, "The contestants were ladies and gentlemen from the cultured circles of society," and while the rivalry among the shooters was keen to the last degree, "an air of such refinement and courteous dignity as is not often witnessed by observers of public games characterized every one connected with the contest."

From the youngest T-ball players to the rough-tough pro footballers, Illinois is absorbed in sport. Though the focus is often on the pros of Chicago, sport permeates every corner of the state. Let's take to the playing field.

- Starting with High School
- Lettering in Football
- Chicago's Oldest Game
- Illinois's Players
- Baseball Hall of Fame
- Follow the Bouncing Basketball
- Pro Football
- And in this Corner
- Olympic Gold
- Flying for Fun
- Ice and Snow
- At Random

STARTING WITH HIGH SCHOOL

And the Wooden Shoes take the field

The high school team of Teutopolis (also called T-Town) is called the Wooden Shoes. A shoemaker of the town, seeking to express his pleasure in the team in 1935, donated a pair of wooden shoes to the coach, J.H. Griffin. The girls, who have almost as good a record as the boys, are called the Lady Shoes. The priest of the local church, discussing the popularity of high school sport in the area, claims, "If they have basketball in heaven, Teutopolis will be in charge."

Other curious team names from Illinois high schools include:

Atwood Rajahs — Girls: Rajenes
Centralia Orphans — Girls: Orphan Annies
Chicago (Maria) Mystics
Chicago (South Shore) Tars — Girls: Tarettes
Chillicothe Grey Ghosts
Cobden Appleknockers
Collinsville Kahoks
Elgin (St. Edward) Greenwave
Fisher Bunnies
Freeburg Midgets

Freeport Pretzels
Hampshire Whip-purs
Kankakee Kays
McLeansboro Foxes — Girls: Lady Foxes
Milledgeville Missiles
Monmouth Zippers — Girls: Zipperettes
Monticello Sages
Tamms (Egyptian) Pharaohs
Valmayer Pirates — Girls: First Mates
Witt Speedboys — Girls: Speedgirls

Where the boys weren't

High school basketball in Illinois started as a girls' sport, not a boys'. In 1895, girls' basketball was organized in three Chicago-area schools: Oak Park, Austin, and Englewood. Tired of playing among themselves, the Austin girls challenged Oak Park, and on December 18, 1896, at Austin High School, the first game took place. Austin won, 16-4. Each year, interscholastic play got more and more serious. However, in 1906, some fuddy-duddy on school board decided that championship basketball was just far too strenuous for "delicate" females and would have to stop. Before the hammer fell, the teams slipped in one more year, including a trip by one team to St. Joseph, Michigan, probably the first interstate game by girls' high school teams.

State champs

Illinois's first state high school basketball championship was held at the Oak Park YMCA in 1908, at the instigation of Lewis Omer, the director of the Y. Rockford was invited to participate but declined over some imagined slight or very real grudge against Oak Park. Peoria finally won the official tournament, while Rockford won a tournament of its own making. A girls' state tournament wasn't held until 1975-76.

The Sweet 16

Illinois has "da Bears," "da Bulls," the Cubs, and the White Sox, and more. That's okay for the people of the Chicago suburbs, but sport needs to be close to home. That's where high school basketball comes in. In Illinois the high school basketball tournament is called the Sweet 16, because 16 schools participate in Champaign, and one comes out the champ. Only in basketball does a team from a little school stand as much chance as a team from a big one. Well . . . kind of, but it happens.

One time it happened

The high school in the little northern stateline town of Hebron has a gym that is only 74 x 34 (8 feet narrower than a regulation court), and yet the boys in that tiny town by the Wisconsin border managed to take the state championship away from bigger schools with bigger gyms in the 1951-52 season. Years after the Hebron team won the state championship, the most noticeable thing one still sees when approaching the town is the water tower, which is painted like a basketball, in honor of the town's proudest moment.

◄ On October 30, 1992, Aurora celebrated a huge anniversary. It was the 100th game in the 100-year-long rivalry between the football teams of Aurora East and Aurora West, the oldest high school rivalry in the state and one of the oldest in the nation.

High school rivalry

LETTERING IN FOOTBALL

◄ Some of the more interesting college team nicknames in Illinois:
- **University of Chicago Maroons** - from a color chosen by the 1894 baseball team for their socks
- **DePaul Blue Demons** - from "D(ePaul)-Men"
- **Illinois Institute of Technology Scarlet Hawks**
- **Lewis University Flyers** - their symbol is a pilot created by cartoonist Milton Caniff of "Terry and the Pirates"
- **Southern Illinois Salukis** - salukis are Egyptian hunting dogs and SIU is in (or at least on the edge of) the region known as Little Egypt
- **Western Illinois Leathernecks** - the coach from 1927-64 was in the Marine Corps Reserves, which gave permission to use its nickname
- **Millikin Big Blue**   • **Sangamon State Prairie Stars**
- **Trinity Christian Trolls**

College nicknames

◄ The first truly professional football coach anywhere was the University of Chicago's Amos Alonzo Stagg—also the longest lasting: he coached for 71 years! After playing football for Yale University, Stagg became the University of Chicago's first sports coach, in both football and basketball. Under the influence of James Naismith, inventor of basketball, Stagg brought the game to Chicago—a fact that put him into the Basketball Hall of Fame in 1959.

The university played its first football game on October 22, 1892, against Northwestern. While coaching at the U. of C. for 41 years, Stagg tried to prevent professional football from developing. He regarded pro football as evil and injurious to the "upbuilding of the present and future generations of clean, healthy, rightminded and patriotic citizens."

Required to retire at 70, Stagg moved to the College of the Pacific in Stockton, California, where he put in many more years. He was even named college coach of the year at 81. He was still active in sports when he died at age 98. The sports stadium at the University of Chicago is named Stagg Field after this grand old man of college sport.

A coach for all seasons —and forever!

The Secret Service wasn't there

Probably the only person ever to play football against two future presidents was George Musso. A future Chicago Bears Hall of Famer, the Collinsville native played against Ronald Reagan (pictured at left) in 1929, when the Dixon boy was playing for Eureka College, and Musso was on the Millikin College team. Six years later, Musso came up against Michigan center Gerald Ford while playing in the College All-Star Game in Chicago.

Waukegan wonder

The son of a Waukegan music teacher, Otto Graham was a lot more interested in sport than in music. While at Northwestern, he became the only person ever to be named All-American in both football and basketball. As a member of the College All-Stars in 1943, he played against the Washington Redskins and intercepted a pass from Sammy Baugh, running it 97 yards for a touchdown. Turning professional, Graham started with the Rochester Royals but quickly moved to the new Cleveland franchise. In 1965, he was inducted into the Pro Football Hall of Fame. Waukegan has given Graham a star on its Walk of Fame.

From the heights to the pits

Robert Zuppke, called the "Little Dutchman," was a German-born, Wisconsin-raised football player who became head coach at the University of Illinois in 1913. In 1922, he introduced the huddle, which became a standard means of communication in the game. Illinois took or tied the Big Ten title seven times during the next fifteen years, including the national championship in 1927. But from there it was downhill. For another thirteen years, alumni waited patiently for more victories, but they never came. In 1941, Zuppke was forced to retire.

The Gipper's mentor

Chicagoan (-turned-Indianan) Knute Rockne has been described as having "sold football to the men on the trolley." Rockne, the son of a Norwegian carriage maker who came to Chicago for the Columbian Exposition and never left, went to Notre Dame as a student and became a chemistry instructor so that he could be free on weekends to play pro ball. Soon, however, he was made head coach, a position he retained for thirteen years, during which the university lost only twelve games and never had a losing season. Rockne was a master of motivation and locker-room speeches. His famous one-liner— "Win just one for the old Gipper"—referred to player George Gipp, who had died several years earlier.

First Heisman Trophy

In 1935, Jay Berwanger, halfback for the University of Chicago, won the first Heisman Trophy. At that time, the Heisman Trophy, given by the Downtown Athletic Club of New York, meant nothing to him. He had received many trophies that year, and the one he prized the most was the Silver Football, the trophy for the Most Valuable Player of the Big Ten Conference. He was more excited about the flight to New York to receive the Heisman than the trophy itself. On his return to Chicago, he had no place to put the large prize so he gave it to his Aunt Gussie, who used it for the better part of ten years as her front doorstop.

Berwanger was a one-man gang on the field. He called the plays, ran, passed, punted, blocked, played defense, kicked extra points, kicked off, returned punts and kickoffs, and played sixty minutes. Other teams knew that in order to beat the U. of C. they only had to beat Jay. One man who tried was future president Gerald Ford. On graduating, Berwanger was drafted by the Chicago Bears, but he never had any desire to play professionally.

There have been no other Heisman winners from Illinois schools.

The coach, not the violinist

Often, a person with a name similar to that of someone famous will change it to avoid confusion. Herbert Crisler, football coach extraordinaire, happily took on the nickname Fritz to enjoy the confusion with famed violinist Fritz Kreisler. Born in Earlville, Crisler got his early coaching experience from the great Alonzo Stagg at the U. of C., then moved on to Minnesota, Princeton, and Michigan. He virtually single-handedly got the NCAA to change some rules in 1958—the first time changes had been made in college football in 46 years.

CHICAGO'S OLDEST GAME

The founding city

Chicago was one of the first cities represented in professional baseball. A Chicago team played from 1871-75 in the first professional league, the National Association of Professional Base Ball Players.

William Hulbert, owner of the Chicago White Stockings in 1876, was angry when the association reversed its decision about who had the right to shortstop Davy Force's services (after the mixed-up kid had signed two different contracts). Hulbert, determined to get his own way, formed the National League of Professional Base Ball Clubs, with rules that gave the owners more power than the players. One of the main reasons for doing so was to abolish gambling in the clubs, thus drawing back the public, which had become disgusted. The new association included teams from Boston, Chicago, Cincinnati, Louisville, Hartford, St. Louis, Philadelphia, and New York. Hulbert outlawed gambling, Sunday games, and allowing a city, regardless of the population, to have more than one franchise from the league.

The American Baseball League, organized in Philadelphia in 1900, included teams from Chicago, Indianapolis, Detroit, Buffalo, Cleveland, Kansas City, Minneapolis, and Milwaukee.

COLLEGE FOOTBALL HALL OF FAME

PLAYERS

University of Chicago
Andrew Robert Wyant, 1894
Clarence Herschberger, 1898
Walter Eckersall, 1906
Walter Steffen, 1908
Paul R. DesJardien, 1914
John Jay Berwanger, 1935

University of Illinois
Bart Macomber, 1915
Charles R. Carney, 1921
Harold Grange, 1925
Bernie Shively, 1926
Alexander Arrasi Agase, 1946
Claude Young, 1946
J. C. Caroline, 1954
Dick Butkus, 1964

Northwestern University
James E. Johnson, 1905
John Leo Driscoll, 1917
Ralph Baker, 1926
Ernest Renter, 1932
Edgar Manske, 1933
Steve Reid, 1936
Otto E. Graham, 1943
Ron Burton, 1959

COACHES

University of Chicago
Amos Alonzo Stagg, 1951
Clark D. Shaughnessy, 1968

University of Illinois
Edward K. Hall, 1951
Robert Zuppke, 1951
George Woodruff, 1963
Robert Blackman, 1987

DePaul University
Edward Anderson, 1971

Northwestern University
Charlie Bachman, 1978

Great Chicago fire bursts pennant bubble

The Chicago White Stockings were in a "pennant" race for the 1871 championship against the Philadelphia Athletics and the Boston Red Stockings when the Great Chicago Fire occurred, destroying the baseball park. The team's competitors helped replace the equipment but did not let the White Stockings win out of sympathy—Philadelphia took the season.

Some baseball firsts

• Chicago of the National League played Cincinnati of the American League in a two-game series in 1882, in what came to be regarded as the forerunner of the World Series. Chicago won.

• The cork-centered baseball was first used in a World Series game in Chicago in 1910. Invented by Pennsylvanian Benjamin Shibe in 1909, it gradually replaced the old solid-centered ball, often called the dead ball. "Shoeless" Joe Jackson of the Chicago White Sox hit the last home run of the dead-ball era in October 1919.

• The first major league All-Star Game was held at Comiskey Park in Chicago on July 6, 1933. The American League won 4-2 because of a home run by Babe Ruth.

Tinker to Evers to Chance

The Chicago Cubs' great threesome, who took the game in the early 1900s and made it their own, were Joe Tinker (shortstop), Johnny Evers (second base), and Frank Chance (first base). Their famed double play was recorded by Chicago columnist Franklin P. Adams.

These are the saddest of possible words:
"Tinker to Evers to Chance."
Trio of Bear Cubs and fleeter than birds,
"Tinker to Evers to Chance."
Ruthlessly pricking one gonfalon bubble,
Making a Giant hit into a double,
Words that are weighty with nothing but trouble—
"Tinker to Evers to Chance."

A gonfalon is a banner or pennant. Chance became the manager of the Cubs in 1905, and in his first year brought home the pennant. He was named to the Hall of Fame in 1946.

Forming the National Negro League

Andrew "Rube" Foster was an African-American ballplayer who played for the Chicago Lelands in 1907, leading that team to a record of 110 wins and 10 losses. The following year he formed the Chicago American Giants, a team that won 129 games and lost only 6 in its first season. He called a meeting of black baseball owners and on February 13, 1920, they organized the National Negro League. It included two Chicago teams—the American Giants and the Chicago Giants—as well as the Indianapolis ABCs, Kansas City Monarchs, St. Louis Giants, Detroit Stars, Dayton Marcos, and Cuban Stars. Attempts at forming a Negro league had been made during the 1800s but all had failed quickly. Foster was president of the NNL until his death in 1930.

The first game held under the auspices of the new National Negro League was held in Indianapolis between the Chicago Giants and the Indianapolis ABCs, on May 2, 1921. The ABCs won.

White Sox owner Charles Comiskey didn't believe in paying the players on his team very much, even when he was raking in the money from the crowds their playing brought to Sox Park. So when underpaid first baseman Chick Gandil told some gamblers that he was certain several members of the team could be bribed to fix the 1919 World Series, he was right. The great Sox team made a miserable hash of the series, letting the Cincinnati Red Sox win. When Comiskey asked Ban Johnson, the head of the American League, to investigate, Johnson called the owner a crybaby. Rumors built, however, and Comiskey continued to pursue the question, until the summer of 1920, when pitcher Eddie Cicotte, feeling desperately guilty for the $10,000 he had taken, fell apart, and went to the grand jury. Then "Shoeless" Joe Jackson joined him, and the conspiracy dissolved. "Yes, kid, I'm afraid it is," replied Jackson to a crying kid who begged to be told "it isn't so" on the day of their indictment on September 28, 1920.

Before the trial, considerable evidence from the grand jury disappeared. The eight players who were tried and acquitted by a very partisan jury included Gandil, Cicotte, Jackson, Swede Risberg, Happy Felsch, Buck Weaver, Lefty Williams, and Fred McMullin. That group, referred to ever after as the Black Sox, never played ball again. Judge Kenesaw Mountain Landis was appointed commissioner of baseball, with the job of making sure that the game stayed straight.

When the White Sox got dirty

The White Sox played . . . and played . . . and played, in the longest baseball game ever, against the Milwaukee Brewers on May 9, 1984. In order to break the tie, 34 innings were played over two days, taking a total of 8 hours and 6 minutes. The final score was Sox, 7-6.

The long distance record

ILLINOIS'S PLAYERS

The game must have been too much for Dan O'Leary on a summer's day in 1883. It was the last half of the 9th with 2 out, against Port Huron. The Peoria player successfully hit a ball that was clearly a home run . . . but then he ran the wrong direction. The umpire counted O'Leary out, but he always had the pleasure (?) of knowing that he was the only player in organized baseball to make a home run the wrong way.

Wrong Way O'Leary

Edward Barrow, born in Springfield, started in baseball managing a semi-pro team in Iowa. From there he moved to the minor leagues and then to the Boston Red Sox, where he worked with Babe Ruth. Owner Harry Frazee solved some financial problems by selling the Babe and other good players to the Yankees. Barrow went with them, and served as general manager for nineteen years, creating what has been called "the mightiest empire baseball has ever known." Barrow's Yankees won 14 pennants and took the World Series 10 times. He was named to the Baseball Hall of Fame in 1953.

Barrow and the Babe

Veeck and the midget

On August 19, 1951, when Chicagoan Bill Veeck was with the St. Louis Browns (before coming to the White Sox), his team was playing the Detroit Tigers. Out walked a pinch hitter, Chicagoan Eddie Gaedel, only 3 feet 7 inches tall, and wearing the number 1/8. The Detroit pitcher, unable to find his range between Gaedel's shoulders and knees, walked the midget. The little Chicagoan was the only midget ever to play in a major league game.

MVP doubled

Milwaukee Brewers outfielder Robin Yount, born in Danville, was chosen the American League Most Valuable Player in both 1982 and 1989. He was the first player since 1940 to be named MVP in two different positions.

Putting girls in baseball

The All-American Girls Professional Baseball League was the brain child of Chicago Cubs' owner and chewing-gum magnate, P.K. Wrigley. Founded in 1943, it was the first professional women's league in the country. Wrigley and his associates, unable to field male teams because of the war, thought the women's league could entertain the "war-weary" public with top-notch female talent. Because Wrigley wanted the women to "Look like women. Play like men," the uniform called for a short skirt. Makeup and sexily swinging shoulder-length hair were required. Spring training included charm school. Wrigley paid all bills for two years and then sold off his interest to his advertising man, Art Meyerhoff. When the league folded in 1954, long after the men had returned from the war, the general public forgot about its accomplishments until the 1992 film, *A League of Their Own*.

In the fall of 1988, the National Baseball Hall of Fame opened its "Women in Baseball" exhibit. At that time, 545 women from the U.S., Canada, and Cuba were honored for their contributions to the league from 1943 -1954.

A Peoria Redwing dodging a tag from a Kenosha, Wisconsin, ballplayer.

Illinois had four teams in the All-American Girls Professional Baseball League: Rockford Peaches (1943-54); Peoria Redwings (1946-1951); Chicago Colleens (1948, official league member in 1948 only - played exhibition games in 1949-50); Springfield Sallies (1948, official league member in 1948 only, played exhibition games in 1949-50.)

BASEBALL HALL OF FAME

◀ Byron-born ballplayer Albert G. Spalding got his start pitching for the Rockford team called Forest City and then moved on to the Boston Red Stockings. America's star pitcher in 1875, he pitched 56 victories, 5 losses, and 3 ties. Moving to the Chicago White Stockings, he won 47 and lost only 14, pitching the team to the 1876 pennant. He and his brother took their accumulated expertise and opened a sporting-goods store, at which he sold uniforms and the game's first standardized ball. He also soon began to publish the official *Baseball Guide*. The chain of stores gradually became a manufacturing company that produced the balls used by the leagues until the 1970s. Becoming president of the White Stockings in 1882, Spalding spent the remainder of his life promoting baseball around the world. On a world tour in 1888-89, the White Stockings played near the Pyramids in Egypt, in Ceylon, and for the Prince of Wales in England. A.G. was elected to the Baseball Hall of Fame in 1939.

The player who became a ball

Shortstop Ernie Banks of the Chicago Cubs, described as a "seven-day-a-week ballplayer," is a Texan who was named to the Baseball Hall of Fame in 1977.

An arm of iron

"Iron Man" Joseph Jerome McGinnity was an Iron Man pitcher, meaning the Rock Island-born hurler spent a lot more time on the mound than modern pitchers do. Five times in his career, McGinnity pitched two complete games in one day. In 1902, he pitched 434 innings and 44 complete games. The following year, he faced 1,658 batters. After playing for Baltimore, Brooklyn, and New York, he managed many minor league teams and the Brooklyn Dodgers. He was named to the Hall of Fame in 1946.

◀ Lou Boudreau, born in Harvey, started out his pro career in basketball rather than baseball. He played for the Hammond (Indiana) All-Americans basketball team in 1938, before choosing to dedicate his talents to baseball. He played the majority of his games with Cleveland where he was the star of the lineup. In 1944, he was batting champion. He also was the top defensive fielder in the league eight times. In 1948, when Cleveland won the World Series, Boudreau won the MVP award before becoming a playing manager. He was elected to the Baseball Hall of Fame in 1970.

Hall of Famer from Harvey

◀ "Red" Ruffing, born in Granville, started his working life in the mines, but that work soon left him minus four toes on his left foot. Unable to do the running that outfielding required, he reluctantly switched to pitching. With the New York Yankees, Ruffing pitched in six World Series, winning three of them. Ruffing was inducted into the Hall of Fame in 1967.

Pitching was second-best

Other Illinois natives in the Baseball Hall of Fame

In addition to the Hall of Famers mentioned earlier, the following players and umpires born in Illinois have been elected to the Baseball Hall of Fame:

- Pioneering player **Will Harridge**, born Chicago 1883, elected 1972
- Umpire **Billy Evans**, born Chicago 1884, elected 1973
- First baseman **Jim Bottomley**, born Oglesby 1900, elected 1974
- Umpire **John "Jocko" Conlan**, born Chicago 1899, elected 1974
- Third baseman **Fred Lindstro**m, born Chicago 1905, elected 1976
- Pioneering player **Warren Giles**, born Tiskilwa 1896, elected 1979
- Umpire **Al Barlick**, born Springfield 1915, elected 1989

FOLLOW THE BOUNCING BASKETBALL

Lots of influence

◀ Henry V. Porter, born in Manito, was a high school basketball coach who ultimately became more involved in establishing the rules of the game. Executive director of the National High School Federation, he helped establish the size of the ball and the shape of the backboard. For 30 years he served on the national rules committee that codified a nationwide system of rules. Porter was elected as a "contributor" to the Basketball Hall of Fame in 1960.

Illinois's top college basketball teams

◀ Loyola of Chicago, under the direction of George Ireland, took the NCAA Division I college basketball championship in 1963. They are the only Illinois college team to do so. The only NCAA Division II Men's national basketball championship (first year of the championship) went to Wheaton College of Wheaton, in 1957.

National Invitation Tournament champions from Illinois are DePaul University in 1945, Southern Illinois University in 1967, Bradley University in 1982.

All-time, top-of-the-heap coach

◀ DePaul University coach Ray Meyer was born and raised in Chicago, part of a family that was large enough to field both a basketball team and a cheerleading squad. After playing basketball for Notre Dame, Meyer returned to South Bend as assistant coach before moving to DePaul in Chicago. In his 42 years there, he led the DePaul Blue Demons to 37 winning seasons, 13 NCAA playoffs, and the 1945 NIT Champ- ionship. Meyer was named to the Basketball Hall of Fame in 1978. His son, Joey Meyer, has followd in his footsteps as the Blue Demons's coach.

◀ The first professional basketball league that included Chicago was the American Basketball League, founded in 1925 by Chicagoan George Halas, owner of the Chicago Bruins, and men from Washington and Cleveland. The first championship, played the following spring, was won by the Cleveland Rosenblums. The Depression proved detrimental to the league. In 1937, the new National Basketball League was formed, with a focus on college-type ball, but the Bruins didn't join it until '39. In 1943, Halas disbanded the Bruins, but the United Auto Workers union local purchased the franchise for the Chicago Studebakers, a racially integrated team which collapsed after a year. The franchise went to the Chicago Gears, which signed all-time college champ, George Mikan.

Chicago's pro teams

The Chicago Bulls' Michael Jordan, a Brooklyn-born hero to most Illinoisans, won two Olympic gold medals for basketball, in 1984 and on the 1992 "Dream Team." He's led the Bulls to two NBA championships. On January 8, 1993, he became the 16th person to hit the 20,000-point mark in NBA history.

Suddenly Chicago was at the top, and in 1947, the Gears won the pro championship.

That should have been the start of pro ball's heyday in Chicago, but instead, Maurice White, owner of the sponsoring American Gear Company, decided he wanted it all—a whole league to himself, and he withdrew the Gears from the NBL. His plans collapsed, the Gears disintegrated, and Mikan went to the Minneapolis Lakers.

◀ While the National Basketball League was entering its final days in 1946, a new league was getting underway—the Basketball Association of America. The Chicago Stadium's entry was the Chicago Stags, coached by Harold Olsen. The NBL became the NBA in 1949.

In the meantime . . .

◀ It wasn't exactly a real start on trotting around the globe, but on January 7, 1929, the members of a new basketball team recently formed in Chicago sweet-talked their jalopy into getting them to Hinckley to play their first game. Chicago sports promotor Abe Saperstein named his "dream team" the Harlem Globetrotters. With the African-Americans winning all their games, local teams were unwilling to invite them back, so they developed comedy routines. Saperstein, an English-born, Chicago-raised sports addict, was too small to play in sports himself, but he was always the boss, and the players called him "Little Caesar." In 1939, the Globetrotters lost to the New York Renaissance Five, a.k.a. "the Rens," in the first professional world championships, held in Chicago. The following year they won against George Halas's Chicago Bruins.

By jalopy to Hinckley

George is the "greatest"

Hall of Famer George Mikan learned to play basketball in a backyard court in Joliet. After he broke his leg, he turned to baseball, for which he had a surprising talent. But Mikan chose a future as a priest and went to DePaul University. The call of the priesthood faded away when he couldn't manage to complete the Greek requirement, but in the meantime he discovered basketball again. The fact that he had to play with his glasses strapped on his head didn't slow him down. Going on to law school and taking his degree, Mikan finally turned to basketball full time, playing briefly for the Chicago Gears and then for the Minneapolis Lakers. He was the first player in history to score 10,000 points, and he led the Lakers to six world championships in seven seasons. In 1950 he was named by the Associated Press as the greatest basketball player of the first half of the century. When the American Basketball Association was formed in 1967, Mikan, then a lawyer in Minneapolis, became the first commissioner.

Illinoisans in the Basketball Hall of Fame

The Basketball Hall of Fame includes people from all categories of sport—high school, college, coaching, pro. Many Illinois natives have been elected:

College coach and official **John J. Schommer**, born Chicago 1884, elected 1959

College player and Minneapolis Laker **George L. Mikan**, born Joliet 1924, elected 1959

High school coach and rule-maker **Henry V. Porter**, born Manito 1891, elected 1960

Andy Phillip, player on several teams who became coach of the St. Louis Hawks, born Granite City 1922, elected 1961

Loyola University coach **Leonard D. Sachs**, born Chicago, elected 1961

College coach **Harlan O. Page**, born Chicago 1887, elected 1962

AAU First-Team All-Tournament player **Robert F. Gruenig**, born Chicago 1913, elected 1963

College and Olympic team coach **Arthur C. "Dutch" Lonborg**, born Gardner 1899, elected 1972

Notre Dame player and coach **Edward W. "Moose" Krause**, born Chicago 1913, elected 1975

DePaul University coach **Ray Meyer**, born Chicago 1913, elected 1978

Amateur official and executive **Louis G. Wilke**, born Chicago 1896, elected 1982

New York Knicks player **Harry "The Horse" Gallatin**, also coach of the St. Louis Hawks, born Wood River 1927, elected 1991

PRO FOOTBALL

In at the start

At a meeting in Canton, Ohio, on September 17, 1920, the American Professional Football Association was formed, with Jim Thorpe as president. Included in the new league were three Illinois teams—the Rock Island Independents, the Racine Cardinals (that was from Racine Avenue in Chicago, not Racine, Wisconsin), and the Decatur Staleys. The Racine Cardinals soon became the Chicago Cardinals, and the Chicago Tigers joined. The first game played by a APFA team took place nine days later at Rock Island, where the Independents beat the non-league St. Paul Ideals 48-0.

◀ Illinois hasn't been shy about starting new professional football teams, but not many have lasted. The Decatur Staleys played in 1920, the Rock Island Independents from 1920 to '26. Chicago had a bunch:

The Who?

Cardinals, 1920-59 (American Professional Football
    Association and National Football League)
Tigers, 1920 (APFA)
Staleys, 1921 (APFA)
Bears, 1922-present (NFL)
Bulls, 1926 (AFL)
Rockets, 1946-48 (All-America Football Conference)
Hornets, 1949 (AAFC)
Fire, 1974 (World Football League)
Winds, 1975 (WFL)
Blitz, 1983-84 (U.S. Football League)

◀ Legend says that after the American Professional Football Association, predecessor of the NFL, was formed in 1920, the Chicago franchise was determined by a game on November 7, 1920. The Chicago Cardinals beat the Chicago Tigers 6-3. The legend may not be true, but the Tigers disbanded and the Cardinals became the champs.

Who represents Chicago?

◀ George Halas, a 25-year-old professional baseball player, was invited in 1920 by A. E. Staley to form a football team in Decatur. The Decatur Staleys team was to belong to the new American Professional Football Association, which Halas helped found.

There's only one Papa Bear

Their first game was against the Moline Tractors (a non-league team) on October 3, 1920, in Decatur. The Staleys won, 20-0. After the season, Staley decided that football wasn't for him, and he paid Halas $5,000 to move the team to Chicago and call it the Staleys for one year. In 1922, the Staleys became the Chicago Bears, and the APFA became the National Football League, at Halas's suggestion. He brought the "T" formation back into prominence, and was named a Charter Member of the Pro Football Hall of Fame in 1939. During his years of coaching he attained a record of 326-151-31 with eight NFL championships. Papa Bear retired from coaching in 1968 but retained active management of the team until his death in 1983.

Papa Bear's luck

When the *Eastland* capsized in the Chicago River in 1915 (see page 151), one of the passengers listed as missing was G. S. Halas. But George, soon-to-be owner of the Chicago Bears, who had booked passage in order to get to Michigan City, Indiana, for a baseball game, had missed the boat. Perhaps one of the luckiest mistakes that has happened to anyone.

So long, so unlucky

The longest losing streak in the NFL happened to the Chicago Cardinals in the 1940s. After losing 29 games straight, their bad luck was broken against another Chicago team, when they beat the Chicago Bears 16-7.

Isn't selling a person slavery?

The Rock Island Independents were one of the professional football teams in the 1920s that competed with the Chicago Bears. It was also one of the first to sell its players instead of just having them leave. In probably the first player deal that used a standardized contract, George Halas bought tackle Ed Healey, for a measly $100 on November 27, 1922. Healey went on to become a Hall of Famer. The Independents later folded.

Number 77

Born in Pennsylvania, Harold "Red" Grange was raised in Wheaton, where, because he worked as an iceman in the summer as part of his conditioning, he became known as the "Wheaton Iceman." At the University of Illinois he became probably the most famous college player ever, especially after he made four touchdowns in the first twelve minutes of a game against the University of Michigan in 1924. The first college player to go professional in a dramatic fashion, Red Grange quit college to go on a tour with "Cash and Carry" Pyle. Then he joined the Chicago Bears with a contract guaranteeing him $30,000—all in 1925. In 1926, however, he and Pyle started the American Football League, which failed financially. As the "Galloping Ghost" (so named by sportswriter Grantland Rice), he was so popular that he was signed for the movies and was even drafted in an attempt to get him to run for Congress. Almost singlehandedly, he made pro football popular.

First — and only

From the time the NFL was started until 1932, the champions of the year were the team with the best record. But in that year, there was a tie between the Chicago Bears and the Portsmouth Spartans, so the first NFL championship game was held. It was scheduled for Wrigley Field on December 17, 1933, but it snowed so hard that the game was moved indoors at the Chicago Stadium, which happened to have a dirt floor because a circus had just been appearing there. With an 80-yard field, they had to alter the rules somewhat. After three quarters with no score, Chicago got a touchdown by bending the rules and then added a safety for a final score of 9-0. The following year the league split into two divisions and regular playoffs began. The Bears beat the New York Giants 23-21.

Broken Rocket

Elroy "Crazylegs" Hirsch of the All-American team of the Chicago Rockets was carrying the ball in a play against the Cleveland Browns on September 26, 1948, when he went down in a mass of arms and legs. Probably someone kicked him by accident, but after two days of yawning and dizziness, he was found to have a skull fracture. He sat out the rest of the year and started again the next fall with the L.A. Rams. Who's heard of the Chicago Rockets lately?

Dick Butkus, born and raised in Chicago, was Prep Football Player of the Year in the nation while at Vocational High School. The linebacker went to the University of Illinois, where he led the team to a 17-7 victory over the University of Washington in the 1964 Rosebowl. A first-round draft pick of the Chicago Bears, Butkus was called "perhaps the best of all time" before knee injuries forced his retirement in 1973. He's now associated with WGN radio and TV in Chicago.

Chicago's own Dick Butkus

◀ Illinois natives elected to the Pro Football Hall of Fame: End/coach/owner of the Chicago Bears George Halas, born Chicago 1895, inducted 1963

Center George Trafton, born Chicago 1896, elected 1964

Quarterback Otto Graham, born Waukegan 1921, elected 1965

Halfback/quarterback John "Paddy" Driscoll, born Evanston 1896, elected 1965

Official Hugh "Shorty" Ray, born Highland Park 1884, elected 1966

Founder of the Chicago Cardinals, Charles W. Bidwill, Sr., born Chicago 1895, elected 1967

Halfback Tony Canadeo, born Chicago 1919, elected 1974

Tackle/linebacker George Connor, born Chicago 1925, elected 1975

Linebacker Ray Mitschke, born Elmwood Park 1936, elected 1978

Linebacker Dick Butkus, born Chicago 1942, elected 1979

Guard/tackle George Musso, born Collinsville 1910, elected 1982

Tackle Mike McCormack, born Chicago 1930, elected 1984

Pro Football Hall of Fame

AND IN THIS CORNER

◀ World light-heavyweight boxing champ throughout the '50s, Archie Moore, often gave his birthplace as Collinsville, Illinois, though he just as often listed Benoit, Mississippi, which has been accepted as the truth, at least by *Encyclopaedia Britannica*. Just as variable was his age. He might have been born in 1913, or perhaps it was 1916. And he got a kick out of people never really knowing for sure how old he was. He was probably almost fifty in 1962 when he lost his title. He tried after that to get out of the "light" heavyweight category and into the "heavy" heavy-weight, but he never made it—getting knocked out by both Rocky Marciano and Floyd Patterson.

Well, we'll stick him here anyway

Food for controversy

One hundred thousand people turned out at Chicago's Soldiers Field on September 22, 1927, to witness the Dempsey-Tunney fight, certain that the popular Jack Dempsey would regain his heavyweight title from Gene Tunney. In the seventh round, Tunney went down. When Referee Dave Barry ordered Dempsey to a neutral corner, he refused to go, so that, according to the rules, the count could not start. When the count finally started, Tunney had had several extra seconds to recover his wits. At the count of "9," Tunney rose, refreshed, and won. He earned $990,000 for 30 minutes work—a mere pittance compared to today's title fights. Boxing fans still argue about the fairness of Tunney's victory.

Some other title fights in Chicago

• World heavyweight boxing champ "Cinderella Man" James J. Braddock stepped into the ring at Comiskey Park in Chicago to give a comeuppance to upstart Joe Louis on June 22, 1937. Eight rounds later, Braddock lay on the mat, knocked out by the "Brown Bomber." Joe Louis kept the title for 12 years, retiring undefeated in 1949.

• When world heavyweight boxing champion Joe Louis retired from the ring on March 1, 1949, the title was open. On June 22, fighting in Chicago, Ezzard Charles defeated "Jersey Joe" Walcott in a match that the National Boxing Association declared a title fight.

• "Pound for pound," many say, Sugar Ray Robinson was the best boxer ever. A middleweight fighter, he regained his title five different times. The last time was in Chicago in 1958, when he took on Carmen Basilio, who had beaten him the previous year.

• Sonny Liston, an ex-con from Arkansas, became world heavyweight boxing champion on September 25, 1962, when he KO'd champ Floyd Patterson in the first round of a match at Comiskey Park. Patterson tried to regain his title, but Liston again got him in a knockout. Liston held the title until February 25, 1964.

"Sting like a bee"

Born Cassius Clay in Louisville on January 17, 1942, Muhammad Ali, a Chicago resident for many years, was the first fighter in history to regain his heavyweight title three times. He became world champ first in 1964 by knocking out Sonny Liston. He lost the title officially (though not popularly) after he refused to be inducted into the army. He regained it after knocking out George Foreman in 1974. In 1978, he lost the championship to Leon Spinks on a split decision, taking it back again in September. He tried twice more to regain the title, in 1980 and '81, but failed. In 1992, Ali's daughter spoke out against boxing because her father is suffering from boxing-inflicted brain damage.

OLYMPIC GOLD

Chicagoan Avery Brundage competed in the 1912 Olympics in the penthathlon and decathlon. Runner Abel Kiviat said of Brundage in *Tales of Gold,* "He was a good athlete, but everybody hated him. Even when he became President of the Olympic Committee they all hated him. He wouldn't talk to anyone, and nobody talked to him." Brundage started a construction company that eventually gave him the funds to become involved in amateur sport—and he meant amateur! He ran the International Olympic Committee with an iron fist for two decades, from 1952 to 1972, maintaining the illusion of amateurism in the Olympic Games. It wasn't until long after his death that American athletes were able to openly participate in the commercialism of sport.

The man with the power

Peter Ueberroth's father traveled a lot, taking his family along with him. He happened to be in Evansville, Illinois, when Peter was born. Perhaps that traveling is what later put Uebberoth into the travel business. When the possibility of a Los Angeles Olympiad was first being discussed in the 1970s, Ueberroth was the owner of First Travel Corporation, the largest travel company in the nation after American Express. Just after L.A. got the games (which almost no other city had wanted due to the 1972 terrorist killings in Munich and the 1976 financial failure in Montreal), Uebberoth was chosen to manage the games for the city. After he accepted the job, the city voted that there would be no public funds available for the task. However, he succeeded. He tells the story of how he did it in his book, *Made in America.* His success with the Olympic Games got him the job of baseball commissioner, one that he gave up fairly quickly. In 1992, Ueberroth was put in charge of rebuilding South Los Angeles after it was destroyed following the acquittal of four policemen for beating black motorist Rodney King.

He gets the big jobs

Chicago was awarded the Third Olympiad, to be held in 1904, but then St. Louis announced its World's Fair, and the "honor" (which was not all that great the first few years) was taken away and given to St. Louis, in the hope that public interest would increase.

Chicago was the loser

• Sybil Bauer of Chicago won a gold medal in the 1924 Olympics 100-meter backstroke, becoming, at the same time, the first woman to break a man's record in an event. She died suddenly at age 24, just before she was scheduled to get married.

• Betty Robinson, born in Riverdale, won the 100-yard dash when track and field events for women were first held, 1928 in Amsterdam. This victory made her the first woman to win a track and field event. Eight years later, she participated in the gold-medal relay, after having been in a plane crash that smashed one leg and arm and cracked a hip.

• Champaign's skater Bonnie Blair became, in 1992, the first woman skater to win back-to-back gold medals in Olympic speed skating. Skating since she was two, she won the gold medal and set a world record for 500 meters in the 1988 Winter Olympics at Calgary. Then, in 1992, she won the gold again in Albertville.

Some Olympic firsts for women

Tarzan at the start

Johnny Weissmuller began his swimming at Fullerton Beach on Lake Michigan. Seeing promise in the 15-year-old boy, Coach Bill Bachrach of the Illinois Athletic Club drilled him in a year-long training regimen. He never lost a major race after those years. Johnny Weissmuller swam into the American spotlight when he won three gold medals at the 1924 Paris Olympic games, beating the famed Hawaiian swimmer, Duke Kahanamoku. In the 1928 Amsterdam

games, Weissmuller won two more gold medals. During ten years of amateur competition, he was undefeated. By 1928, he had won 52 national titles and set 67 world records. The Associated Press named him the "Swimmer of the Half-Century." He was described as "half human, half hydrofoil." He was also called "the great dramatizer of swimming." He became a Hollywood star when he played Tarzan in *Tarzan, the Ape Man.* He said of his role, "It was up my alley. There was swimming in it, and I didn't have much to say." He is shown here in the 1932 movie.

One against many

Babe Didrikson was just one lone woman from Texas in 1932, representing Employers Casualty Company in the Olympic track and field trials. She singlehandedly won 30 points in the competition, beating the total record of the 22-woman Illinois Athletic Club.

The minister pole-vaulter

Two-time Olympic gold medal (1952 and 1956) pole vaulter Bob Richards, born in Champaign in 1926, was already an ordained minister when he joined the U.S. track team. He worked as a full-time minister, sermons and all, at a Church of the Brethren in Long Beach, California, while he trained full-time, too—not an easy thing to do. After his success at setting world records, he became a spokesman for Wheaties. His story was told on the DuPont Television Theater in a play called *Leap to Heaven.*

Determination

Evanston swimmer John Naber was taken—fortunate little boy—to Greece when he was 9 and he saw Olympia. Right then he became determined to someday win an Olympic gold medal. In fact, he won four of them at the Montreal games in 1976, as well as one silver.

Swimmer by chance

Twenty-one-year-old Nelson Diebel, a resident of Western Springs, won the 1992 Olympic gold medal for the 10-meter breaststroke. But it's amazing that it happened, because he admits to having been a "loser, dirtbag, borderline suicidal." When his parents divorced in the '80s he "came unglued"—broke into a school gym, cheated, lied, smashed windshields, and had trouble with drugs and alcohol. He credits swimming and his coach at the Peddie School in Hightstown, New

Jersey, with saving him. When he entered Peddie, he lied on his application, saying that he was an experienced swimmer. Coach Martin's strenuous four-hour-a-day swim practices changed his attitude, his experience level, and his life.

Babe Didrikson's successor

Jackie Joyner-Kersee, born in East St. Louis, has been called the "greatest woman athlete of the second half of the twentieth century" (Babe Didrickson gets the title for the first half). She started running at age 9 and soon moved into the long jump. Her success inspired her brother Al to also become an athlete, and the two of them have joined the few brother-and-sister pairs in history to win gold medals in the Olympics. Jackie went to college on a basketball scholarship but concentrated her efforts on track events, especially the heptathlon (7 events). The first woman to score more than 7,000 points in the event, she won the 1988 Olympic gold and then repeated in 1992, when she also won a bronze in the long jump.

FLYING FOR FUN

Pioneer on the dunes

Civil engineer Octave Chanute, who was born in Paris and worked all over the world, became fascinated, when he was already in his sixties, with the idea of aeronautics. He moved his office to Chicago in 1883 and frequently camped out on the Lake Michigan sand dunes to test various ideas of how to build a flying machine. Wilbur and Orville Wright consulted Chanute in 1901 and many say that his advice helped the Wrights decide to build a biplane, which they successfully flew in 1903. Chanute Air Force Base at Rantoul is named for Octave.

Flying the poles

It helps to be wealthy if you have an idea that will cost a lot to implement. Chicago-born scientist, aviator, and adventurer Lincoln Ellsworth was able to finance two expeditions. In 1926 he went with Italian explorer Umberto Nobile on a dirigible crossing of the North Pole. Nine years later, having already flown to Antarctica several times, he flew the entire width of that continent, including crossing the Pole. Part of Antarctica is now called Ellsworth Land. In between, among other fun things, he made a canoe trip 800 miles into Labrador.

Wrong-way Falconi

Some people just never know which way is up. On August 28, 1933, a pilot named Tito Falconi flew a single-engine plane 250 miles from St. Louis to Joliet, upside down. Apparently he landed right side up.

**By the skin
of their balloon**

◄ Rockford-born Ben Abruzzo led the team that flew a balloon across the Pacific Ocean for the first time, in 1981. *The Double Eagle V*, with crew Larry Newman, Ron Clark, and Rocky Aoki, was launched from Nagashima, Japan. In less than four days it traveled the 5,070 miles to Cavelo, California. Toward the end of the flight, the bag began to leak, and Abruzzo had to make a crash landing on shore in order to survive.

ICE AND SNOW

**First to appear
on a TV tradition**

◄ The Norge Ski Club in Fox River Grove, founded in 1905, is one of the oldest ski-jumping organizations in North America. Originally founded in Chicago by immigrants, the club's first tournaments were held in Humboldt Park; it later moved to Fox River Grove. In 1922, when the day of a scheduled championship arrived, there was no snow. The club had it brought in by train from Baraboo, Wisconsin. In 1939 and '56, jumping competitions were held at Soldiers Field in Chicago. How? They constructed a plywood scaffold over the seats and columns. The very first episode of ABC's "Wide World of Sports" featured the Norge Ski Club. Today the club has four hills, along with Olympic-sized scaffolds, from which intrepid skiers can soar more than 200 feet.

**Curse of the
Blackhawks**

◄ When Chicago Blackhawks coach Pete Muldoon was fired in 1927, he cursed the team with a future in which they never won the Stanley Cup. The curse worked for 35 years. It wasn't until 1962, when Bobby Hull was a member of the team, that they won the coveted trophy.

**One Hull of a
hockey player**

◄ In 1957, at the age of 18, Canadian-born Bobby Hull signed with the National Hockey League's Chicago Blackhawks. He played center his first two seasons. During his third season, he switched to left wing, where he soared. He was named to the All-Star team twelve of his fourteen seasons. He was named the Associated Press "player of the decade" for the 1960s. In 1966 Hull became the first NHL player to score 50 goals in a season. His shot was clocked at 120 mph. A rival who stopped one of his shots said, "It felt like I had been seared by a branding iron. His shot once paralyzed my arm for five minutes. It's unbelievable." His blurring speed, clocked at 29 mph, and his hard shot combined for a total of 604 goals, when he retired in 1972. Then he signed a contract for $2.75 million to be player-coach of the Winnepeg Jets. He played until 1978, finishing his career off with an additional 400 goals for a total of 1,012 career goals. Bobby Hull was elected to the Hockey Hall of Fame in 1983.

AT RANDOM

The buffalo hunter

◄ First he was a buffalo hunter, in the days when there were plenty of buffalo. Then he became a showman, challenging any and all to match him in shooting glass balls and birds. Many would-be champion marksmen from both Europe and the United States accepted Winslow-born

W. F. "Doc" Carver's challenge, but they all failed. In the 1880s, Buffalo Bill Cody asked Carver to join his show, and the two ex-hunters appeared in and ran the show as it traveled the world for twenty or more years. In a shooting exhibition before the Prince of Wales, Doc Carver broke 100 glass balls in a row without faltering, and then did almost as well from the back of a speeding horse.

World champ at billiards

Monmouth-born Ralph Greenleaf turned leisure-time billiards into a championship sport that grabbed headlines. At 12, the boy who had been given a small billiards table when his health wouldn't allow him to play strenuous sports, beat the world champ. He himself became the world champ when he was 19 years old, without losing a single game in the match! He held the championship for most of the next forty years.

George Hancock, a reporter for the Chicago Board of Trade in 1887, unwilling to give up baseball for the duration of winter, devised a game using a larger, softer ball for indoor use. The first game was played at Chicago's Farragut Boat Club on November 30, 1887. Calling the game softball, he and his friends formed the Mid Winter Indoor Baseball League of Chicago. They worked on the rules and equipment (which evolved from a broomstick and a boxing glove), finalizing and accepting them in 1889.

The boxingball glove

Most references say that the first car race was the *Chicago Times-Herald* newspaper's race on Thanksgiving day in 1895, won by the Duryea brothers (see page 163). However, contestants who were on hand earlier and were not chosen to participate in the main event were offered a consolation race, which was held on November 2. It followed a 92-mile route from Chicago to Waukegan and back. The only car to complete the course was a modified Benz driven by Oscar B. Mueller of Decatur, which averaged 10 miles an hour.

The first auto race

In the early part of the century, Elgin was the focus of all eyes in the auto racing world each August when the Elgin National Road Race was held. The first race, held August 27, 1910, was won by Ralph Mulford at an impressive speed of 62.5 mph over the 8.5-mile course along gravel country roads. Another Ralph, DePalma, won three times. The first Indy-500 winner, Ray Harroun, took part, as did Barney Oldfield and Eddie Rickenbacker. Except for the war years, races were run each year, from 1911 to 1920.

Elgin in the racing world

Roller skating for the masses

After roller skating's introduction in 1863, it became increasingly popular. The Casino in Chicago was one of the largest rinks ever built. The facility had room for 1,000 skaters on the hard maple floor and 3,000 spectators. On opening day in 1884, 5,000 people came. There was racing, dancing, and "fancy" skating, which included the Picket Fence, Dude on Wheels, and Philadelphia Twist.

Did "ja" know?

The first 18-hole golf course in the United States was built at Wheaton in 1893, by the Chicago Golf Club.

**The first roller derby,
pre-TV style**

◀ Leo Seltzer was a Chicago entrepreneur who sought ways to bring crowds out of their Depression, preferably ones that put their hard-won dollars into his hands. In 1935, building on the idea of the six-day race, he established the first roller derby, Seltzer's Trans-Continental Derby, in which teams of skaters had to skate the distance from New York to San Francisco. Individuals on the teams would take turns skating while others rested and ate. Not wanting to let the audience in the Coliseum get bored, he incorporated occasional sprints, which allowed the audience to place bets and the skaters to get experience at jabbing with their elbows and knocking each other down.

Copycat in curls

Wrestler George Arena claimed to be the original "Gorgeous George." With blond shoulder-length hair and a primping routine fans loved to hate, Gorgeous George entered the ring in 1936 and wrestled under that name for 20 years. He was born in Chicago, raised in Racine, Wisconsin, and spent much of his career wrestling in Milwaukee. With the advent of TV, George Wagner, also known as Gorgeous George, became the most famous "Gorgeous George" and Arena took him to court for using the name. The judge ruled that it couldn't be copyrighted, but Arena always claimed the other man was a copycat.

**The tennis player
par excellence**

◀ Jimmy Connors, hero of the tennis world, was born in East St. Louis in 1952. After being introduced to the game by his mother, he entered national championship play when he was eight. He began winning international tournaments in 1974, ultimately winning the U.S. singles championship four times, in 1976, 1978, 1982, and 1983. He won the 1982 Wimbledon singles, and the doubles in 1975 with Ilie Nastase.

World champ

◀ The chess player with an ego to match his talent, Bobby Fischer, was born in Chicago in 1943 but raised in Brooklyn. At 15 he became the youngest grand master ever. At 18, he turned down the opportunity to play in the U.S. championship contest because the prize money wasn't worth his effort. So they raised the ante, he played, and he won. In 1972, Fischer became the Chess Champion of the World by beating the Soviet Union's Boris Spassky. In 1992, Fischer and Spassky took each other on again in a series of matches held in Yugoslavia. Fischer won again and earned $3.2 million in prize money.

**Around the world in
22 months**

◀ African-American Bill Pinkney, a former marketing executive from Chicago, set out to sail around the world alone in 1990. The experienced sailor's journey was sponsored by Armand Hammer and Bill Cosby; Motorola of Schaumburg gave him communications equipment; and a Boston firm organized a non-profit campaign that purchased his sailboat. At various stages throughout the 32,000 miles aboard his boat called the *Commitment,* Pinkney spoke to 150 schools, by radio or in person, to give schoolchildren his message—"Once you have made a commitment, you don't give it up, no matter what." He began the trip from Bermuda in 1990 and returned there in May 1992. He anchored once in Tasmania to fly home to Chicago for a visit with his wife, Ina.

CRIME AND HARD TIMES

In 1854, Abraham Lincoln was the defense attorney in a murder case tried at Beardstown which was called the "Almanac Murder Trial." He was able to convince the jury that the prosecution's eyewitness really couldn't have seen Duff Armstrong kill James Metzker by the light of the moon, as had been alleged. Lincoln produced an almanac that proved the moon had been setting and the night too dark.

Lincoln himself—at least his body—was the focus of a later case. Ben Boyd, an adept counterfeiting engraver of Big Jim Kenealy's gang, had been sentenced to a long term in prison. Kenealy came up with the bright idea of kidnapping Lincoln's body and holding it until Boyd had been released. The Secret Service learned of the plan and was waiting in ambush for the gang to sneak into Springfield's Oak Ridge Cemetery. A rousing good example of ineptness on the part of officials allowed the gang members to escape at that time, but they were later caught and imprisoned.

Crime and disaster are an inevitable part of life and death in any populous state, but Illinois (especially Chicago) seems to have had more than its share. Much of it downright awesome. Take a look.

- Crime among the Settlers
- Assassins
- Murder I
- The Capone Era
- Murder II
- Death Afloat and Aloft

AMONG THE SETTLERS

Crime is nothing new

🔫 The old town of Kaskaskia, which would later be the first capital of the state, was taken over by a marauder from Connecticut in 1780. John Dodge and his men moved into Fort Kaskaskia and forcibly took control of the isolated and widespread French settlers. For six years, they stole, raped, and burned as they wished. There was no law to stop them because the area was temporarily under no nation's control.

Banditti

🔫 An organized gang known as the "Banditti of the Prairie" ruled the area around Oregon in the 1830s and '40s. The main horse thieves and murderers were John Driscoll and his four sons. They were the prime reasons that the local noncriminal element formed a vigilante force known as the Regulators in 1841. Ultimately, 111 Regulators caught and shot to death two of the sons. When the Regulators themselves were tried for murder, they were acquitted by a jury consisting mostly of other Regulators.

Such an honor

🔫 Elizabeth Reed was convicted of poisoning her husband with arsenic-laced sassafras tea so that she could marry another man. She was tried, convicted, and imprisoned, but then tried to escape the Palestine jail by burning it down. Moved to Lawrence County jail in Lawrenceville, she was hanged on May 23, 1845, before a crowd of 20,000 people—the first female executed by hanging in Illinois.

The excursion train

🔫 At midnight on August 10, 1887, an excursion train belonging to the Toledo, Peoria & Western Railroad struck a burning culvert, wrecking the train and killing about 85 of the 500 passengers who were on a trip from Peoria to Niagara Falls. It was a very long and crowded train,

with 20 wooden cars, because the price of the special journey was so cheap—$7.50 round trip.

Earlier in the day, a road gang was burning high prairie grass near the tracks because sparks from passing trains often ignited the grass. The boss failed to notice that the fire was still smoldering when he left. A strong wind came up, turning smoldering grass into a raging fire that burned the supports of the old bridge. The train, not equipped with airbrakes due to cost-cutting measures taken by the railroad, could not stop in time. Some trapped victims were never identified.

Set it up, bartender!

🔫 If a guy intent on doing evil wanted a way to knock a person out quickly in the 1890s, he could always count on getting help at the Lone Star Saloon in Chicago. There, the owner/bartender would mix a drink that was guaranteed to send the customer into unconsciousness for hours, if not days. The bartender proudly attached his own name to the drink with its mysterious ingredients. That name, Mickey Finn, became part of our language.

The Birger-Shelton gang war terrorized southern Illinois, especially Williamson and Franklin counties, in the 1920s. The Sheltons—Carl, Earl, and Bernie—thought the territory around East St. Louis was theirs for the distribution of moonshine, but then outsider Charlie Birger

The Birgers and the Sheltons

arrived and established his own gang, determined to take over the territory. No one was safe. At least fourteen murders took place within a few short years, with Joe Adams, the mayor of West City, among the dead. Seems Adams had switched his allegiance from Birger to the Sheltons.

The Sheltons even dropped bombs from an airplane on the Birger home at Egypt. Charlie was finally caught, tried, and hanged in 1928, even though the state had switched to the electric chair as of July 1, 1927. The widespread Shelton family carried on their criminality into the 1940s. Carl was killed on the Shelton farm in Fairfield in 1947, and Bernie in a Peoria tavern the next year. Earl was shot in the Farmers' Club in 1949 but recovered; Ray was killed on his tractor in Wayne County in 1950. A sister and her husband were machine-gunned in 1951, but they, too, were lucky and survived. Finally, in 1951, the Shelton home exploded and burned to the ground. The photo was taken when the Birgers decided to be recorded for posterity.

Violence had never startled people in Williamson County. In fact, there may have been as many as 50 murders there between 1839 and 1876. At the turn of the century, labor troubles in the coal mines started, often resulting in bloodshed from gunfire and explosions. But in the 1920s, the county really earned its nickname of "Bloody Williamson."

"Bloody Williamson"

It started in 1922 with the Herrin Massacre (see pg.168) and gathered strength when the Ku Klux Klan controlled the county. Most of the area had been able to ignore Prohibition because of the large number of moonshine stills located in the woods. But when the Catholic immigrants got involved in illegal liquor sales, the Protestant-white-supremists in the Ku Klux Klan decided it was time to act. In 1923, they brought in S. Glenn Young from Kansas, a man not afraid to use his guns (and who had lost his job with the feds because of it). He got a friendly federal agent to deputize the Klansmen and then turned them loose on the county. The Klan higher-ups expelled him from the Klan because of the viciousness with which he went after bootleggers, but they weren't able to wrest control of the county from his hands . . . until a January day in 1925, when a deputy sheriff (who had previously been a bootlegger arrested in one of the Young-led raids) entered a Herrin store, where Young and two other men were arguing. In all the gunfire that followed, no one survived. Efforts began in the county to wrest control out of the bigoted hands of the KKK.

ASSASSINS

The professional malcontent

Nothing ever seemed to be right for Charles Guiteau, a native of Freeport. He tried the law, he tried marriage, he tried a religious commune, but nothing pleased him. The professional malcontent would never have entered history except for one fact: he also tried politics. He became a devoted follower of presidential candidate James A. Garfield, speaking up for him wherever he went. When Garfield won, Guiteau expected to get some recognition—after all, didn't he single-handledly get Garfield elected? Actually, the recognition he wanted was an ambassadorship. But Garfield probably never even knew who the political hanger-on was, except maybe as one of the many people who freely entered his office (a far cry from today's White House).

Gradually, Guiteau convinced himself that this man who ignored him should be eliminated—in fact, that God was telling Guiteau to get rid of Garfield. Finally, on July 2, 1881, the lunatic wrote an obituary of Garfield and went to the train station as the president was leaving on a well-publicized trip. As Garfield and his party walked toward the main waiting room, Guiteau shot him in the back. The assassin was quickly caught and arrested. Garfield lived until September 19, 1881, with a bullet in his abdomen that could not be removed. Guiteau was tried, pleading insanity, found guilty, and hanged on June 30, 1882.

Taking justice into his own hands

Born and raised Jacob Rubenstein in Chicago, Jack Ruby became an entrepreneur, hanging around the fringes of the Chicago gangster world. In his thirties he moved to Dallas, where he ran a strip joint. The police knew of him, and paid no attention when he slipped into the basement of the Dallas Police headquarters on November 24, 1963. When Lee Harvey Oswald, the suspected assassin of President John F. Kennedy, was being relocated, Ruby stepped forward and shot him. Ruby was found guilty of murder and sentenced to death, but an appeals court overturned his conviction. Ruby, however, died of an embolism before another trial could take place, still implying that there were hidden causes behind the murder.

"Some difficult days ahead"

For hours the man crouched in a rooming-house bathroom, waiting for just the right moment. It came in the early evening, when James Earl Ray's long-awaited target stepped out onto his motel balcony, chatting casually with the Reverend Jesse Jackson. Suddenly, civil rights leader Martin Luther King, Jr., lay on the concrete, dying, a bullet through his jaw and neck. It was April 4, 1968, and the Reverend King was in Memphis, Tennessee, to give a speech at the Mason Street Temple. There were, indeed, difficult days ahead, because riots occurred through major U.S. cities in response to the killing.

King's killer, James Earl Ray, was an Alton-born man who had escaped from prison in Missouri the previous year. Apparently he had been following King for several months, living in fairly high style. Whether or not there was a group of conspirators who paid Ray to kill King has never been settled. But Ray, who confessed to the killing, was sentenced to 99 years in prison.

One who should know

When John W. Hinckley, Jr., attempted to kill President Reagan on a Washington, D.C., street in 1981, the most serious injury was sustained by Reagan's White House Press Secretary, James S. Brady. Brady, a Centralia native, was shot above his left eye. The bullet fragmented, sending metal into his brain. After five hours of surgery, Brady began a long, slow recovery. Brady and his wife became very vocal advocates of gun control, testifying wherever and whenever they could, as people who know just how devastating handguns can be. Brady's story was told in a 1992 TV movie, *Without Warning: The James Brady Story.*

MURDER I

Daniel Welsh of Buffalo, New York, already had a wife when he showed up in Chicago and fell in love with a respectable young woman named Rose. Discovering after their marriage that he was already married, Rose left him and arranged for him to lose his job. Welsh, furious, shot her. He was found guilty and sentenced to hang on December 10, 1869. Many people felt he should be reprieved because Rose's death was basically her own fault, so Welsh's lawyers managed to get enough signatures on a petition to force the governor to grant a reprieve. Welsh lived at Joliet prison for 25 years.

"She brought it on herself"

Herman Mudgett, one of America's most revolting serial killers, was born in Gilmanton, New Hampshire, and later left his first wife and child there when he moved on to medical school and, eventually, a career in murder in Chicago under the name H.H. Holmes. He began in the 1880s by killing an inconvenient landlady of a drugstore he wanted to own in suburban Englewood. After several years, he constructed a strange new "hotel" at 63rd and Wallace. It was a carefully designed masterpiece of a building, directed toward one end—the murder and disposal of bodies, without arousing suspicion in the neighborhood, because something special was going on nearby—the Columbian Exposition.

The Murder Castle and the Columbian Exposition

Young women were flocking to the city, hoping to earn a living. Instead, they earned their deaths by answering Holmes's ads. They readily fell for the handsome man they met and agreed to marry . . . after signing over their life savings or insurance policies. Then they died, usually in as gruesome a manner as possible. The bodies were disposed of in a limepit or were cut up and burned. However, when Mudgett decided it was time to eliminate some of the accumulating skeletons, he tried to burn down the hotel. From then it was only a matter of time. When he persuaded his Chicago assistant to pull a swindle in Philadelphia, Detective Frank P. Geyer gradually uncovered the history of Herman Mudgett and his "Murder Castle." The man may have killed as many as 200 people, but he was convicted in Pennsylvania of the lone murder of his assistant and was hanged in 1896.

The sausage maker

Adolph Louis Luetgert, president of a large Chicago sausage company, was known for his sexual pursuits. His wife became so jealous that Luetgert decided to get rid of her nagging by dissolving her in a chemical bath at his factory. He was arrested in 1898 for her murder and was convicted by the testimony of several of his mistresses who had heard him threaten to dispose of her. He always proclaimed his innocence, but when all that remained of Mrs. Luetgert—her friendship ring, pieces of bone, and her teeth—were recovered, Adolph's fate was sealed: life in prison.

Chicago Bluebeard

By the time he married his final victim in Chicago in 1904, German-born Johann Hoch had already wed, poisoned, and collected insurance on an untold number of women, from San Francisco to New York. There were perhaps as many as 50, but communications among police departments were inadequate at the time, and a tally was never made. However, the police were already watching him because of a tip from a West Virginia minister when he married Chicagoan Marie Walcker. She died within days and Hoch moved on to New York. There, his landlady recognized his photograph in the newspaper and he was extradicted to Chicago. Hoch was found guilty and hanged on February 23, 1906.

Darrow for the defense

University of Chicago students Nathan Leopold and Richard Loeb kidnapped 13-year-old Bobby Franks on May 22, 1924. In a note signed "George Johnson," they asked for $10,000 ransom as a cover. In reality they weren't concerned about money. Instead, they were trying to demonstrate that they were, in some way, superior to the common run of people. They had already killed Bobby and were quickly caught because they weren't as bright and superior as they had thought; their own mistakes revealed them. Famed attorney Clarence Darrow defended the two students, who would surely have gone to the electric chair if he had not been successful in convincing the jury that Leopold and Loeb were insane. Richard Loeb was murdered in a homosexual episode in prison in 1936. Nathan Leopold was paroled from prison in 1958 and went to a service job in Puerto Rico where he died in 1971.

THE CAPONE ERA

The man who started it all

A major era in organized crime in Chicago began with the arrival from Italy of teenaged James Colosimo in 1895. Within a few brief years he had control of Chicago's huge prostitution business. Later, when he ran into trouble in 1909, he sent for his nephew, John Torrio, from New York. The two worked well together for a number of years, until Torrio saw the potential for the bootlegging business when Prohibition was about to start. Colosimo disagreed; he was willing to stick to the old ways, and he was in charge. So Torrio decided to do something about that. He, too, sent for help from New York—in the form of a young killer named Alphonse Capone. On May 11, 1920, Big Jim Colosimo died at his restaurant, with a single bullet in the back of his head. Al Capone was on his way up.

After that, the ambitious Capone advanced from bartender and shill at Torrio's saloon to taking increasing control of the Chicago's bootlegging, prostitution, gambling, and dance halls. At age 26, Al Capone inherited the underworld of Chicago from Torrio, who returned to New York after serving a brief prison sentence in Waukegan. From then on, others did most of Capone's killing for him, especially Frank "The Enforcer" Nitti. Capone's business card called him simply a "Second-Hand Furniture Dealer."

On the morning of November 10, 1924, a customer at Schofield's Flower Shop on North Clark Street in Chicago found the florist dead among the colorful blossoms that he loved to arrange. The florist was bootlegger Dion O'Bannion, an Aurora-born gang leader who controlled North Side crime. His major opponents were Johnny Torrio and his protegé, Al Capone. Torrio called for O'Bannion's death, and Capone arranged it. Arrested the next day, the two men were quickly released because, of course, they had alibis. O'Bannion received a funeral worthy of one so famous and powerful! The procession was headed by an open car with a life-size statue of O'Bannion followed by 26 flower-laden cars—as much as $10,000 worth.

One way to take over

The St. Valentine's Day Massacre

Throughout the years after Capone took control, his gang and the one controlled by Bugsy Moran and Joey Aiello sniped back and forth at each other, killing one man here, another there. In early 1929, Capone demanded that all of his adversaries be taken care of. Nitti arranged for several killers, dressed as policemen, to go to Moran's headquarters in a garage on North Clark Street on February 14. They found seven gangsters, lined them up against a wall, and killed them all. As it happened, Moran was not there. When he heard of the murder method, he exclaimed, "Only Capone kills like that!" To which Capone, who was safely in Florida at the time, replied, "They don't call that guy 'Bugs' for nothin'." Capone thought he was making Chicago safe for his own people. Instead, the St. Valentine's Day Massacre set the federal government even more firmly on his trail.

The FBI agent who became a legend

☛ There was nothing shy about young Chicago Prohibition officer Eliot Ness. When he was given the assignment in 1929 of making life tough for Al Capone and his boys, Ness set up a group of nine agents, whom he called the "Untouchables," thus telling his adversaries from day one that his men could not be tempted or bribed. It was his job to make sure that the bootlegging business was hindered at every turn, and that the newspapers knew all about it. Such activities made the business of being a gangster much tougher. TV programs to the contrary, Ness, as he admitted in his autobiography, *The Untouchables,* never actually met Al Capone. But then, who wants to destroy a good myth?

A matter of taxes

☛ The only way the government could get to Al Capone was to charge him with income tax evasion. A federal court in Chicago found him guilty on October 17, 1931, and sentenced him to 11 years in prison, along with a fine of $80,000. He was quoted as saying, "Let the worthy citizens of Chicago get their liquor the best they can. I'm sick of the job—it's a thankless one and full of grief. I've been spending the best years of my life as a public benefactor." Capone was released in 1939 suffering from syphilis. He died on his Florida estate in 1947.

The "Terrible" Touhy

☛ The Chicago area's own home-grown gangster of the Prohibition Era was Roger "The Terrible" Touhy, born in Chicago and raised in Downers Grove, where he was an altar boy at the local church. By 1926, Touhy and his brothers were using their trucking business to distribute bootleg liquor in the northwest suburbs, where one of the best customers was Al Capone. However, Capone decided he wanted the territory. Touhy pretended through negotiation sessions to be a man who wouldn't hestitate to kill, thus earning the nickname "The Terrible." Ultimately, Touhy and his cohorts were convicted of a kidnapping that Capone's men had performed. Sent to Joliet prison for 199 years, Touhy spent ten years trying to prove his innocence before escaping and being put on the FBI's Most Wanted List. Free only briefly, Touhy was returned to Stateville. After 26 years in prison, Touhy published his story in a book, *The Stolen Years.* The book may have played a role in convincing a judge in 1959 that the kidnapping for which he had been convicted was faked. Three weeks after he was released and had gone to live with his sister in Chicago, Touhy was killed by shots in the night.

The Dillinger question

☛ Most of John Dillinger's bank-robbing saga took place in neighboring Indiana and Ohio, but his death was one of the more famous moments in Chicago history—or was it? Dillinger had escaped from an Indiana lock-up using a hand-carved wooden "gun," and then fled to Chicago, which he knew well. Declared "Public Enemy #1" by the FBI, he was betrayed by a brothel keeper named Anna Sage, who became known as the infamous "Lady in Red." On the night of July 22, 1934, Dillinger, Sage, and another woman attended a showing of *Manhattan Melodrama,* starring Clark Gable and Myrna Loy, at the Biograph Theater on Lincoln Avenue. Waiting outside were more than twenty FBI agents, headed by the famed lawman, Melvin Purvis. As the trio came out of the theater, the women hung back, and Dillinger was shot.

Or was he? Chicagoan and true-crime writer Jay Robert Nash spent several years investigating the entire Dillinger story and is convinced that the death of a not-very-good lookalike was arranged by Dillinger himself so that he could be free to spend his loot and not be hounded wherever he went.

Chicago crime scene, in literature
American Gothic by Robert Block, 1974 - horror and murder at the Chicago World's Fair, based on Mudgett
Compulsion by Meyer Levin, 1956 - novel of the Leopold-Loeb murder
True Detective by Max Collins, 1984 - Chicago crime during Prohibition
Little Caesar by William Riley Burnett, 1929 - story based on Al Capone
Knock on Any Door by Willard Motley, 1947 - how a Chicago boy turned gangster
The Man with the Golden Arm by Nelson Algren, 1949 - the story of a slum resident
The Scott-Dunlap Ring by George LaFontaine, 1978 - true novel of Chicago safecrackers in 1900

Baby Face in Barrington

George "Baby Face" Nelson (original name: Lester Gillis) lived out his life and death in the Chicago area as a member of John Dillinger's gang. After Dillinger's apparent death in Chicago, Nelson got the rank of "Public Enemy #1," especially after he tried to rob as many banks as he could. But he wasn't bright enough to carry off the spree, and on November 27, 1934, he was cornered by FBI agents in a field at Barrington. They put 17 bullets in or through him, yet he still had the energy to get away. His body, clad only in underwear, was found the next day in a ditch near Niles.

Dr. Carl Holmberg, a chemistry professor at Syracuse University in New York, vanished from his office in 1955. Rockford paint-factory worker Verne Hansen was arrested on February 4, 1961, for drunk driving. A routine check showed the driver's fingerprints to match those of the missing professor. "I suppose I will have to go check up to see if the story is true," Hansen acknowledged when told of his true identity. He remembered nothing of his previous life.

A change in lifestyle

MURDER II

Valerie, one of the 21-year-old twin daughters of Senator Charles H. Percy, was murdered during the early morning hours of September 18, 1966, in an upper-floor bedroom at Percy's Kenilworth mansion. She suffered severe knife wounds to her chest, stomach, eye, and face as well as having her skull bashed in. There was no immediate arrest. However, in 1973, Francis Leroy Hohimer, who was serving 30 years for armed robbery in the Iowa State Penitentiary, told authorities that a deceased partner of his, Frederick Malchow, may have done the job. Malchow had died from a fall after breaking out of a Pennsylvania prison. Nothing was ever proved, and no other solution was found.

Unsolved

A terrible kind of groupie

Eddie Waitkus, first baseman of the 1949 Philadelphia Phillies, returned to his room at Chicago's Edgewater Beach Hotel and found a note saying a Ruth Ann Burns must see him at once. When the 29-year-old unsuspecting ballplayer knocked on her door, he was invited in by a woman he'd never seen before, secretary Ruth Ann Steinhagen. She pulled out a rifle and shot him in the chest, saying only, "For two years you have been bothering me, and now you are going to die."

But Eddie survived because Steinhagen then called the front desk. Ruth Ann, infatuated with the ballplayer, had brooded about him for two years, and without Waitkus's knowledge, she decided that if she couldn't have him, no one could. She was committed to Kankakee State Hospital. Novelist Bernard Malamud used the incident as the basis for his book, *The Natural,* which became a movie.

"Born to raise hell"

Those words were tattooed on the arm of killer Richard Speck, born in Kirkwood, Illinois, and raised in Texas. In 1966, Speck was in the Chicago area trying to get a job on a cargo ship. When there were no jobs, he started drinking and shooting drugs. On the night of July 13, he went to a house near the South Chicago Community Hospital, where nurses lived, dormitory style. One by one, he took eight women and stabbed or strangled them, raping one. A ninth woman, Corazon Amurao, a student nurse from the Philippines, managed to hide under a bed until far into the next day. Speck was arrested on July 17, after having self-inflicted cuts on his arms sewn up at Cook County Hospital. A jury found Speck guilty in less than an hour. He died in prison in 1992.

> Illinois's second-worst mass murder occurred in the late hours of January 8, 1993, when the two owners and five employees of a Brown's Chicken restaurant in Palatine were murdered. No solution was immediately forthcoming.

Clown of death

Contractor John Wayne Gacy, Jr., of Norwood Park near Des Plaines, was known as a man who would dress as a clown and perform at children's parties. What was not known was that after he picked up young men he molested, even tortured them, murdered them, and buried them under his house. One youth who got away told the Chicago police, but they refused to act. Then on December 11, 1978, a Des Plaines woman reported that her son had not returned after going to visit Gacy. A week later, police investigating Gacy's house noticed a peculiar smell. They soon located the bodies of 29 boys. Four more bodies found in nearby rivers were attributed to him. Gacy was tried, found guilty of 33 murders on March 13, 1980, and sentenced to 21 consecutive life terms and 12 death sentences. He is still on Death Row.

Tylenol murderer still unknown

One unknown person instigated a revolution in consumer items. He or she placed cyanide in some Tylenol capsules, placed a few capsules in each of several bottles, and returned the bottles to the shelves of several stores in the Chicago suburbs. Starting on September 29, 1982, several people had occasion to take some pain reliever . . . and they died, in great pain. A seventh-grader from Schaumburg, a brand-new mother in Winfield, a working mother in Lombard, three members of an Arlington Heights family, and a flight attendant were stricken. Within hours of an investigator putting together the fact that they had all taken Tylenol, every bottle of Tylenol in the country was taken off the shelves. But there were no clues. One man, James W. Lewis, tried to extort $1 million from the makers of Tylenol and went to prison for two consecutive 10-year terms. Many law officers think that Lewis was guilty of the original tampering, but there is no proof. No other solution has been found. Instead, every over-the-counter medicine made in America is now packaged in tamper-proof bottles, tubes, and plastic.

Twelve-year nightmare

"Getting involved" drastically changed the life of Oak Park resident Steven Linscott. In 1980, a young nursing student, Karen Anne Phillips, was found dead in her apartment near Linscott's home. Linscott reported to police that he dreamed about a young woman, her clothing pushed up, being beaten to death. The police assumed that Linscott was really confessing. He was arrested, tried, convicted, and sentenced to 40 years in prison. On July 15, 1992, just five days before a retrial was to begin, the prosecution announced that new scientific evidence had weakened the case and he was released.

DEATH AFLOAT AND ALOFT

☛ It was July 24, 1915. The employees of the Hawthorne Works in Cicero were looking forward to their annual outing. They were taking the excursion boat *Eastland* from the Chicago River out into Lake Michigan for a day on the water. More than 2,500 eager people had boarded the boat at the Clark Street bridge when some foolishness made most of the crowd rush over to one side of the big boat. It suddenly flipped, hull up, in the river, drowning 812.

The Eastland excursion

☛ The *Lady Elgin* was a steam sidewheeler that regularly made the journey on Lake Michigan between Chicago and Milwaukee. Early in the wee hours on September 8, 1860, the luxurious boat left from Chicago with its regular passengers and crew, plus 300 members of the Union Guards who had been at a fund-raising gala to support presidential candidate Stephen A. Douglas. Rain obscured the captain's vision of the schooner *Augusta of Oswego*, running without lights. The two boats collided off Winnetka. Of the 385 people on board, 98 people made the ten-mile swim to shore and 287 persons were drowned.

Death on Lake Michigan

In 1989, a diver, Harry Zych, discovered the remains of the *Lady Elgin* in Lake Michigan off Waukegan. He petitioned a court to declare the boat his property, but the State of Illinois historic preservation agency fought that decision and won.

☛ September 1961 was a bad time for airliners in the Chicago area. On September 1, a TWA Constellation crashed near Hinsdale, killing 78 passengers, making it the fourth worst air disaster in American history up to that time. Then, on September 17, a Northwest Orient Electra II crashed on takeoff from Midway Airport in Chicago. Thirty-seven people were killed in an accident that was caused by poor maintenance.

A very bad September

Fame and the airship   One of the most famous moments in public broadcasting occurred when the German Zeppelin *Hindenburg* exploded and burned as it was being attached to its mooring at Lakehurst, New Jersey, on May 6, 1937. Broadcasting about the arrival was Chicago newscaster Herb Morrison of WLS Radio. When the majestic vehicle burst into flames, Morrison continued to broadcast through his moans of horror and his tears. Amazingly, only 36 of the 97 people on board died, because the giant ship was close to the ground.

A record that must not be broken   The worst airplane disaster in American history occurred at Chicago's O'Hare International Airport on May 25, 1979. A fully loaded American Airlines DC-10 bound for California failed to get airborne on takeoff and crashed, killing all 279 people on board.

The Effingham fire   Incompetent hospital personnel failed to heed a visitor's warning about smelling smoke. The result was 77 dead from the fire at St. Anthony's Hospital in Effingham on April 5, 1949. The fire started in a basement laundry chute and quickly spread through the "fireproof" building. Twelve newborn babies were left in a room alone to die. None of the fire escapes was used. Many people died in their beds, unable to get out of restraints or traction apparatus. One writer noticed that "numerous press photographs show dozens of able-bodied citizens gaping at the spectacle without any effort at rescue work."

Fires and more fires

• On February 13, 1875, a Chicago *Sun* reporter predicted that a horrible theater fire was going to happen—there were too many unsafe conditions in the city's theaters. Twenty-eight years later, Chicago's Iroquois Theater—only 38 days old and billed as "absolutely fireproof"—fulfilled that prophetic warning when it was destroyed by fire on December 30, 1903. The 2,105 patrons who had come to see Eddie Foy in *Mr. Bluebeard* were unaware that sparks from an electric arc lamp used as a floodlight had ignited the bottoms of the scenery backdrops. The fire rapidly spread through the theater, killing about 600—most of them women and children. This second (and even more deadly) "Great Chicago Fire" led to the passage of a better fire code, and every theater in the United States installed an asbestos or iron curtain.

• A food plant explosion killed 42 in Pekin on January 3, 1924.

• A fire on February 8, 1934, at the state arsenal in Springfield, where numerous state records were kept, caused $850,000 damage and destroyed records that couldn't be duplicated.

• An ordnance plant explosion at Elwood killed 49 in 1942.

• During rush hour on May 25, 1950, a CTA streetcar was rerouted and hit a gasoline truck carrying 8,000 gallons of gas. Both vehicles ignited, killing 33 on the streetcar; eight surrounding buildings were destroyed by fire and many cars were demolished. This was the worst streetcar accident ever recorded.

• Airborne magnesium and aluminum dust ignited by a polishing machine in Haber Corp.'s Chicago metalwork plant resulted in a fiery explosion that killed 35 workers on April 16, 1953.

• A fire at a Chicago Catholic school called Our Lady of the Angels killed 87 children and 3 nuns on December 1, 1958.

THE BUSINESS OF BUSINESS

On January 11, 1837, young attorney Abraham Lincoln, in an address to the Illinois legislature, observed, "These capitalists generally act harmoniously, and in concert, to fleece the people." His views of businessmen hadn't changed by 1861, when he said to the U.S. Congress, "A few men own capital, and that few avoid labor themselves."

Lincoln's opinion notwithstanding, Illinois has become one of the major centers of business in America—and it isn't all Chicago. There's Caterpillar in Peoria, Archer-Daniels-Midland in Decatur, State Farm in Bloomington, Outboard Marine in Waukegan, and more.

Numerous businesses known worldwide were started in Illinois, by inventors and other people with ideas. And almost every place in the state can call itself the "capital" of something!

Come on in. The business climate's fine!

- A Quick Trip Around
- Down on the Farm
- Snackin' Time
- Inventors with Awesome Ideas
- Inventing Fun
- Tell It to America
- Workers Unite!
- Illinois Underground
- Shopkeeper to the World

This must be the Capital of the World!

$ A quick history of Illinois enterprise via town nicknames:

Abingdon - Wagon Capital of the World
Batavia - Rock City (from its limestone quarries)
Cairo - Goose Capital of the World
Centralia - Oil Center of Illinois
Chicago - Hog Butcher for the World (from Carl Sandburg but no longer true)
Decatur - Soybean Capital of the World
East Moline - Farm Implement Capital
Eureka - Pumpkin Capital of the World
Galesburg - World's Greatest Mule Market
Harvard - Milk Capital of the World
Kewanee - Hog Capital of the World
Monmouth - Prime Beef Capital of the World
Peoria - Whiskey Town (from huge Hiram Walker distillery)
Sparta - Comic Book Capital of the World (Spartan Printing Company used to print huge quantities of comic books)
Steger - Piano Center of America (the piano factory changed to radio cabinets long ago and then to TV cabinets)

A QUICK TRIP AROUND

Harvesting the river at Meredosia

$ After steamboats started running on the Mississippi River in 1826, Meredosia became a button center. Mussel shells, used in making pearl buttons, were collected each day from the river by people called shellers, and sold to the four button factories in town. The Boyd Button Company, which closed in 1948, was the last independent button-cutting plant in the country.

It was hard to keep a good train running

$ Early railroads in Illinois just couldn't make it. By 1837, Illinois had only 24 miles of railroad track. The state owned the Northern Cross, the first railroad pulled by a steam engine west of the Allegheny Mountains and north of the Ohio River. Because the engine required huge amounts of water and fuel, passengers were expected to carry water and load wood. The inadequate metal rails mounted on wood planks often curled and pierced the train-car floors.

In 1850, the Illinois Central Railroad received the first federal land grant for the purpose of constructing a railroad. The grant was for 2,700,000 acres of land on each side of the route, which was planned to go from Chicago to Cairo. On September 27, 1856, the final spike was driven in the 705-mile system. As in most Midwestern states, much of the state's development occurred along the railway routes. By 1901, the IC had a $32 million income, served 13 states, and had 4,200 rail miles.

It was an Illinois Central train, the Cannonball Express from Chicago to New Orleans, that brave engineer Casey Jones saved in real life and in the folk song.

Crossroads of America

In the 1940s, Chicago had 7 railroad stations, into which trains belonging to 41 different railroads converged. It was virtually impossible to go anywhere in the U.S. without transferring in Chicago. On any one day, 1,700 trains moved passengers, while an even greater number distributed freight.

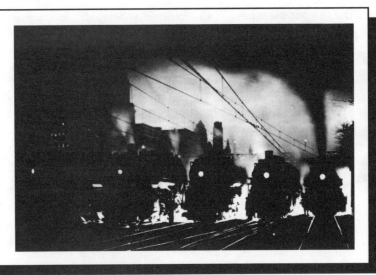

Pinkerton, Private Eye

⑤ Allan Pinkerton, the world's first "private eye," came from Scotland to Chicago, then Dundee, in 1842. He worked as a cooper (barrel-maker) before becoming a crime stopper. He was first the deputy sheriff of Kane County, then of Cook County. Pinkerton formed a detective agency that eventually became famous worldwide. This was helped when he prevented an assassination attempt on Abraham Lincoln soon after Abe's election to the presidency. After working for the Union during the Civil War, Pinkerton served as the tough guy for management in union battles around the country, giving him a bad name with many people. Pinkerton's firm used stationery that featured a picture of an eye with the slogan "We never sleep," which is thought to be where the term "private eye" comes from.

An Elgin watch was a precious possession

⑤ Chicago watchmakers, Benjamin Raymond and John C. Adams, founded Elgin National Watch Company in 1864. Absorbed in perfecting every detail, they didn't produce their first watch until 1867, priced at $117, an incredibly high price at that time. But by 1881, production had gone up to 2,000 watches a day and the price went down. Elgin watches were known for accuracy and durability. Competition from the Swiss in the 1960s forced the company to change its manufacturing and marketing strategies and leave their 13-story building in Elgin after a hundred years. Going where the experienced watchmakers were, Waltham Watch Company later moved into Elgin.

Conquest of the blob

⑤ It was one of the 1960s' more memorable fads—and it's come around again in the '90s. What is it? The Lava Lite. It's a lamp filled with a fluid in which a nebulous blob bubbles and oozes in response to the heat of the bulb. It comes in many colors, often quite garish. But watching the continuous motion had a tranquilizing effect. And many have been the conversations—nay, arguments—about how the lamp works. The Chicago firm that makes it, Lava Simplex Internationale, refuses to say, except that it's not oil and water but a mixture of 11 different chemicals.

Double your pleasure

ⓢ   William Wrigley, Jr., learned early that he had what it took to be a successful salesman. Selling both his father's soap and other products, he first discovered chewing gum as a premium, given away to help sell baking powder. Soon people were asking for the gum and ignoring the baking powder. He quickly reversed the procedure and started giving away other premiums to persuade retailers to buy his gum. In 1893, he started manufacturing his own gum, introducing Wrigley's Spearmint and Juicy Fruit. He always advertised heavily, saying that it was necessary to "Tell them quick and tell them often." Today the Wrigley Company sells about half of America's chewing gum. (See p. 126)

Not necessarily a pretty read

ⓢ   Six novels of Chicago's business world:

The Chute by Albert Halper, 1937 - work in a Chicago mailing house

Danger! Keep Out by Edward Nichols, 1943 - gas, oil, and cars: industry in 1920s' Chicago

The Foundry by Albert Halper, 1934 - 1920s' industry

The Jungle by Upton Sinclair, 1906 - exposé of the stockyards

The Pit by Frank Norris, 1903 - protest of Chicago's wheat market

Tomorrow's Bread by Beatrice Bisno, 1938 - sweatshops and the labor development in Chicago

The phantom whitewasher

An unidentified man calling himself Mandrake ran a one-man crusade against tobacco and liquor billboards in Chicago's innercity in the 1980s. Apparently fed up with companies targeting African-Americans and Hispanics, he decided to destroy their advertising by painting over it. Describing himself as a 54-year-old concerned professional, Mandrake said he thought he had a moral obligation to fight back. Lung cancer rates are four times higher for blacks than whites and the incidence of drinking-related illnesses in minority groups is skyrocketing.

Zenith: The first and the last

ⓢ   Chicago Radio Laboratory was established in 1915 by two Chicago ham operators, R.H.G. Mathews and Karl Hassel. A wealthy investor, Eugene F. McDonald, came on board in 1921 as sales agent and helped to form the new Zenith Radio Corporation. Zenith is the last independent manufacturer of color TV and picture tubes in the country. Competition from Japan has become tough, but the company's future may lie in the development of high-definition television.

> Zenith made the:
> first portable radio in 1924
> first push-button radio in 1927
> first black-and-white TV
> first remote control device
> first color TVs.
> And if you're a stereo FM radio listener, you listen to a system introduced by Zenith and approved by the Federal Communications Commission as the national system.

DOWN ON THE FARM

What Illinois farmers grow

Farming began in Illinois with the first settlers clearing the land for crops. Today, the state is reaping the harvest of their toil. Illinois ranks #1 in the nation in soybeans, and #2 in both corn and hogs (Iowa is #1). McLean County is #1 in the nation in corn production, Henry County in hogs, and Champaign County in soybeans.

The five main crops grown on Illinois farms are (according to 1990 statistics):

Corn - $2.768 billion
Soybeans - $2.059 billion
Hogs - $1.206 billion
Cattle - $802 million
Dairy Products - $357 million

💲 In 1831, Cyrus McCormick, age 22, from Rockbridge County, Virginia, publicly demonstrated a reaper, a device that would take the back-breaking labor out of harvesting wheat. Although the elements in the machine had been separately invented by other people, he had incorporated them into one working reaper. Throughout his life, however, other inventors would challenge his accomplishment. Convinced that the West was his future market, McCormick moved to Chicago in 1851 and opened a factory to produce his "Virginia reaper." By 1856, he was building 15 mechanical reapers per day. In 1879, Cyrus McCormick was elected by the French Academy of Sciences to their list of great achievers, saying he had "done more for agriculture than any other living man."

A man with one idea— and that a good one

Conquest of the midwest soil

John Deere moved from Rutland, Vermont, in 1837 to start a blacksmith business in Grand Detour. The clay soil in the area was rich, but instead of sliding off plow blades, it stuck, and farm equipment was always in Deere's shop for repair. At a sawmill, he found a broken steel sawblade, took it home, and began experimenting with the polished steel to make a plow that soil wouldn't stick to. Deere and his partner, Leonard Andrus, were able to produce only ten "self-scouring" Grand Detour plows in 1839. In 1846 Deere found a Pittsburgh steel mill that could supply him with the polished steel he needed. By 1857 Deere had moved to Moline and was producing 10,000 plows each year.

Illinois created the image of the American farm

$ Responsibility for the Dick-and-Jane image of the American farm stems from silos and windmills. Storage silos used to be pits in the ground covered with boards. Then, in 1873, Spring Grove farmer Fred L. Hatch looked for a way to stop grain being spoiled by rain and ground seepage. Get it out of the ground, ran his logic. So he did, by lining a square hole inside a barn with rocks and mortar and then carrying the liner up into an above-ground building. But the corners caused problems because it was hard to get the air out of them. A Wisconsin scientist suggested that Hatch make the thing round, and, lo, the silo seen round the world was born. The Hatch family used that first silo for 46 years before taking it down.

Most of the classic windmills came from Batavia. Before 1940 (when rural electrification became widespread), Batavia's name was known far and wide, because it appeared on metal plates attached to the electricity-generating windmills that three Batavia manufacturers turned out by the thousands for many decades.

Barbed wire goes to court

$ Jacob Haish, Joseph F. Glidden, and Isaac L. Ellwood attended the De Kalb County Fair in the spring of 1873 where Henry Rose, a Clinton Township farmer, displayed his "fencing attachment." His patented invention consisted of small wooden strips with random metal wires protruding from them. These strips were to be fastened onto regular fences, wire or wood, to keep animals from breaking through them. Each of the three men worked on a better way to make such "barbed" wire. Each applied for a patent between October 1873 and February 1874. Haish received his on January 20, 1874, but his wire was never made. Glidden and Ellwood built a factory for the Barb Fence Company in 1875. Each accused the other of stealing the idea.

The matter of who actually invented barbed wire became of vital importance as its sales took off. However, until the patent ownership was settled, there was the possibility that individual farmers might be sued by other inventors claiming royalties. The issue was settled on February 29, 1892, when the U.S. Supreme Court decided that ". . . it was Glidden, beyond question, who first published this device; put it on the record; made use of it for a practical purpose; and gave it to the public." De Kalb became the Barbed Wire Capital of the World.

Bet-A-Million Gates

$ At age 21 in 1876, Chicagoan John Warne Gates started selling for a barbed-wire maker in De Kalb. The ranchers he met in the West saw no point in the wire until he fenced 25 Texas longhorns into a San Antonio plaza and told ranchers to see if they could stampede them through the wire. When they failed, his reputation was established and his order book filled. Within a month, he had more orders for barbed wire than the factory could fill, so he bought the factory.

His nickname of Bet-A-Million was acquired after he discovered the joys of gambling by betting $70,000 on a horse race and winning $600,000. After that, he'd bet on anything, whether it moved or not. Eventually, billions of dollars moved through his hands, both coming and going. In later years, Gates—by then the virtual owner of Port Arthur, Texas—was involved in the beginnings of Texaco Oil.

Ⓢ The oldest herd of cattle in North America still owned by the same family still lives where it was founded, in Creston, Illinois. No, that doesn't mean the cows are ancient; it means that the herd has continued to reproduce itself, generation after generation. The famed herd of Angus cattle was started in 1881 by B.R. Pierce, who brought the animals from Scotland.

He knew a good thing when he saw it

The farmer with the magic voice

Iroquois County farmer Walter Hasselbring produced the highest-yielding corn crop seven times in the years from 1975 to 1990, according to the National Corn Growers Association. His 296-bushel-per-acre yield was more than twice the average for the rest of the farms in Iroquois County. There are several secrets to Hasselbring's success. He uses 300 pounds of nitrogen per acre and adds a "lot of bull"—manure from his 105-animal buffalo and cattle herd. But the real secret ingredient is his singing—Hasselbring croons as he strolls through his cornfields and says he "can almost see them grow."

AWESOME

Ⓢ Caterpillar is the #1 producer of earth-moving equipment in the world. The British designed an armored tank in 1915, nicknamed "caterpillar" because of the continuous metal track on which it ran instead of wheels. Benjamin Holt of Stockton, California, saw how efficient such a machine was and modified a farming tractor by using a gasoline engine and putting crawler tracks on it. In 1925, Best Tractor merged with Holt's company, and in 1928, the company, now called Caterpillar, moved its headquarters to Peoria. A Caterpillar tractor is shown here moving coal, another of Illinois's major products.

At the sign of the Cat

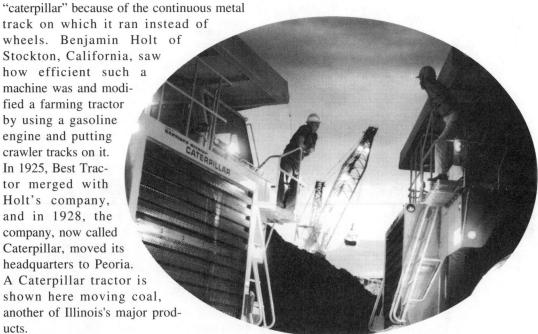

Ducks, ducks, everywhere

⑤ Hanover is the international center for mallard duck production. Whistling Wings Duck Hatchery ships over 200,000 birds each year to game preserves all around the world. Many birds are released directly into the Mississippi Flyway, under which Hanover is located.

Life, for many, focused on the stockyards

⑤ When the meat-packing industry was centered at Chicago's Union Stock Yards, 12 million animals were shipped there each year by rail. The Union Stock Yards was organized in 1865—and opened on Christmas Day—by John B. Sherman who had had a stockyard in Chicago since 1848. The new square-mile yards quickly attracted Swift, Armour, Morris, and others who built plants nearby. Generation after generation of Chicagoans were employed by the stockyards. But working conditions were horrendous and unsanitary. Upton Sinclair's muckraking novel, *The Jungle,* was written to protest these conditions, causing the public to demand an investigation, which led to the federal inspection of meat. Ira Victor Morris's 1952 novel, *The Chicago Story,* is the saga of German immigrants among the meat-packing industry.

As the railroad industry was slowing, more and more meat was being packed farther west, closer to the ranges where the cattle lived, especially in the Kansas City area. By July 30, 1972, the long-term Chicago industry had died and the stockyards were closed.

⚜ Today's Lunch Menu ⚜

Peanut butter sandwich
Peter Pan Peanut Butter from Swift-Eckrich of Downers Grove.
Pepperidge Farm bread, also from Downers Grove.

Bologna and cheese sandwich
Miracle Whip salad dressing, invented by Chicagoan Max Crosset and sold to Kraft Products for $300.
Cheese from Kraft General Foods in Northfield, started by James Kraft, a Chicago cheese wholesaler, and Thomas H. McInnerney, a pharmacist who became more interested in ice cream than drugs.
Bologne from Swift-Eckrich or Oscar Mayer Company, started in 1883 by three brothers with a sausage shop in Chicago.

Dessert
From Sara Lee, which was founded and located in Deerfield for many decades, or goodies from Elmhurst, where the Keebler elves' tree is located.

SNACKIN' TIME

The margarine smugglers

Margarine—a fake "butter" made first from animal fats and then from vegetable oils—was patented in the U.S. in 1873. But the states that depended heavily on their dairy industry promptly objected—especially Illinois's neighbor, Wisconsin. For many decades—until the 1950s, in fact—a big business along the northern border of Illinois was supplying the margarine smugglers, people who drove in from Wisconsin to clandestinely purchase large quantities of the illegal spread and hurry it home to their refrigerators.

⑤ In 1954, Ray A. Kroc of Oak Park, a distributor of milkshake mixers, was visiting Dick and Mac's McDonalds in San Bernardino, California, when his curiosity was aroused by the large number of mixers the brothers bought for their restaurants. The brothers were running their kitchen like an assembly line in order to handle the many orders for hamburgers, fries, and milkshakes. Their motto was, "If you want fancy, go somewhere else. If you want a simple good meal and you want it fast, come to us."

"You deserve a break today!"

Kroc became the national franchise agent for the McDonald brothers. The franchise agreement called for a percentage of sales. On April 15, 1955, Ray Kroc opened his first McDonald's in Des Plaines (photo). That same year "Speedee," a little hamburger man, became the company symbol. In 1961, Kroc bought out the McDonald brothers for $2.7 million after annual sales hit $54 million. He also changed the company's logo to the Golden Arches. With the chain in hand, Hamburger University was opened in Elk Grove Village, and Bachelor of Hamburgerology degrees were awarded to the first graduating class. When Ray Kroc died on January 14, 1984, there were 7,778 restaurants and 45 billion hamburgers had been served. By 1993, 100 billion was in sight.

Sweet dreams in hamburger land

McDonald's Corporation, which is headquartered in Oak Brook, installed a 700-gallon hamburger-shaped waterbed on which executives can brainstorm. Do you suppose that if one of them falls asleep, he or she will dream of the Hamburglar?

AWESOME

⑤ Otto Schnering of Chicago, founder of Curtiss Candy Company, produced a 5-cent bar that combined peanuts, caramel, chocolate, and fudge, which he called Kandy Kate. The candy bar became so popular that he had to hire 125 additional people just to fill orders. When he decided to hold a rename-the-candy-bar contest, the winner was "Baby Ruth," after President Cleveland's oldest daughter who had died of diphtheria at age 12. It didn't hurt that many people thought the bar was named for Babe Ruth, who hit 54 home runs in 1920. When the baseball star tried to market a candy bar in his own name in 1930, Schnering took him to court and kept the baseball star from cashing in on his own name.

Baby Ruth conquers the Babe

Chuckles, Jelly Bellys, and Ronald Reagan

ⓢ In addition to Curtiss, the Chicago area is home to several other biggies in the world of candy. Brach, founded by Chicagoan Frank Brach, makes all those interesting little things such as chocolate-covered peanuts, candy corn, and toffee that you find sold in bags just about everywhere. Leaf of Bannockburn makes, among other familiar candies, Heath bars, Chuckles, and Milk Duds. And, lest we forget, there's Jelly Bellys, made famous by President Ronald Reagan's sweet tooth. He ordered several cases every month of the elegant little jelly beans that come in flavors nature never intended. Jelly Bellys are made by the Goelitz Confectionery Company of North Chicago.

"That's Crackerjack!"

ⓢ The people who regularly passed F.W. Rueckheim's popcorn stand in Chicago in the 1890s knew that his carmelized popcorn-and-nuts was something special, but it took a particularly enchanted customer in 1896 to exclaim, after tasting his first bite, "That's crackerjack!" Rueckheim took the comment as the new name for his product and soon began to box the popcorn and sell it in baseball stadiums. He put tiny prizes in the box along with the popcorn and nuts to give an added excitement to the product. Little has changed about the product since, to the delight of nibblers everywhere.

INVENTORS WITH AWESOME IDEAS

Lincoln wasn't just a lawyer

ⓢ Abraham Lincoln was awarded a patent in 1849 for inflatable cylindrical devices that would help boats float over rocky shoals. The shipping industry, however, took little note of his great invention, and he was a little too busy to pursue it.

The man who couldn't play his own invention

ⓢ Evanston-born experimenter Laurens Hammond had the good fortune (family fortune, that is) to be able to follow his own curiosity. After inventing an electric clock, he turned his skills to imitating the sounds coming from a phonograph. The result was the first electronic keyboard, aka: Hammond organ, which he couldn't even play. Pipe-organ manufacturers objected—not to his lack of playing talent, but to his claims that the instrument could reproduce the sounds of a traditional organ—but the Federal Trade Commission agreed that the Hammond machine, could, indeed, match the more expensive machines. Hammond also invented a not-so-popular electric bridge table that automatically shuffled and dealt cards.

💲 George M. Pullman, a Chicagoan by choice, developed a special railroad car in which people could sleep on long journeys. However, no one was particularly interested because the car was higher and wider than the usual car—until tragedy turned into good luck for Pullman. Abraham Lincoln was assassinated in Washington, D.C., and Illinois wanted its own hero brought home in style. A luxurious Pullman car was added to the funeral train carrying his body from Chicago to Springfield. Overnight, the modifications needed on the line—from bridges being raised to roadways widened—were made. Thousands along the route saw Pullman's special car, and his fortune was made.

Traveling in style

💲 J. Frank Duryea and his brother, Charles, originally bicycle-shop owners from Peoria, moved to Springfield, Massachusetts, where they worked on developing new-fangled automobiles. They built a gasoline-powered car, the Duryea Motor Wagon, that won first prize in America's first major auto contest—often called a race, though it wasn't really. Sponsored by Herman H. Kohlsaat, publisher of the *Chicago Times-Herald,* on Thanksgiving Day in 1895, the event was meant to demonstrate that automobiles might soon replace horses. Kohlsaat's PR man, however, managed to turn it into the "Race of the Century." The Duryea car completed a "sustained ride of 40 miles, from Jackson Park to Evanston and back" in only 9 hours, an average of 6.6 mph over the very snowy course. Only one other of the six entrants was gasoline-powered.

And the winners are the Duryeas!

💲 Illinoisans in the National Inventors Hall of Fame include:
Cyrus McCormick for his reaper and John Deere for his plow (see page 157).
Lewis Hastings Sarett (born Champaign), for developing a way to synthe size compounds from materials that don't occur naturally.
Marvin Camras (born Chicago) for developing magnetic recording.
Arnold O. Beckman (born Cullom), for inventing equipment to measure acidity of materials (he also started Beckman Instruments).

National Inventors Hall of Fame

INVENTING FUN

💲 Moses Gerrish Farmer of Chicago, an imaginative electrician with a bent for play, demonstrated in 1843 that it was possible to run a toy train by electricity. However, he did nothing to turn this idea into a commercial enterprise.

Toy trains too early

A nightmare or a welcome voice!

Technasonic of Lincolnwood markets a "talking" scale that is able to keep track of your weight. The first time you use the scale, you're given a memory number. Then, each time you step on the scale, it can tell in both digits and voice how much you've lost or gained since you last weighed yourself. It's bad enough to have to read the result, but to hear it, too?!

Inventors who believed in fun
Illinoisans who invented items for life on the lighter side:
- Ball-bearing roller skate, by Levant Richardson of Chicago.
- Pinball game, invented in 1930 by Chicago's In and Outdoor Games Company.
- Portable movie projector, by Chicagoan Herman DeVry.
- Self-healing cord bicycle tire, invented by John F. Palmer of Chicago and produced by B. F. Goodrich. And the bicycle that you stop by back pedaling was invented by Freeport's Daniel Stover and William Hance.
- Solar-powered radio receiver, invented by the Admiral Corporation in Chicago in 1955, using newly invented transistors.
- Vacuum cleaner that worked by suction, patented by Chicagoan Ives McGaffrey—whoops! That doesn't belong here! It's not fun!
- Zipper, invented by Chicagoan Whitcomb Judson, especially fun for people who hated hooks and eyes.
- Ferris wheel, invented by George Washington Gale Ferris of Galesburg (see p. 74).

Tinkering around

⑤ Good ideas can come from anywhere. An Evanston stonemason invented one of the classic toys made of wood (at least it used to be; now it's plastic). Charles Pajeau, after watching children play contentedly for hours with empty thread spools and sticks, put together a set of simple wooden pieces that children could tinker with. Tinker Toys went on the market in 1913 and promptly sold a million sets.

Thinking on a different scale

⑤ Frank Lloyd Wright wanted to build the biggest skyscraper in the world. His son, John Lloyd Wright, had a lot more fun out of miniature logs that children could use to construct things. In 1916, the J.L. Wright Company began producing the now-famous Lincoln Logs, which allowed children to construct any idea they could come up with. Wright's company merged with Playskool in 1943. The logs are now produced in Walla Walla, Washington, from Ponderosa pine—one of the few toys left made of wood.

TELL IT TO AMERICA

A Pulitzer in Mexico

Usually a Pulitzer Prize-winning journalist is regarded as a serious individual who covers important events, but Chicago-born Stan Delaplane (who won his Pulitzer in 1942) gained most of his renown on international junkets that filled his newspaper columns. The man who earlier introduced Irish coffee into the United States set out in 1961 to locate the skull of Mexican revolutionary hero-cum-bandit Pancho Villa, which had been missing from his grave since 1926. Delaplane got together a group of pilots in small planes, who called themselves Delaplane's Dorados. And, while Mexican farmers dug up the ground near the Chihuahua Desert, they zoomed overhead, supposedly keeping an eye out for the small object. No luck but plenty of publicity.

$ The first newspaper published in Illinois was Kaskaskia's *Illinois Herald* published by Matthew Duncan beginning in 1814. Duncan was a Kentuckian who had come to Illinois as a hanger-on of the territorial governor, Ninian Edwards. A year later, Duncan was responsible for the first book printed in Illinois, *Laws of the Territory of Illinois*. It later came to be called *Pope's Digest* after Nathaniel Pope, who persuaded the legislature to authorize its printing.

The first newspaper in Illinois

$ For a time in the 1940s and '50s, Hollywood, its image and its industry, was virtually controlled by three women who were essentially gossip columnists and broadcasters. One was Hedda Hopper, the second was Sheilah Graham, and the other was Freeport-born Louella Parsons (real name: Louella Oettinger). A snide comment from one of them in the press could destroy a career, while frequent mentions of others might build their careers.

The power of an inquisitive woman

Actually, Louella started the whole business, by writing the very first movie column, which was published in the *Chicago Herald* in 1914. Forever after attached to the papers of William Randolph Hearst, she moved from New York to Hollywood in 1925, where she quickly became a power with her radio interview show, "Hollywood Hotel."

$ archie, the literary cockroach who can't manage a shift key on a typewriter and so writes everything in lower case, and mehitabel, rowdy queen of alley cats, are the creations of walnut-born don marquis. he began his career by writing for joel chandler harris's *uncle remus's magazine*. the philosophic cat and cockroach first appeared in his immensely popular column, "the sun dial," for the new york *evening sun*. marquis's first book, archy and mehitabel, was first published in 1927.

a cat, a cockroach, and no capitals

$ John H. Johnson moved to Chicago from Arkansas as a teenager, when his mother decided he would get a better education there. After attending DuSable High School, he worked for a black-owned insurance company where he had an idea to produce a magazine just for African-Americans. Working with a loan of $500, Johnson produced the first *Negro Digest* in 1942. He sent a mailing to the 20,000 customers of the insurance company, and 3,000 of them subscribed. That success lead quickly to the creation in 1945 of *Ebony,* the magazine that became the backbone of Johnson Publishing Company, then *Jet,* in 1951, and *EM*, in 1985. Johnson Publishing Company is the most successful black publishing company in the world. It is involved in magazine and book publishing, as well as cosmetics, hair care, and broadcasting.

Publishing for African-Americans

The presidency of Johnson Publishing Company has been passed on to Linda Johnson Rice, who has become one of the first women in the U.S. to run a major publishing company.

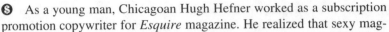

The publisher in the plain brown wrapper

ⓢ As a young man, Chicagoan Hugh Hefner worked as a subscription promotion copywriter for *Esquire* magazine. He realized that sexy magazines had a real market. Starting with a $600 investment, he developed a men's magazine that was to be called *Stag Party*. Before it went to press, however, he changed its name to *Playboy*. The first issue, published on December 10, 1953, featured a picture of Marilyn Monroe, nude.

As the magazine zoomed in popularity, Hefner realized that he could capitalize even further on the concept, and the first of what eventually became 22 private-membership Playboy Clubs worldwide opened in Chicago in 1960, featuring service by luscious Playboy "bunnies." For some years, Hefner had a late-Saturday-night TV program on which nubile women meandered through a cocktail-drinking crowd while name entertainers sang or played. Called the "#1 sexcess story," Hefner's business has recentlysuffered great losses as women's roles have been changing in America. Recently, people have blamed (praised?) Hefner for virtually single-handedly changing the mores of America by establishing the principle that "romance and marriage are . . . deadly enemies." Chicago columnist Len O'Connor called Hefner the "Christopher Columbus of soft porn." He has recently settled down, marrying one of his centerfolds and fathering a son. His adult daughter has taken charge of Playboy Enterprises.

What a library!

ⓢ Playboy Enterprises reference library in Chicago is the most unusual in the world. The shelves contain over eight thousand volumes and three hundred periodicals, most of which you would never see at a public library. A professional librarian and three assistants serve cocktails and make sure no one is clipping pictures. One of the most unusual holdings is a complete collection of *Playboy* magazines in Braille. Do library users read the articles or feel their way over the centerfolds?

Give that man a big cigar!

ⓢ Chicago-native William Paley, excited at the sales results when his father's cigar company advertised on early radio, bought a small, existing group of radio stations that he turned into the communications giant, Columbia Broadcasting System.

Stand by . . . for news!

His picture may not look like it, but this man, ladies and gentlemen, this Paul Harvey, listened to by millions on ABC Radio from Chicago, was arrested in 1951 for scaling a fence at Argonne National Laboratory in Lamont to demonstrate the lack of laboratory security. Now, this Oklahoma-born newsman contents himself with getting up very early in the morning to begin concocting his popular amalgam of news, opinion, commercials, and "The Rest of the Story."

WORKERS UNITE!

⑤ Clyde Bolton, an assembly line worker at Ford Motor Company's Chicago plant, was recently named "best dressed." Bolton showed up for work in ruffled shirts with pink collars, white suits, and/or tuxedos. Bolton's simple explanation was that he felt "better when" when he was well dressed.

Making a personal statement

⑤ The 1867, a new Illinois law declared that "eight hours of labor . . . shall constitute and be a legal day's work, where there is no special contract or agreement to the contrary." To get around the law, special contracts were devised and many employers, often banding together, simply told workers they would be fired if they didn't work as they were told. Other employers "leased" convict labor. For example, in 1884, the average yearly wage for a shoemaker in Illinois was $355; the same work could be done for $159 by convict labor.

New to the nation: the 8-hour day

⑤ The United Mine Workers had managed to get an 8-hour day and a fairly hefty increase in pay for the coal miners of southern Illinois in 1897, but then the Chicago-Virden Coal Company dropped out of the agreement. With the miners on strike, the company brought a large number of black miners from the South, along with 75 armed guards. On October 12, 1898, the two groups clashed. Ten miners and six guards were killed and numerous other men were injured. A monument to the slain men stands at Virden.

The Virden Massacre

⑤ Mary Harris Jones, famed union organizer, came to Chicago as a child from Ireland. She worked as a dressmaker at various times, both before and after she became a widow and lost four children to yellow fever. Losing all her possessions in the Great Chicago Fire of 1871, she found herself being helped by men of the Knights of Labor, whose hall wasn't totally destroyed. She gradually became more and more committed to the labor cause, helping strikers across the country. She rarely settled down after that, living where the action was.

The mother who refused to stay home

"Mother" Jones's short, white-haired figure became a familiar sight at strikes, especially among miners. She helped the United Mine Workers organize in the various mining areas of West Virginia and Colorado. She also began to lecture widely, often bringing tears to the eyes of her audiences by drawing upon often-suppressed horror stories of massacres and riots. She was always able to gain publicity for her causes, because of both who and what she was. At 100 years old, still fighting for what she believed in, congratulations poured in, even from industrialists who had previously been her sworn enemies. At her own request, Mother Jones was buried in the Union Miners Cemetery at Mount Olive, Illinois, among the miners who had been killed in the Virden Massacre. Almost 15,000 people attended her funeral.

The miners weren't always the good guys

⑤ In the early 1920s, mines all over the country were reducing wages their men earned for the dangerous work. At Herrin, where the striking miners controlled the area, a number of gun-toting miners convinced a large group of nonunion miners that they would be granted safe conduct out of town. As the eager "scabs" tried to leave, however, the union miners yelled at them to run if they valued their lives. They ran, and the miners shot them in the back. Twenty-one men were killed. This was just one of a series of episodes that caused Herrin's county to be called "Bloody Williamson" (see p. 143).

The first industrial health expert in America

⑤ Other nations concerned themselves with the health of their workers a hundred years ago, but the United States did not, until Dr. Alice Hamilton (sister of Greek scholar Edith Hamilton and friend of Jane Addams) began to investigate the curious belief that because American workers were paid well, their jobs couldn't make them ill. A professor of pathology at Northwestern University, in 1910, she was appointed to the Occupational Disease Commission in Illinois, the first body charged with investigating industry-related diseases. The result of her work was the first workmen's compensation legislation. She next undertook the same kind of investigation for the federal government.

ILLINOIS UNDERGROUND

The salt of the earth

⑤ Proof that seas once covered Illinois lies in the salt deposits of Gallatin County. One of the earliest salt works west of the Allegheny

Mountains was near the present-day town of Equality. The French and Indians were producing salt before any major white settlement began. In 1803, the Indians signed over the "great salt springs" to the federal government. At its height, the area produced 500 bushels of salt per day from brine. Although slavery was prohibited everywhere in Illinois by the Northwest Ordinance, slaves and indentured servants were allowed in these salt-manufacturing operations. There were 239 slaves in Gallatin County in 1820.

Getting the lead out

⑤ In the early 1700s, Nicholas Perrot was the first white man to see Indians operating galena mines. Discovering that lead taken from galena ore could be used for bullets, he spread the word. By 1807, the federal government was in control of the mines, and miners from Europe, especially Cornwall, England, began to pour into the area. The town of Galena became a boomtown—at least for the men. Women entered at their own risk. There were so few of them that any female, 13 or older, female entering town could be married within hours. In 1845, 45 million pounds of lead were shipped out, 80 percent of the nation's total.

Illinois and coal

$ Great deposits of soft, or bituminous, coal were laid down across southern Illinois during the Pennsylvania Period of geologic history. The first coal mining in Illinois occurred at the Big Muddy River bluffs by Murphysboro. The supply was on the surface and little digging was required to reach the useful mineral. Now coal is transported all over, and the main mines are in Perry, Franklin, Jefferson, St. Clair, and Williamson counties. At the heart of the coal region is the town of—appropriately enough—Carbondale.

Illinois has more coal reserves (dark area on map) than any other state except Montana—an estimated 78 billion short tons. Coal mining is not a thing of the past. In fact, in 1991, Illinois produced about 60 million short tons, more than two-thirds of the amount produced in the historical peak year of 1918. About 10,000 people are still employed in coal mining of both strip mines and underground mines in Illinois.

A history of disaster

$ A small explosion in the Moweaqua coal mine on December 22, 1932, was ignored. Gases built up, and on Christmas Eve, an explosion killed 54 of 56 miners who entered the shaft. The dead included two sets of sons and fathers, two bridegrooms, and seven sets of brothers.

When a mine explosion at Centralia killed 111 men on March 25, 1947, United Mine Workers President John L. Lewis demonstrated his power by shutting down all U.S. soft-coal mines for a week in their memory. The company was fined only $1,000 for the accident.

When inspectors twice asked for safety improvements at a West Frankfort mine, the superintendent said they weren't going to get made. On December 21, 1951, a huge methane explosion killed 119 miners.

The Cherry Mine disaster

The worst industrial accident in Illinois occurred on November 13, 1909, when 259 men (including 12 rescue workers) lost their lives in a mine fire and subsequent explosion at the St. Paul Coal Mine in Cherry. A load of hay, intended for the mules at the bottom of mine, caught fire from a leaking kerosene torch, and fire swept through the tunnels. Rescue operations continued for 36 hours.

SHOPKEEPER TO THE WORLD

"Give the lady what she wants"

⑤ Retailer and merchant Marshall Field quit school at the age of 16 to clerk in a store. After moving to Chicago in 1856, he was employed as a traveling salesman for a wholesale firm. Six years later, the ambitious Field was a general partner. In 1865 he and two other men formed Field, Palmer, and Leiter. Marshall had bigger plans than his partners, however, and he bought them out in 1881 when he established Marshall Field and Company. Field introduced innovative retailing practices such as marking the price of an item on the item, allowing customers to return things they were dissatisfied with, opening a bargain basement, creating beautiful window displays, and making a special effort to attract female customers. A marketing genius, Field created the slogan "Give the Lady What She Wants," and then made sure that his store backed it up. Field was also very philanthropic with his wealth. He contributed the ten acres on which the University of Chicago was built and gave $10 million to establish the Field Museum of Natural History.

A store without a window

⑤ Young Montgomery Ward worked for Marshall Field until 1872, when he took his carefully saved $2,400 and a partner named George R. Thorne, and started a new type of business, selling things through a catalog and shipping them to the customer by mail. Ward's first catalog consisted of only one page. The enterprise bloomed because suddenly country people could buy affordable products without having to go long distances to stores.

An advertising man for Ward, Robert L. May, developed a Christmas promotion featuring a reindeer with a red nose, which he named Rudolph. The company distributed two million brochures with the story of Rudolph saving the day when Santa's other reindeer couldn't see through the foggy night. Cowboy singer Gene Autry turned the story into a popular record. It hit the charts on December 2, 1949, and has become a Christmas standard.

America's first pregnant doll

⑤ Judith Corporation in Lake Forest received the Turkey of the Year Award for 1992 by the Evanston/North Shore National Organization for Women. The award goes to companies who have excelled in sexist or degrading things. Apparently, Judith's pregnant doll, named Judy, fit the bill. A baby can be found beneath mom's pop-off stomach. Instantly, she looks slim and trim when a flat postpartum tummy is attached. The company is not disillusioned by so dubious an honor. "Judy" has a daddy-to-be partner, Charlie, and plans are underway to introduce a new doll to the family, one that is expecting twins.

⑤ Aeronautical pioneer William Stout, a native of Quincy, founded the first passenger service airline—Stout Air Services—in 1926. The airline flew between Detroit and Grand Rapids, Michigan. Among his other inventions were an all-metal Sky Car, a high-speed railplane, and a fiberglass car whose engine was in the rear.

First in the air, with passengers

⑤ Minnesotan Richard Warren Sears, having sold watches to railway men, moved his business to Chicago, where he hired a young watch repairman named Alvah C. Roebuck. Their first catalog, produced in 1887 (15 years after Montgomery Ward's), still went to station agents, but the following year they began to distribute their wares to the general public. In 1895, Roebuck sold his interest in the company to Julius Rosenwald who developed the firm into the giant it became. Sears himself resigned from the firm in 1909.

From watches to the biggest retailer in the world

Springfield-born Julius Rosenwald established a multimillion-dollar fund to be used to improve the education of African-Americans. The fund built more than 5,000 schools in the South. Rosenwald also funded the creation of the Museum of Science and Industry in Chicago.

⑤ The man who has been called the "Father of the Modern Drugstore," Charles R. Walgreen, was born near Galesburg in 1873. He became a pharmacist in Chicago, and in 1901 borrowed $2,000 from his father to open a drugstore. Eight years later he sold a half interest in his first store to raise funds to open a second, into which he incorporated a soda fountain and lunch counter, the first time such innovations had appeared in what had formerly been dark, medicinal-smelling shops. By 1916, nine drug stores were formed under one corporation, Walgreen Company. By the time of his death in 1939, there were almost 500 Walgreen stores nationwide.

A revolution in drugstores

⑤ Brooding on the north side of the Chicago River is the Merchandise Mart, for decades the largest commercial building in the world. Started by Marshall Field, the two-block-long building took several years to complete. The 95 acres of floor space were ready to serve the wholesale-buying business by 1930. Later the building became one of the major investments of the Joseph P. Kennedy family. Since 1991 it has had a major retail shopping mall on several floors. In the photograph shown here, the building was under construction in 1929.

Part of the Kennedy fortune

CALENDAR OF EVENTS DAY BY DAY

If there is an asterisk (*) after an item, check the index for where more information can be found in this AWESOME ALMANAC.

JANUARY

1 Political leader Melvin Price born 1905 in East Saint Louis

Pro Football Hall of Famer George Connor born in Chicago 1925

Pulitzer Prize-winning author Philip Joseph Caputo born 1941 in Chicago

From this date mining companies in Illinois had to restore land after strip mining coal, 1962

2 Basketball Hall of Fame contributor Henry V. Porter born Manito 1891

Chicago Sanitary and Ship Canal opened 1900 *

Chicago Cardinals football player Anthony Blazine born Canton 1912

3 Food plant explosion kills 42 in Pekin in 1924

Chicago Portage National Historic Site designated in River Forest 1952

4 Senator Stephen A. Douglas introduced the Kansas-Nebraska Act 1954 *

Long-time Illinois senator Everett McKinley Dirksen born 1896 in Pekin

Four elevated-train cars fell off tracks in Chicago Loop, killing 12, 1977

15-cent Everett Dirksen stamp issued at Pekin 1981

5 Illinois stopped being a county of Virginia and was without government 1782 *

Musician-composer Joe Marsala born 1907 in Chicago

Mr. Green Jeans of "Captain Kangaroo," Hugh Brannum, born in Sandwich 1910

Mike Ditka, coach of the Chicago Bears, fired 1993

6 Poet and Pulitzer Prize-winning author Carl Sandburg born in Galesburg 1878 *

Publisher Joseph Medill Patterson born 1879 in Chicago

A new constitutional convention convened at Springfield 1920

Novelist/film producer Noel Behn born in Chicago 1928

Psychologist Kenneth Keniston born in Chicago 1930

13-cent Carl Sandburg stamp issued at Galesburg 1978

7 Chicagoan William H. Burton patented procedure to make gasoline 1913

The Globetrotters played their first game, at Hinckley 1927 *

8 John G. Neihardt, poet laureate of Nebraska, born in Sharpsburg 1881

Psychologist/author, founder of "encounter group" therapy Carl R. Rogers born 1902 in Oak Park

Great opera base Georgio Tozzi born in Chicago 1923

Country-western singer Christy Lane (real name: Eleanor Johnston) born 1940 in Peoria

Black author/poet Gwendolyn Brooks appointed poet laureate of Illinois 1968 *

Chicago Bulls star Michael Jordan reached a career point total of 20,000 1993 *

9 Author Henry Blake Fuller born 1857 in Chicago

10 Famous operatic baritone Sherrill Milnes born Downers Grove 1935

Electronic organ inventor Laurens Hammond born Evanston 1895 *

Founder of Mercury Records Berle Adams born Chicago 1917

12 Football coach Fritz (Herbert) Crisler born Earlville 1899 *

Three-time National League batting leader Ricky Van Shelton born in Chicago 1952

14 Artist Robert MacCameron born Chicago 1866

Jewish reformer Hannah Greenebaum Solomon born Chicago in 1858 *

John Dos Passos, author of the trilogy *U.S.A.*, born Chicago 1896

15 Lincoln and his partner William Berry bought a store in New Salem 1833

Dancer Loie Fuller born Fullersburg 1862 *

Bandleader-drummer Gene Krupa born 1909 in Chicago *

Religious leader Paul Casimir Marcinkus born 1922 in Cicero

16 Illinois went "dry" as the 18th Amendment started Prohibition in 1920, opening the floodgates to Chicago's criminal era

2-cent Pulaski stamp was issued at Chicago 1931

Chicagoans Benny Goodman and Gene Krupa recorded jazz on the stage of Carnegie Hall in New York City 1938 *

17 Loyal Davis, father of Nancy Reagan, born Galesburg 1896

Emmy-winning actress Betty White of "The Mary Tyler Moore Show" and "Golden Girls" born 1922 in Oak Park

Chester resident E.C. Segar introduced Popeye in his comic strip as a minor character 1929 *

19 Rock and Roll Hall of Famer Phil Everly of the Everly Brothers born 1939 in Chicago

Broadcast journalist Ann Compton born 1947 in Chicago

20 "Little Orphan Annie" cartoonist Harold Gray born Kankakee 1894 *

Swimmer John Naber, winner of four gold medals and one silver in the 1976 Olympics, born in Evanston 1956*

Kaskaskia Island in the Mississippi River was declared by U.S. Supreme Court to belong to Illinois, not Missouri, 1970

21 Chewing gum executive William Wrigley born Chicago 1933

551-mile oil pipeline from Texas ending at Norris City completed 1943

22 Singer-musician Sam Cooke born 1935 in Chicago *

23 Territorial senator Nathaniel Pope introduced bill moving northern boundary of Illinois into Wisconsin, 1818 *

Pulitzer Prize novelist Ernest Poole born Chicago 1880

Children's author Virginia Snider Eifert born 1911 in Springfield

Actress Arlene Golonka born Chicago 1936

24 Baseball Hall of Fame radio/TV announcer Jack Brickhouse born 1916 in Peoria

Death of S. Glenn Young stops KKK control of "Bloody Williamson" County 1925 *

"Saturday Night Live" comedian and actor John Belushi born Chicago 1949 *

25 Famed Chicago gangster Al Capone died in Florida 1947 *

Dance great Irene Castle, who started Orphans of the Storm, died in 1969 in Deerfield *

26 Movie critic Gene Siskel, man of the other thumb, born in Chicago 1946

Worst snowstorm in Chicago history started, dumping 23 inches, 1967

Chicago Bears win Super Bowl XX, defeating New England Patriots 46-10, in 1986

27 Rock Island was incorporated and become county seat of Rock Island County 1841

First black pro football coach, Fritz Pollard, born Chicago 1894

28 Baseball pitcher Emil O. Yde born at Great Lakes 1900
U of Chicago invented lettering in football 1904 *
Nobel Prize biochemist Robert Holley born in Urbana 1922 *

29 Basketball Hall of Fame college coach John J. Schommer born Chicago 1884
American League, including a Chicago team, was organized 1900 *

30 Oscar-winning best supporting actress Dorothy Malone, for *Written on the Wind,* born Chicago 1930
Journalist Robert Markus born Chicago 1934
Singer/dancer Jody Watley, 1988 Grammy winner as Best New Artist born 1961 in Chicago

31 Actor John Agar, Shirley Temple's first husband, born in Chicago 1921
Psychologist Mary Robbins Haworth born Chicago 1931
First daytime TV soap opera started broadcasting from Chicago 1949 *

FEBRUARY

1 Edward Baker Lincoln, second child A. Lincoln, died at Springfield after 52-day illness 1850
Illinois became the first state to ratify 13th Amendment, outlawing slavery, 1865
Artist Doris Emrick Lee born 1905 in Aledo
Broadcast journalist Bob Jamieson born 1943 in Streator
25-cent Ida B. Wells stamp issued at Chicago 1990

2 Chicago became one of the founding teams in the National League 1876
Johnston McCulley, creator of Zorro, born in Ottawa 1883*
Comedian Charles J. Correll, who played "Andy," born 1890 in Peoria *
Founder/owner of the Chicago Bears, George Halas, was born in Chicago 1895 *
Basketball Hall of Fame player Edward W. "Moose" Krause born Chicago 1913
Hall of Fame second baseman Red Schoendist born in Germantown 1923

3 U.S. Congress approved creation of Illinois Territory, which included Illinois and Wisconsin, 1809 *
Clarence E. Mulford, creator of Hopalong Cassidy, born in Streator 1883 *
Comedian-actor Shelley (Sheldon Leonard) Berman born 1926 in Chicago

4 Baseball player Herman "Germany" Schaefer born Chicago 1878
Discoverer of Pluto, astronomer Clyde Tombaugh, born Streator in 1906 *
NOW founder and feminist writer Betty Friedan born Peoria 1921 *

5 Governor and presidential candidate Adlai Stevenson II born in Chicago 1900 *
Best-selling novelist-priest Andrew Greeley born in Oak Park 1928

6 President Ronald Wilson Reagan born Tampico 1911 *

8 William D. Boyce founded the Boy Scouts of America in Ottawa 1910 *
Springfield fire destroys state records 1934
"Different Strokes" actor Gary Coleman born Zion 1968

9 Political leader-soldier John Alexander Logan born 1826 in Murphysboro *
White Sox owner Bill Veeck, the "Clown Prince of Baseball," born Chicago 1914 *
Nation's first nuclear power generator turned on at Argonne National Laboratory, 1957

10 The legislature voted for a constitutional convention to bring up the issue of slavery 1823
Giving up in Illinois, the first Mormons set out westward from Nauvoo, 1846 *

Illinois Central Railroad chartered 1851 *
Hall of Fame baseball umpire Billy Evans born Chicago 1884 *

11 Lincoln delivered his "Farewell Address" to the people of Springfield at the Great Western Railroad Station 1861
Musician-conductor Louis Persinger born 1888 in Rochester
Popular novelist and Oscar- and Tony-winning playwright Sidney Sheldon born Chicago 1917

12 Waukegan (Potawatomi way of saying "trading post") incorporated 1849
$1.00 stamp commemorating the Lincoln Memorial issued at Springfield 1923
6-cent Illinois Statehood stamp issued at Shawneetown 1968

13 President Grant's friend and secretary of state, John Aaron Rawlins, born East Galena 1831
Cartoonist Sidney Smith, creator of "Andy Gump," born 1877 in Bloomington
Oilman Rawleigh Warner, Jr., born in Chicago 1921
Actress Kim Novak born Chicago 1933 ^

14 Ferris Wheel inventor George W. Gale Ferris born Galesburg 1859 *
Frontiersman and showman "Pawnie Bill" Gordon William Lillie born Bloomingdale 1860
Comedian Jack Benny born Benny Kubelsky in Waukegan 1894 *
Seven killed in St. Valentine's Day Massacre as Capone's men gun down rivals in Chicago 1929 *

15 First train reaches Springfield on tracks of Northern Cross Railroad 1842
Presidential candidate John B. Anderson born Rockford 1922
Chicago mayor Anton J. Cermak shot in Miami, while traveling with President Franklin D. Roosevelt, 1933*
Bengals quarterback Ken Anderson born Batavia 1949

16 Bandleader/waltz king Wayne King born 1901 in Savanna
Ventriloquist Edgar Bergen born Chicago 1903 *

17 Surveyor Abraham Lincoln finishes surveying the town of Petersburg 1836
Billionaire oilman H. L. Hunt born Vandalia 1889

18 Jean Marie Auel, author of *The Clan of the Cave Bear,* born 1936 in Chicago
Archbishop Samuel Stritch elevated to cardinal 1946 *
Styx musician Dennis DeYoung born in Chicago 1947

19 Astronaut Joseph P. Kerwin born in Oak Park 1932 *
First started by 10-year-old boy destroyed State Arsenal and its records 1934

20 The president's son, Willie Lincoln, died in the White House 1862
Artist Ivan Albright born in North Harvey 1897
Jazz musician Jimmy (James Edward) Yancey born 1898 in Chicago
Cartoonist Don Hesse born Belleville 1918
Two-time Olympic gold medal pole-vaulter Bob Richards born Champaign 1926 *
Model Cindy Crawford born in De Kalb 1966
The 22-cent Du Sable stamp was issued at Chicago 1987

21 Jazz musician Stew Pletcher born Chicago 1907

22 Actor Robert Young of "Father Knows Best" and "Marcus Welby, M. D.," born in Chicago 1907
Tallest known human Robert Wadlow born in Alton 1918

23 First Confederate POWs, 2,000 of them, arrived at prison camp in Springfield 1862
Oscar-winning director (for *Skippy* in 1930) Norman Taurog born in Chicago 1899
Author-journalist William L. Shirer born 1904 in Chicago
"Conspirators" (Rotary International) founded in Chicago 1905

"Bluebeard" Johann Hoch hanged for final murder in Chicago 1906 *

8-cent Rotary International stamp issued at Chicago 1955

24 State legislature at Vandalia votes to move state capital to Springfield 1837 *

Actress Marjorie Main (real name: Mary Tomlinson Krebs) born 1890 in Acton

Cartoonist Scott Long born Evanston 1917

25 Tony-winning costume designer Patricia Zipprodt born in Evanston 1925

"M*A*S*H" writer and producer Larry Gelbart born in Chicago 1928

Black Muslim leader Elijah Muhammad died in Chicago 1975

26 Broadcast journalist Robert Novak of "Evans and Novak" born Joliet 1931

27 Novelist James T. Farrell, creator of the "Studs Lonigan" trilogy, born 1904 in Chicago

Novelist and *New Yorker* magazine writer Peter De Vries born Chicago 1910

28 Oscar-winning director (for *Gigi*) and Liza's father Vincente Minnelli born Chicago 1910

MARCH

1 Virginia relinquished claim to Illinois territory 1784

Martin Luther King, Jr., assassin James Earl Ray, born 1928 in Alton *

Actor Robert Conrad (Falk) born Chicago 1935

Samuel Cardinal Stritch became first American named to Papal Curia 1958 *

2 Illinois Industrial College (now University of Illinois) opened at Urbana in 1868

Political leader Robert H. Michel born 1923 in Peoria

3 Bandleader Ina Ray Hutton born 1916 in Chicago

First WWII naval vessel built in Illinois, mine sweeper YMS-84, launched in the Chicago River 1942

Three German-American couples sentenced for treason in Chicago 1942

Chicago's Cardinal Stritch banned rock and roll from Catholic school functions 1957

Olympic gold medal athlete Jackie Joyner-Kersee born East St. Louis 1962 *

4 State representative Abraham Lincoln's only term ended 1849

Abraham Lincoln, the first president from Illinois, inaugurated in Washington 1861

American Automobile Association formed in Chicago with 1,000 members, in 1902

Actress Barbara McNair born Chicago 1937

3-cent American Automobile Association stamp issued at Chicago 1952

The *Chicago Daily News* ceased publication, after 103 years, 1978

5 Pioneer Texas cattleman Charles Goodnight born Macoupin County 1836

Nobel Prize-winning economist James Tobin born Champaign 1918

TV actor James Wainwright born Danville 1938

6 Supreme Court ruled in the Dred Scott case 1857 *

William Bell, soap opera creator, born Chicago 1927 *

7 President Jackson appointed A. Lincoln postmaster of New Salem 1833

The official State Motto adopted 1867 *

Bantamweight boxing champ Jimmy Barry born Chicago 1870

Basketball Hall of Fame college player Andy Phillip born Granite City 1922

8 Pulitzer Prize-winning journalist Edgar Ansel Mowrer born 1892 in Bloomington

Actor David Cryer born Evanston 1936

Actress Jamie Lyn Baur of "The Young and the Restless" born Chicago 1949

Actor Aiden Quinn born Chicago 1959

9 Lincoln announced his candidacy for the Illinois State Assembly from Sangamon County in 1832, a contest which he lost

Metal sculptor David Smith born Decatur 1906

Political activist George Lincoln Rockwell born 1918 in Bloomington *

TV journalist Charles Gibson born in Evanston 1943

First American world chess champ Bobby Fischer born in Chicago 1943 *

10 Edward Baker Lincoln, second son of Abraham Lincoln, who died at 4, born in Springfield 1846

11 Ground was broken for new capitol building in Springfield 1868 *

12 Basketball Hall of Fame player Robert "Ace" Gruenig born in Chicago 1913

Robert Gottschalk, founder of Panavision movie process, born Chicago 1918

Writer Daniel Cohen born in Chicago 1936

13 John Wayne Gacy, Jr., convicted of murdering 33 young men between '72 and '78, 1980 *

14 Golfer Bob Goalby born in Belleville 1931

Quincy Jones, most award-winning musician, born Chicago 1933 *

Astronaut Eugene Cernan born Chicago 1934 *

Musician Walter Parazaider, of the group Chicago, born 1945 in Chicago.

Actor Adrian Zmed born in Chicago 1954

Minnesota Twins outfielder Kirby Puckett born in Chicago 1961

15 Socialist and heiress Marjorie Merriweather Post born in Springfield 1887

Basketball player Terry Cummings born in Chicago 1961

16 Aviation pioneer William Bushnell Stout born Quincy 1880 *

Basketball Hall of Fame coach Arthur C. "Dutch" Lonborg born Gardner 1899

17 Oscar-winning actress Mercedes McCambridge for *All the King's Men*) born in Joliet 1918

Astronaut Thomas Mattingly II born in Chicago 1936 *

18 The "Great Tornado" struck in three states, including Illinois, killing 695 people, 1925

Actor Smiley Burnette, Gene Autry's sidekick, born in Summun 1911

19 Lawman Wyatt Berry Stapp Earp, "Wyatt Earp," born in Monmouth 1848 *

"Silver Tongued Orator" and presidential candidate William Jennings Bryan born in Salem 1860 *

Hall of Fame pitcher "Iron Man" Joe McGinnity born in Rock Island 1871

Surgeon Evarts A. Graham born in Chicago 1883

Best-selling author Irving Wallace (Irving Wallechinsky) born 1916 in Chicago

"Amos 'n Andy Show" first broadcast by WMAQ in Chicago 1928

Tornado hits Shelby, Bunker Hill, and Gillespie, killing 33 in 1948

13-cent Commercial Aviation stamp issued Chicago 1976

$2 William Jennings Bryan stamp from the Great Americans series issued Salem 1986

20 Basketball Hall of Fame college player Harlan O. Page born Chicago 1887

Chicago's worst tornado hit, killing 28, in 1920

Joseph Zangara, assassin of Mayor Anton Cermak, executed 1933 *

21 Broadway showman Florenz Ziegfeld born Chicago 1869 *

Baseball player Owen Lacey Friend born Granite City 1927

22 Nobel Prize physicist Robert Andrews Millikan born Morrison 1868 *

23 Bill Mosienko of the Chicago Black Hawks scored 3 goals in 21 seconds 1952

24 George William Mundelein elevated to the College of Cardinals 1924 *

Baseball player Denny McLain born Chicago 1944

25 Famed knuckleball pitcher Emil John "Dutch" Leonard born Auburn 1909

Huge floods caused by heavy rains hit southern Illinois 1913

Mine explosion in Centralia killed 111 workers 1947

Sugar Ray Robinson beat Carmen Basilio in Chicago 1958

10-cent Haym Salomon Revolution Bicentennial stamp issued at Chicago 1975

26 Bob Woodward, journalist of Watergate fame born at Geneva 1943

27 Silent and not-so-silent film actress Gloria Swanson born Chicago 1899 *

Oregon beat Ohio State to win first NCAA basketball championship, in Evanston 1939

28 "Copperhead" mob attacks Union regiment returning to front at Mattoon 1864 *

Editor and author Norman Hapgood born Chicago 1868

Nobel Prize physicist Jerome I. Freidman born Chicago 1930 *

5-cent Frances E. Willard stamp of the Famous Americans series issued at Evanston 1940

30 Singer Frankie Laine born Chicago 1913

White House Press secretary James Brady shot in presidential assassination attempt, 1981 *

31 Frank Lloyd Wright, Jr. (called Lloyd) born in Oak Park 1890 *

Jazz musician Red (Kenneth) Norvo born 1908 in Beardstown

Emmy- and Tony-winning actor Richard Kiley born Chicago 1922

Author John Jakes born in Chicago 1932

APRIL

1 Basketball player Kevin Duckworth born in Harvey 1964

2 Actor and dancer Buddy Ebsen (real name: Christian Rudolf Ebson, Jr.) born 1908 in Belleville

Jazz musician Marty Marsala born in Chicago 1909

Baseball Hall of Fame umpire Al Barlick born in Springfield 1915

Writer Edward Dorn born in Vella Grove 1929

Journalist-author Georgie Anne Geyer born in Chicago 1935

3 Cartoonist Bud (real name: Harry Conway) Fisher born 1885 in Chicago *

Mine explosion killed 49 at Ziegler mine in 1905 *

Chicago's first female mayor, Jane Byrne, elected 1979 *

4 Thomas "Tad" Lincoln, fourth son of Abraham, who lived to be 18, born in Springfield 1853

5 Horror and science fiction writier Robert Block born Chicago 1917

St. Anthony's Hospital blaze killed 77 at Effingham in 1949

Richard J. Daley elected mayor of Chicago, a position he held 21 years, 1955 *

George M. Pullman received patent forsleeping car1864*

Harold Washington elected Chicago's first African-American mayor 1983

6 Black Hawk lead Sac and Fox followers across Mississippi back into Illinois, violating treaty 1832 *

The cornerstone of the Mormon temple at Nauvoo was laid 1841 *

Joseph Smith III ordained head of Re-organized Church of Jesus Christ at Amboy 1860 *

Nobel Prize geneticist James Watson born Chicago 1928 *

Actress Marilu Henner born Chicago 1952

Figure skater Janet Lynn born in Rockford 1953

8 Father Marquette arrived at Kaskaskia village 1675 *

Bacteriologist William Henry Welch born 1850 in Bloomington

Pulitzer Prize novelist Margaret Ayer Barnes born in Chicago 1886

Pro Football Hall of Famer George Musso born in Collinsville 1910 *

First Lady Betty (Elizabeth Anne Bloomer) Ford born 1918 in Chicago

1970 Pulitzer Prize journalist Seymour Hersh born 1937 in Chicago

9 20-cent U.S.-Germany stamp issued at Germantown 1983

10 Springfield, established near spring in Kelly's fields, became temporary county seat in 1821

The Illinois and Michigan Canal opened 1848 *

Kent family adopted Clark (superboy) in Smallville *

11 Tornadoes hit Illinois and adjoining states, killing 271, in 1965

12 Musician Robert Fizdale born 1920 in Chicago

Author/dramatist Jack Gelber born 1932 in Chicago

Grammy-winning jazz pianist-composer Herbie Hancock born 1940 in Chicago

Philip K. Wrigley, owner of the Cubs for 45 years, died at Chicago 1977 *

13 Jazz musician Bud (Lawrence) Freeman born 1906 in Chicago

Early soap opera creator Roy Winsor was born in Chicago in 1912 *

Singer Howard Keel, on Broadway in *Carousel* and in movies in *Annie Get Your Gun* and *Showboat,* born 1917 in Gillespie

Baseball player Bret Saberhagen born Chicago Heights 1964

Manmade flood hits Chicago's Loop 1992 *

14 President Lincoln killed by John Wilkes Booth at Ford's Theater in Washington 1865 *

Musician Norman Luboff, founder of the oft-recorded Norman Luboff Choir, born in Chicago 1917

Jazz saxophonist "Jug" Ammons born Chicago 1925

15 Lincoln moved to Springfield from New Salem in 1837

Radio performer Marian Driscoll Jordan of "Fibber McGee & Molly" born 1897 in Peoria

Harold Washington, first African-American mayor of Chicago, born in Chicago 1922 *

Ray Kroc opened first McDonald restaurant in fast-food chain in Des Plaines 1955 *

16 Donner Party set off from capital grounds 1846 *

Steamer *Prairie State* exploded, killing many, at Pekin 1852

Chicago's Haber Corp. metalwork plant caught fire, killed 35, in 1953

17 Grierson's Raiders' heroic raid through Mississippi began 1863

Oscar-winner William Holden (real name: William Franklin Beedle, Jr.) (for *Stalag 17*) born 1918 in O'Fallon

TV journalist Roger O'Neil born Chicago 1945

18 Actress Barbara Hale, Perry Mason's secretary, born De Kalb 1922

First black named chief justice of a federal court, J. B. Parsons, 1975

19 Government official Eliot Ness of "The Untouchables" born 1903 in Chicago *

E. F. White made the first nonstop flight from Chicago to New York 1919

Teacher Annie Louise Keller died protecting White Hall students from tornado 1927 *

20 Pontiac, Ottawa chief, killed by a drunk Peoria Indian at Cahokia 1769

Botanist Mary Agnes Chase born Iroquois County 1869

Firestone mogul Harvey Samuel Firestone, Jr., born Chicago 1898

Supreme Court Justice John Paul Stevens born in Chicago 1920

21 First train crossed the Mississippi River, at Rock Island, to Davenport, Iowa, 1856

Tornadoes hit Illinois and Midwest, killing 52, and destroying 500 homes in Hometown, in 1967

22 A. Lincoln enlisted in militia at Richland Creek, Sangamon County, 1832

Movie and TV actor Eddie Albert (real name: Edward Albert Heimberger) of "Green Acres," born in Rock Island 1908

Architect of prefab aluminum homes, Edward Larrabee Barnes, born in Chicago 1915

Playwright Mark Medoff, winner of a Tony for *Children of a Lesser God,* born in Mount Carmel 1940

23 The first boat passes through the Illinois & Michigan Canal 1848

Hall of Fame first baseman Jim Bottomley born in Oglesby 1900

Author Charles Richard Johnson born 1948 in Evanston

25 Chicago was approved by Congress as the site of the 1893 World's Columbian Exposition 1890 *

Train hit from behind at Naperville, killing 45, in 1946

Basketball player David Corzine born in Arlington Heights 1956

26 Grand Master mystery writer Dorothy Salisbury Davis born 1916 in Chicago

Tony Award-winning actor Russell Nype born in Zion 1924

Basketball Hall of Fame player Harry " The Horse" Gallatin, born in Wood River 1927

10-cent Jane Addams stamp of the Famous Americans series issued at Chicago 1940

27 Steamboat bound for Cairo exploded on Mississippi, killing almost 2,000, 1865

28 Pi Beta Phi Sorority founded in Holt House, Monmouth College 1867

Peoria native Scott Heimdall abducted in Ecuador 1990 *

29 Laredo Taft, American sculptor of monumental works, born Elmwood 1860 *

The first Decoration Day observed at Woodlawn Cemetery in Carbondale 1866 *

Journalist Melvin Durslag born Chicago 1921

"Saturday Night Live" comedienne Nora Dunn born in Chicago 1952

30 First boat to pass through St. Lawrence Seaway arrived in Chicago 1959

Basketball player Isaiah Thomas born Chicago 1961

MAY

1 The British tried to retake Cahokia but failed, with heavy casualities, 1779

Writer of *Ruggles of Red Gap* and *Merton of the Movies,* Harry Leon Wilson, born in Oregon 1867

The World's Columbian Exposition formally opened in Chicago by President Grover Cleveland 1893 *

UFO consultant and astronomer J. Allen Hynek born Chicago 1910 *

2 Comedian George Gobel, Emmy winner in 1954, born 1919 in Chicago

Chicago Giants lost to Indianapolis ABCs in first game of National Negro League 1921 *

First Baha'i Temple in Western Hemisphere dedicated in Wilmette 1953

3 Lincoln's Funeral Train reached Springfield at 9 A.M. 1865

Hall of Fame pitcher "Red" Ruffing born in Granville 1905 *

Oscar-winning actress Mary Astor born Quincy 1906 *

Musician Virgil Fox born Princeton 1912 *

Founder and director of the Modern Jazz Quartet, jazz pianist John A. Lewis, born in La Grange 1920

Basketball player Jeffery Hornacek born Elmhurst 1963

Sears Tower topped off 1973 *

4 Bridge over Rock River collasped Dixon in 1873, killing 42 people *

"Poet of the open road" Richard Hovey born in Normal 1864

Haymarket "Riot" in Chicago 1884; 8 died when a bomb went off *

Writer Jane Temple Howard born Springfield 1935

Pulitzer Prize columnist and TV personality George F. Will born 1941 in Champaign

5 Attorney Jill Wine Volner of Watergate fame born in Chicago 1943

6 Baseball player Dick Wakefield, the first bonus baby, born in Chicago 1921

Short story writer Jack Sharkey born in Chicago 1931

Herb Morrison of Chicago's WLS reported the explosion of the *Hindenburg* 1937 *

7 Division Act separates Northwest Territory in half, putting Illinois in Indiana Territory 1800 *

Lincoln won for the defense in the Almanac Murder Trial at Beardstown 1858 *

Poet and Librarian of Congress Archibald Macleish born in Glencoe 1892 *

Al Capone killed his own gunmen in Cicero with a baseball bat 1929

8 John"Bet-A-Million" Gate, who made fortune in barbed wire, born Turner Junction 1855 *

Religious leader-author Bishop Fulton John Sheen born 1895 in El Paso *

Novelist Harold Sinclair, who used Bloomington for his background, born in Chicago 1907

Illinois's only four-time governor, Republican James R. Thompson, born in Chicago 1936

18-cent Savings & Loan stamp issued at Chicago 1981

9 The White Sox played the longest baseball game ever, against Milwaukee Brewers, 1984 *

10 Prophetstown destroyed by Illinois militia volunteers,staring the Black Hawk War 1832 *

Shawneetown native James Wilson's unit captured Confederate President Jefferson Davis 1865 *

Hall of Fame baseball manager and executive Edward G. Barrow born Springfield 1868 *

11 Chicago gangster Big Jim Colosimo shot, probably by Capone, 1920 *

Adler Planetarium, first planetarium in U.S., opened in Chicago 1930 *

U. of Illinois wins first intercollegiate gymnastics team championship 1840

Author Mark Vonnegut born 1947 in Chicago

12 Explorer Lincoln Ellsworth, first person to fly over both poles, born in Chicago 1880 *

Actor Bruce Boxleitner born in Elgin 1951

13 Erik Jansson, Swedish founder of Bishop Hill, a utopian colony, murdered 1850 *

Cyrus Hall McCormick, inventor of the mechanical reaper, died in Chicago 1884 *

14 Lewis & Clark Expedition to explore the Louisiana Purchase set off from Illinois 1804 *

First battle of Black Hawk War fought near Byron 1832, with the Indians winning *

Col. Elmer Ellsworth of Springfield was first Illinois soldier killed in the Civil War 1861

15 George Rogers Clark began campaign to claim the Illinois area for Virginia in 1778 *

Captain U.S. Grant mustered 21st Illinois Infantry in Mattoon 1861

Long-time Chicago mayor Richard J. Daley born in Chicago 1902 *

Jockey Jim Berger rode five winners in a row at Sportsman's Park 1941

16 Joseph Medill McCormick, editor of the *New York Daily News,* born Chicago 1877 *

17 John Deere, inventor of self-scouring steel plow, died Moline 1886 *

Al Capone pleaded guilty to carrying a concealed weapon, sentenced to one year in prison, 1929

18 Abraham Lincoln nominated for the presidency by Republicans on the 3rd ballot meeting in Chicago 1860

Nobel Prize chemist Vincent DuVigneaud born in Chicago 1901

Irene Hunt,1967 Newbery Medalist for *Up a Road Slowly,* born in Pontiac 1907

Science fiction writer Fred Saberhagen born in Chicago 1930

Baseball player Jim Sundburg born in Galesburg 1951

19 Chautauqua director Arthur Bestor born in Dixon 1879

LA publisher's wife and society mover and shaker Dorothy "Buffie" Chandler born Lafayette 1901

Pulitzer Prize biographer Ernest Samuels born in Chicago 1903

Pulitzer Prize playwright Lorraine Hansberry, author of *A Raisin in the Sun,* born in Chicago 1930 *

20 Illinois declared a territory of second grade 1812

Indian Creek Massacre, with 15 settlers killed, 1832

Pulitzer Prize biographer Allan Nevins born in Camp Point 1890 *

Supreme Court justice John Marshall Harlan born in Chicago 1899 *

21 Actor Mr. T (Larence Tero) born in Chicago 1952

Mr. T. celebrated his 35th birthday by cutting down all the trees on his Lake Forest property 1987

22 Abraham Lincoln—inventor—awarded patent 1849 *

13-year-old Bobby Franks kidnapped by Leopold and Loeb, and killed in Chicago 1924 *

23 First women executed in Illinois, Elizabeth Reed, hanged in Lawrenceville in 1845 *

24 U.of C. baseball team appeared in maroon socks, giving rise to the school nickname, 1894

Jane Byrne, first woman mayor of Chicago, born in Chicago 1934 *

25 Jazz musician-composer Miles Davis born 1926 in Alton

The 1-cent and 3-cent Century of Progress stamps issued at Chicago 1933

Chicago Transit Authority streetcar hits gasoline truck killing 33 in 1950

American Airlines DC-10 crashed after takeoff at O'Hare, killing 278, 1979 *

22-cent Ameripex '86 stamp issued at Rosemont 1985

26 Congress passed Stephen A. Douglas's Kansas-Nebraska Bill 1854 *

Illinois hit especially hard by series of tornadoes beginning this day, 53 people killed in Mattoon, 1917

7.1-cent Tractor stamp issued at Rosemont 1989

27 A. Lincoln enlisted as private in Elijah Iles' company at Ottawa in 1832

Entertainer/frontiersman Wild Bill Hickok born 1837 in Troy Grove *

Century of Progress International Exposition (aka: 1933 World's Fair) in Chicago opened *

Musician-composer Ramsey Lewis, Jr., born 1935 in Chicago

Chicago Bears coach George Halas retired 1969

28 National League president for many years Warren C. Giles born Tiskilwa 1896 *

Astronomer who started search for E.T., Frank Drake, born Chicago 1930 *

4-cent coil Abraham Lincoln stamp issued at Springfield 1966

29 Abraham Lincoln delivered his famous" Lost Speech" in Bloomington 1856

5-cent John Ericsson Statue stamp issued 1926 at Chicago

Buck O'Neil became the major league's first black coach, in Chicago 1962

Tornadoes hit southern Illinois, killing 12, in 1982

30 Actress and one-woman show Cornelia Otis Skinner born in Chicago 1902

Cubs' Frank Chance hit by pitched ball five times in one game 1904

Bandleader-clarinetist Benny Goodman born 1909 in Chicago

Illinois-born sculptor and architect Henry Bacon's Lincoln Memorial in Washington, D.C., dedicated 1922 *

Flack and Heathcote traded between games of a double header 1922 *

Actor Clint Walker born in Hartford 1927

"Memorial Day Massacre" when 10 striking steel workers were killed by police in Chicago 1937

Baseball catcher and manager John Felske born Chicago 1942

31 Decoration Day invented by Benton resident Mary Cunningham Logan *

First African-American woman ambassador, Patricia Roberts Harris, born Mattoon 1924 *

Nobel Prize physicist John Robert Schrieffer born in Oak Park 1931

NBC broadcast journalist Fred Briggs born in Chicago 1932

Actor Tom Berenger born 1950 in Chicago

3-cent International Geophysical Year stamp issued at Chicago 1958

Street in Silvis changed to Hero Street U.S.A. 1971 *

JUNE

1 Comiskey Park opened July 1, 1910, and closed 80 years later when new one was built

Actress June Haver, once Mrs. Fred MacMurray, born 1926 in Rock Island

Track star Brian Oldfield born in Elgin 1945

2 Author-naturalist Edwin Way Teale, 1966 Pulitzer winner for *Wandering through Winter,* born 1899 in Joliet

Olympic gold medal swimmer and actor Johnny Weissmuller born in Chicago 1904 *

Musician Michael Anthony (member of Van Halen) born 1955 in Chicago

3 Oscar-winning screenwriter James Goldman (for *Lion in Winter*) born 1927 in Chicago

Composer Florence Beatrice Price became the first black woman to have major orchestral works performed 1953 *

First Illinois astronaut, Jim McDivitt, launched into space for first time 1965 *

4 Cardinal adopted as State Bird 1929 *

Actor Bruce Dern born 1936 in Chicago

German submarine, now on display at the Museum of Science and Industry, captured 1944 *

5-cent Swedish Pioneers stamp issued at Chicago 1948

Tennis star Andrea Jaeger born in Chicago 1965

5 Mystery writer Georgiana Randolph, who wrote under name Craig Rice and others, born in Chicago 1908
Singer/soap star Bill Hayes born Harvey 1926
Ordnance plant explosion at Elwood killed 49 in 1942
Cardiss Collins elected from Chicago 1973; went on to become longest-serving African-American woman in Congress *

6 Chicago's elevated train, the "L," had its first run in 1892

7 Constitutional convention began at Springfield 1847
Bandleader Glen Gray (real name: Glen Gray Knoblaugh) born 1906 in Roanoke
Tony-winning (for *Carnival in Flanders*) singer Dolores Gray born in Chicago 1930

8 Chicago inventor Ives McGaffrey patented the vacuum cleaner 1869
Midget baseball player Eddie Gaedel born in Chicago 1925 *

9 Wedding song "O Promise Me" premiered in the show *Robin Hood* in Chicago 1890
Children's author Mildred Geiger Gilbertson born 1908 in Galena
Leader of first balloon to fly the Pacific, Ben L. Abruzzo, born in Rockford 1930 *
Bill Pinkney, first African-American to sail around the Earth alone, returned to U.S., 1992 *

10 A. F. Callahan of Chicago patented the window envelope 1902
Actress Julie Haydon (real name: Donella Donaldson) born Oak Park 1910
Astronaut Jim McDivitt born in Chicago 1929 *
Former Secretary of Transportation Samuel Knox Skinner born in Chicago 1938
Pulitzer Prize-winning cartoonist John McCutcheon *

11 Journalist Ruth Shick Montgomery born in Sumner 1912
Football player Gary Fencik born in Chicago 1954

12 Emmy-winning TV producer Russ Bensley born in Chicago 1930
Cheap Trick drummer Bun E. Carcos born in Rockford 1951

13 Pulitzer Prize poet and critic Mark Van Doren born 1894 in Hope *

14 The French claimed Illinois in a ceremony at Sault Ste. Marie, Michigan, 1671 *
Folksinger and Oscar-winning actor Burl Ives born Hunt 1909 *
Children's author Janice May Udry born 1928 in Jacksonville
Actress Marla Gibbs born Chicago 1931

15 Baseball player Eddie Waitkus shot in Chicago by an obsessed fan 1949 *
Actor Jim Belushi born in Chicago 1954 *

16 Republicans meeting at Springfield nominated Abraham Lincoln for U.S. Senate 1858; he gave "House Divided" speech
Actress Laurie Metcalf, who plays Roseanne's sister, born in Chicago 1955

17 First NCAA track and field championships held at U. of Chicago in 1921
Abraham Lincoln's redesigned tomb was dedicated by President Hoover at Springfield 1931
State's largest tree victim of high winds in Grundy County 1992 *

18 Newspaper publisher,founder of UPI, Edward Wyllis Scripps, born 1854 in Rushville
Basketball Hall of Famer George Mikan born Joliet 1924 *
Sociologist Lester Frank Ward born in Joliet 1841
Pulitzer Prize movie critic Roger Ebert (in fact, the only one) born Urbana 1942 *
Actress Constance McCashin born 1947 in Chicago

19 Sears Roebuck founder Alvah Roebuck born Chicago 1848 *

Author-publisher Elbert Green Hubbard born 1856 in Bloomington *
Illinois women granted first right to vote, in school board elections, 1891
Developer of synthetic rubber/Nobel Prize winner Paul John Flory born in Sterling 1910 *
Sam Giancana, due to testify before the Grand Jury, shot in his Oak Park home, 1974

20 Pere Marquette and Louis Jolliet, canoeing down the Mississippi, probably got their first sight of Illinois 1673 *
First Eucharistic Congress opened in Chicago, over a million attend, 1926

21 Naturalist and writer Donald Culross Peattie born in Chicago 1898
Historian Wayne Gard born in Brocton 1899
Actor Michael Gross born in Chicago 1947
Musician-singer-songwriter Nils Lofgren of the E Street Band born 1951 in Chicago
The governor signed bill reinstating death penalty for 16 categories of murder 1977

22 Influential African-American dancer and choreographer Katherine Dunham born in Chicago 1910 *
Dancer/choreographer Gower Champion born in Geneva 1921 *
Miners and strike breakers clashed in Herrin Massacre, killing 20, 1922 *
Actor Richard Allan born in Jacksonville 1923
Illinois Waterway completion heralded by arrival of barges from New Orleans 1933 *
Joe Louis wins world heavyweight boxing title at Chicago 1937 *
5-cent Poland stamp issued at Chicago 1943
Ezzard Charles beat Jersey Joe Walcott in a Chicago fight for the championship 1949 *

23 First Illinois law requiring school attendance passed 1883
Paul Butler, founder of Butler Aviation and Oak Brook, born Chicago 1892 *
Eleven buildings destroyed by fire in Shawneetown 1904
John McDermott won the U.S. Open at Chicago Golf Club, first American golfer to do so, 1911
Oscar- and Tony-winning choreographer and director Bob Fosse born Chicago 1927 *
Jonathan Livingston Seagull author Richard David Bach born 1936 in Oak Park

24 Elizabeth founded because of defense of Apple River Fort by a woman 1832 *
Mobster John Gotti began serving life sentence in maximum security penitentiary at Marion 1992

25 Jock Hutchison becomes first American to win British Open in 1921

26 1952 Caldecott Medal winner for "The Biggest Bear," Lynd Ward, born 1905 in Chicago
Edward H. Levi, attorney general under President Ford, born in Chicago 1911
Illinois women became first women east of the Mississippi to get the right to vote in a presidential election, 1913
Bandleader Richard Maltby born in Chicago 1914
Pianist Leonid Hambro born 1920 in Chicago

27 Mormon prophet Joseph Smith killed by mob at Carthage in 1844 *
First cosmetics "queen" Harriet Hubbard Ayer born Chicago 1849 *
Bruce Johnston of the Beach Boys, who replaced founder Brian Wilson, born in Peoria 1944
Basketball player Craig Hodges born in Park Forest 1960
Route 66 from Chicago to Santa Monica officially decertified 1985

28 Radical journalist/novelist Floyd Dell born in Barry 1887
Anthropologist Donald Carl Johanson born in Chicago 1943

Actor John Cusack born 1966 in Evanston

29 First woman to head a federal agency, Julia Lathrop, born in Rockford 1858 *

Educator and historian James Harvey Robinson born in Bloomington 1863

Idaho Senator William E. Borah born at Fairfield 1865

Astronomer and observatory builder George Hale born in Chicago 1868 *

Director Jo Anne Akalaitis born 1937 in Chicago

Zion loses Supreme Court case—religious city seal designed by founder must go, 1992 *

30 First woman to graduate from law school, Ada Kepley of Effingham, in 1870 *

O'Hare International Airport opened 1949 *

The TV longest-running soap opera, "Guiding Light," started broadcasting from Chicago 1952 *

Football player Elmer Layden, one of Notre Dame's "Four Horsemen," born Chicago 1903

31 Black Hawk and people abandoned village to cross Mississippi as militia approached 1831 *

JULY

1 World's first juvenile court established in Cook County 1899

State Flower of the violet went into effect 1908 *

Comiskey Park in Chicago opens—White Sox lose to St. Louis Brown 2-0, 1910

Children's author/illustrator Martin Provenson born 1916 in Chicago

Airmail service from New York to Chicago began 1919

Hanging was outlawed in Illinois as of this date in 1927; electric chair took over

Second state flag designed by Mrs. Sanford Hutchinson of Greenfield approved 1970 *

Illinois law requiring front seat belts to be used went into effect 1985

2 Ornithologist Robert Ridgeway born Mount Carmel 1850*

New constition ratified by the voters 1870 *

Astronomer Seth Barnes Nicholson born Springfield 1891

3 Journalist/TV personality Dorothy Kilgallen born in Chicago 1913

4 Illinois "liberated" from the British when George Rogers Clark entered Kaskaskia and Cahokia 1778

Illinois became part of the new Indiana Territory 1801

Work began on the Illinois and Michigan Canal, at Bridgeport (Chicago) 1836 *

Cornerstone of the first Capitol at Springfield laid 1837 *

Eads Bridge across the Mississippi, first steel bridge in the world, officially opened 1874 *

Exposition at Chicago celebrated 75th anniversary of Emancipation Proclamation in 1940 *

5 Steamer *Columbia* hit submerged stump and sank in the Illinois River at Pekin, killing 87, 1918

Football player George Kunz born in Fort Sheridan 1947

6 Federal troops and railway strikers clashed in nationwide railway dispute 1894

State Flag adopted 1915 *

First major league All-Star game held at Comiskey Park in Chicago 1933 *

Singer Gene Chandler (born Eugene Dixon) born in Chicago 1937

20-cent Babe Ruth stamp issued at Chicago 1983

7 Writer Frank Ramsay Adams born 1883 in Morrison

Former Senator Alan Dixon born in Belleville 1927

Mother Frances Xavier Cabrini named as the first American saint 1946 *

Fluorite officially named State Mineral 1965 *

8 William Jennings Bryan made famed "Cross of Gold" speech at Democratic convention in Chicago 1896 *

Head of many power projects, David Eli Lilienthal, born in Morton 1899

Walter Kerr, Pulitzer Prize-winning drama critic, who was married to humor writer Jean Kerr, born in Evanston 1913

Author James Farl Powers born 1917 in Jacksonville

9 Nobel Prize physicist Ben Mottelson born inChicago 1926

Mattoon-born Patricia Roberts Harris sworn in as ambassador to Luxembourg 1965 *

Teenage actor Fred Savage born in Highland Park 1976 *

10 Williams James Chalmers, co-founder of Allis Chalmers farm equipment, born in Chicago 1852

Pullman Strike ended when Eugene Debs surrendered to federal troops, 1894 *

12 Eleven people killed when steamer *Frankie Folsom* capsized at Pekin 1892

Rioting among blacks on the West Side starts and goes on three nights 1966

13 Original "Today" show host Dave Garroway born in Chicago 1913

Actor Harrison Ford of "Indiana Jones" fame born in Chicago 1942

14 Washing machine manufacturer Frederick Lewis Maytag born in Elgin 1854

Pulitzer Prize-winning journalist/poet Paul Scott Mowrer born 1887 in Bloomington

TV journalist John Chancellor born in Chicago 1927

Chicago 7 defendant Jerry Rubin born in Chicago 1938 *

Richard Speck murdered eight students nurses in Chicago 1966 *

15 Steven Linscott murder case dropped after 12 years and prison time 1992 *

16 Mary Todd Lincoln died at home of sister in Springfield 1882

17 Jessie Sumner, first Illinois congresswoman elected in her own right, born in Milford 1898 *

Architect Bertrand Goldberg born in Chicago 1913

Hall of Fame shortstop and Cubs announcer Lou Boudreau born in Harvey 1917 *

Race riots began on Chicago's beaches, killing 38, 1919 *

18 Oscar-winning (for *Ordinary People*) actress Elizabeth McGovern born 1961 in Evanston

19 First baseman Phil Cavarretta born in Chicago 1916

Nathan Leopold and Richard Loeb pleaded guilty to the murder of Bobby Franks 1924 *

20 Artist and feminist Judy Chicago (Judy Cohen) born in Chicago 1939 *

The Railroad Fair, celebrating 100 years of railroads, opened in Chicago 1948

21 Illinois Central wood-burning trains began operation from Chicago in 1856

Nobel Prize-winning novelist Ernest Hemingway born in Oak Park 1899 *

Goodyear blimp burned over Chicago, crashing into bank, killing 13, 1919 *

Actor/comedian Robin Williams, who won 1979 Grammy for *Reality, What a Concept!* born 1952 in Chicago

22 Author Odell Shepard born 1884 in Rock Falls

Young adult novelist Rosamond du Jardin born in Fairland 1902

Gangster John Dillinger apparently killed by FBI outside Chicago's Biograph Theater in 1934 *

Ice skater David Santee born Park Ridge 1957

Poet laureate Carl Sandburg died 1967

23 Hard-boiled detective novelist Raymond Chandler, creator of Philip Marlowe, born 1888 in Chicago *

Oscar-winning director (for *Bridge over the River Kwai*) Carl Foreman born 1914 in Chicago

First Telstar satellite relayed live television from the US to Europe including Cubs game 1962

24 Steamer *Eastland* rolled over at Clark Street bridge in Chicago, drowning 812, 1915 *

Towns of Zion and Rolling Meadows asked U.S. Supreme Court to reconsider letting them keep seals that include crosses 1992

25 Second City comedienne and actress Barbara Harris born Chicago 1937

26 Oscar- and Tony-winning actor Jason Robards, Jr., born Chicago 1922

Jazz drummer Louis Bellson (and the late Pearl Bailey's husband) born in Rock Falls 1924

Author/actor Jean Parker Shepherd born 1929 in Chicago

27 Lincoln gave "You can fool some of the people" speech at Clinton in 1858

Journalist Vincent Canby born 1924 in Chicago

Actor Jerry Van Dyke born Danville 1931

28 "First citizen of Chicago" John Kinzie made justice of the peace 1825

Novelist and poet Kenneth Fearing born in Oak Park 1902

Ship *Favorite* capsized off North Avenue in Chicago in 1927, killing 27

Guitarist-singer Mike Bloomfield born 1944 in Chicago

Basketball player Doug Collins born in Christopher 1951

29 3,000 square miles of northern Illinois ceded by Potawatomi, Ottawa, and Chippewa 1829

Lincoln and Douglas met at Bryant Cottage to arrange debates Bement 1858 *

Dramatist, poet, humorist Don Marquis born in Walnut 1878 *

New York Giants' good luck charm, Charlie Faust, born in Chicago 1911

30 *Chicago Tribune* publisher Col. Robert McCormick born in Chicago 1880 *

The Union Stock Yards in Chicago closed down after 115 years, 1971 *

Tickets went on sale for the state's first lottery 1974

31 Detective-story writer Davis Dresser (pseud.: Brett Halliday) born 1904 in Chicago

Baseball outfielder and manager Hank Bauer born in East St. Louis 1922

First woman to head a major film studio, Sherry Lee Lansing, born 1944 in Chicago *

AUGUST

1 Robert Todd Lincoln, only son of Abraham Lincoln to live to maturity, born in Springfield 1843

Magazine publisher William Ziff born in Chicago 1898

Military leader William Frishe Dean born 1899 in Carlyle

Actress Tempestt Bledsoe, Vanessa on "The Cosby Show," born in Chicago 1973

2 Final defeat of Indians in Black Hawk War at the Battle of Bad Axe in Wisconsin 1832 *

The original "torch singer," Helen Morgan, born 1900 in Danville

A Chicago jury acquitted the "Black Sox" of defrauding the public 1921 *

Musician James Pankow of the group Chicago born 1947 in Chicago

3 Running for the Whig party, Abraham Lincoln was elected to the U.S. House of Representatives 1846

Pulitzer Prize historian Vernon Louis Parrington born in Aurora 1871

Writer Albert Halper born in Chicago 1904

Film director John David Landis born 1950 in Chicago *

4 Abraham Lincoln was elected to the Illinois House of Representatives from Sangamon County on his second try at office 1834

5 Chicago incorporated as a town, with population 200, in 1833

Chicago passed ordinance that outlawed storing feed hay downtown 1835

Geraldine Stutz, president of Henri Bendel at 33, born in Evanston 1924

6 Hollywood gossip columnist and broadcaster Louella Parsons born Freeport 1893 *

7 Basketball Hall of Fame coach Leonard D. Sachs born in Chicago 1897

8 Supreme Court Justice Arthur Goldberg born in Chicago 1908

Actor Carl Switzer (Alfalfa in "Our Gang" comedies) born 1926 in Paris

8 Lights are turned on for the first time at Wrigley Field, allowing night games, 1988

10 Railway wreck at Chatsworth in 1887 killed 85 people *

Pilot William P. Odum arrived Chicago, after flying around the world in 73 hours, 5 minutes, in 1947

11 Two-time Pulitzer Prize-winning cartoonist Vaughn Richard Shoemaker born 1902 in Chicago

TV talk-show host and singer Mike Douglas born in Chicago 1925

12 Chicago's legal existence marked by first meeting of Board of Trustees 1833

Sears, Roebuck developer and philanthropist Julius Rosenwald born in Springfield 1862 *

Hall of Fame catcher Ray " Cracker" Schalk born in Harvey 1892

Dr. Richard Lawler, who performed the first successful kidney transplant, born in Chicago 1895 *

Oscar-winning screenwriter William Goldman born 1931 in Chicago *

13 Actor Neville Brand born 1921 in Kewanee

First roller derby began in Chicago in 1935 *

Composer-singer Dan Fogelberg born 1951 in Peoria

14 Pulitzer Prize-winning journalist Charles Bartlett born in Chicago 1921

Novelist and screenwriter Frederic Raphael born in Chicago 1931

15 Fort Dearborn Massacre, in 1812 *

Hall of Famer and baseball club owner Charles Albert Comiskey born 1859 in Chicago *

Former governor Otto Kerner born in Chicago 1908

Violinist Florian Zabach born 1921 in Chicago

16 Author William Maxwell born 1908 in Lincoln

Actress Lois Nettleton born in Oak Park 1931

5-cent Emancipation Proclamation stamp issued at Chicago 1963

17 Pulitzer Prize-winning dramatist Jesse Lynch Williams born in Sterling 1871 *

Author-poet Janet Lewis born 1899 in Chicago

Emmy-winning TV producer Harve Bennett born in Chicago 1930

18 Basketball player Rickey Green born in Chicago 1954

Lincoln Home National Historic Site authorized in Springfield 1971

19 Writer Ring Lardner, Jr., born in Chicago 1915

Pulitzer Prize novelist (for *Guard of Honor*) James Gould Cozzens born in Chicago 1930

20 Work began on Eads Bridge across the Mississippi, first steel bridge in the world, 1867 *

Actress Joan Allen, winner of a Tony for *Burn This* in 1988, born in Rochelle 1956

21 First Lincoln-Douglas debate, held at Ottawa 1858 *

Pulitzer Prize-winning historian Don E. Fehrenbacher born in Sterling, 1920

Dramatist/actor/composer Melvin Van Peebles born 1932 in Chicago

22 Melville E. Stone, founder of the now-defunct *Chicago Daily News,* born in Hudson 1848

Musician Maud Powell born in Peru 1868

Writer Ray Bradbury born Waukegan 1920 *

The Barker gang robbed a Federal Reserve mail truck in Chicago 1933 *

6-cent Edgar Lee Masters stamp issued at Petersburg 1970

23 First women Olympic track and field gold medalist Betty Robinson born in Riverdale 1911 *

Musician-actor Tex Williams born 1917 in Ramsey

24 Author Alice Hastings Bradley Sheldon born 1915 in Chicago

Dr. Fager set a new horse-racing record in the mile of 1 minute, 32 1/5 seconds at Arlington Race Course 1968

25 Ann Rutledge, a legendary early love of Abraham Lincoln, died in Sand Ridge at age 22 in 1835

26 1-cent stamp in the LIberty series issued at Chicago 1954

27 Second Lincoln-Douglas debate, held at Freeport 1858 *

First Elgin National Road Race held, in and around Elgin, won by Ralph Mulford, 1910 *

4-cent Lincoln-Douglas Debates stamp issued at Freeport 1958

10-cent Pan American Games stamp issued at Chicago 1959

28 Country singer Billy Grammer born in Benton 1925

Singer, actor, dancer and straight-man for a talking mule, Donald O'Connor, born in Chicago 1925

Tito Falconi flew upside-down from St. Louis to Joliet 1933

Musician Danny (Daniel Peter) Seraphine of the group Chicago born 1948 in Chicago

Anti-Vietnam War demonstrators protested Democratic Presidential nomination 1968 *

Tornadoes hit northern Illinois killing 25 in 1990

29 Oscar-winning screenwriter and director Preston Sturges (real name: Edmund P. Biden) born Chicago 1898 *

Modeling and talent-agency owner Harry Conover born in Chicago 1911

Oscar-winning film director (for *The French Connection*) William Friedkin born in Chicago 1939

James Brady, President Reagan's press secretary, born Centralia 1940 *

Chicagoan Arthur J. Goldberg appointed to Supreme Court by President Kennedy in 1962

30 "Inside" writer (*Inside Europe, Inside Africa,* etc.) John Gunther born in Chicago 1910

"Heavy" actor turned "My Three Sons" dad, Fred MacMurray, born Kankakee 1908 *

Nobel Prize physicist Edward Purcell born in Taylorville 1912

SEPTEMBER

1 National Prohibiton Party formed in Chicago 1869

"Tarzan" creator and cartoonist Edgar Rice Burroughs born 1875 in Chicago *

Chemist Karl Folkers, who isolated vitamin B12, born in Decatur 1906

First meeting of the Communist Party in America, at Chicago 1919

TWA Constellation crashed near Hinsdale, killing 78, 1961

2 Capturer of Jefferson Davis, James H. Wilson, born Shawneetown 1837 *

Baseball Hall of Famer and sporting-equipment manufacturer Albert G. Spalding born Byron 1850 *

Water-color painter, etcher, lithographer George Overbury Hart born Cairo 1868

Upton Sinclair, author of *The Jungle,* which led the establishment of Pure Food & Drug Act of 1906, born in Chicago 1878 *

Manager of big projects Peter Ueberroth born Evansville 1937 *

Tennis star Jimmy Connors born in East St. Louis 1952 *

3 "Wide World of Sports" broadcaster Bill Flemming born in Chicago 1926

Pulitzer Prize novelist Alison Lurie born in Chicago 1926

4 Rocky Mountain explorer Stephen H. Long born 1864 in Alton

Nobel Prize biochemist Stanford Moore born in Chicago 1913

Dancer and *South Pacific* star Mitzi (Francesca) Gaynor born in Chicago 1931

5 Television ratings company founder Arthur C. Nielsen born in Chicago 1897

TV sit-com actor and comedian Bob Newhart of "Buttoned-Down Mind" fame born in Oak Park 1929 *

Singer Carol Lawrence (Laraia), star of *West Side Story* and Robert Goulet's wife, born Melrose Park in 1935

6 First American woman to win the Nobel Peace Prize, Jane Addams, born 1860 in Cedarville *

TV personality Norman Mark born in Chicago 1939

3-cent Civil Engineers stamp issued at Chicago 1952

8 *Lady Elgin* collided with *Augusta of Oswego* off Winnetka, drowning 287, in 1860

First recorded sextuplets, born to Mr. and Mrs. Bushnell of Chicago 1866

Basketball player Maurice Cheeks born in Chicago 1956

9 Abraham Lincoln received his license to practice law 1836

Author and anthropologist Mary Hunter Austin born 1868 in Carlinville

10 Astronomer James Keeler born in LaSalle in 1857 *

Pulitzer Prize biographer Carl Van Doren born in Hope 1885 *

It rained fish in Cairo on this day in 1890

Jim Crowley, one of Notre Dame's "Four Horsemen," born in Chicago 1902

Baseball player and coach Ted "Big Klu" Kluszewski born in Argo 1924

Nathan Leopold and Richard Loeb sentenced to life in prison for murdering Bobby Franks 1924 *

Waukegan's Walk of Stars dedicated 1992 *

11 Educator Robert Bernard Martin born in LaHarpe 1918

Journalist David Broder born in Chicago Heights 1929

12 Pitcher Bob Groom born Belleville 1884

Racing driver Tony Bettenhausen born in Tinley Park 1916

Linebacker Dick Butkus born in Chicago 1942 *

Comic actor Peter Scholari born in New Rochelle 1954

Basketball player Tim Hardaway born in Chicago 1966

Chicagoan Dr. Mae Jemison became first black woman in space, aboard the Endeavor, 1992 *

13 Mormon author-lecturer Ann Eliza Webb Young born 1844 in Nauvoo

Composer Ray Charles (Charles Raymond Offenberg) born 1918 in Chicago

Jazz singer/composer Mel Torme born in Chicago 1925*

Singer/musician Peter Cetera born 1944 in Chicago

14 Winnifred Mason Huck, first Illinois congresswoman, born Chicago1882 *

Oscar-winning movie producer Hal B. Wallis born 1899 in Chicago *

"Lone Ranger" Clayton Moore born Chicago 1914 *

Actor Walter Koenig born 1936 in Chicago

15 Third Lincoln-Douglas debate held at Jonesboro 1858, drawing the smallest crowd *

Pianist Bobby (Robert Waltrip) Short born 1926 in Danville

The first Secretary of Veterans Affairs, Edward J. Derwinski, born in Chicago 1926

"Blondie" by Chic Young first published in Chicago in 1930 *

16 Milwaukee Brewers center fielder Robin Yount, who signed a $3.2 million contract in 1992, born in Danville 1955

Unsolved murder of Valerie Percy in Kenilworth 1966 *

17 Three days of polling started for first Illinois election, resulting in Shadrach Bond as first governor, in 1818

Elizabeth Enright, winner of 1939 John Newbery Medal for *Thimble Summer,* born in Oak Park 1909

American Professional Football Association formed including teams from Illinois 1920 *

Poor maintenance causes Northwest Airliner crash at Chicago, 1961

18 Fourth Lincoln-Douglas debate, held at Charleston 1858 *

Jane Addams founded Hull House in Chicago 1889 *

CBS began broadcasting with William S. Paley's 16 stations 1927 *

Astronaut Charles Veach born in Chicago 1944

O'Hare Airport named after Edward "Butch" O'Hare- Congressional Medal of Honor winner, in 1949 *

CTA "L" collision injured 276 people, 1969

Cubs' Ryne Sandberg signed a $30.5 million contract, more than the *Tribune* paid for the whole team in 1981, 1992

19 Pulitzer Prize-winning columnist Mike Royko born 1932 in Chicago

Pulitzer Prize-winning journalist Lois Jean Wille born in Arlington Heights 1932

20 Baseball coach and manager (Dodgers, Yankees, Senators) Charlie Dressen born in Decatur 1898

21 Sac and Fox Indians agree to stay west of Mississippi, ending Black Hawk War 1832 *

Runner Charles Pores set distance world's record that lasted a long time 1918

Comedian/actor Bill Murray born 1950 in Wilmette

22 Dempsey-Tunney fight in Chicago resulted in famed "long count" 1927 *

Singer Joni James (real name: Joan Carmella Babbo) born in Chicago 1930

FarmAid concert held in Champaign to give financial help to U.S. farm 1985 *

23 Richard S. Rhodes of River Park patented first hearing aid 1879

Cubs' Johnny Evers involved in famed "Merkle's Boner" 1908

24 Botanist and suffragist Mary Agnes Chase born Iroquois County 1869

The first 6-day bicycle race in U.S. was begun in Chicago 1879

Pulitzer Prize novelist Robert Lewis Taylor born in Carbondale 1912

Trial of the Chicago 8— Black Panther leaders who incited riots in Chicago—began 1969 *

25 Sonny Liston knocked out Floyd Patterson in Chicago 1962 *

26 The Treaty of Chicago signed 1833 *

The first Nixon-Kennedy debate was held in Chicago 1960

Chicago Sting win 1981 NASL soccer title defeating New York Cosmos 1-0

27 Illinois Central Railroad completed 1856 *

Magician Harry Blackstone (Henri Bouton) born 1885 in Chicago

Long-time Republican whip Leslie Cornelius Arends born 1895 in Melvin

28 Avery Brundage, long-time head of the International Olympic Committee, born in Chicago 1887 *

Founder of CBS, William S. Paley, born Chicago 1901 *

Eight Chicago White Sox players indicted for throwing the 1919 World Series 1920 *

29 Explorer and naturalist Frederik Schwatka, who mapped the Yukon River, born in Galena 1849

Basketball player Hersey Hawkins born Chicago 1965

Unsolved murders committed through poisoned Tylenol bottles began, 1982 *

30 Novelist Elizabeth Corbett born in Aurora 1887

Pitcher Robin Roberts born near Springfield 1926

OCTOBER

1 The University of Chicago started classes 1892 *

Actor-composer Oscar Brown, Jr., born 1926 in Chicago

Tony-winning actor Tom Bosley of "Happy Days" and "Murder She Wrote" born 1927 in Chicago *

Babe Ruth pointed his finger and made a home run for the first time, in Chicago, 1932 *

2 Florida congresswoman and ambassador to Denmark Ruth Bryan Owen born in Jacksonville 1885 *

Actor William Christopher born Evanston in 1932

3 Decatur Staleys' first game, against the Moline Tractors, 1920 *

Singer Grace Wing Slick of Jefferson Airplane born 1943 in Chicago

Chicago Sting wins 1984 NASL soccer title defeating Toronto Blizzard 3-2

4 Art critic and author Alfred V. Frankenstein born 1906 in Chicago

Railway collision between two trains outside Staunton kills 36 in 1910

Oscar-winning actor (for *Ben-Hur*) Charlton Heston born in Evanston 1922

Woodstock cartoonist Chester Gould invented "Dick Tracy" in a comic strip that debuted this day in 1931 *

5 Ray Kroc, developer of McDonald's fast-food chain, born in Chicago 1902 *

Actor Skip Homeier born 1930 in Chicago

Actress Karen Jane Allen born 1951 in Carrollton

1.5 million people attended an open air mass celebrated by Pope John Paul II 1979

6 Billionaire Abram Pritzker born in Chicago 1896

Singer Kevin Cronin born in Champaign 1951 *

7 Rosa Smith Eigenmann, first prominent woman fish scientist, born Monmouth 1858

Fifth Lincoln-Douglas Debate at Knox College in Galesburg 1858 *

First American-born, American-trained symphony conductor Alfred Wallenstein born Chicago 1898

Jazz musician Jo Jones born 1911 in Chicago

Walter Payton of the Chicago Bears set new lifetime NFL rushing record of 12,400 yds. in 1984

8 Automotive pioneer J. Frank Duryea born in Washburn 1869 *

The Great Chicago Fire began 1871 *

Novelist Meyer Levin born Chicago 1905 *

9 Charles Walgreen, drugstore mogel, born in Knox County 1873 *

Explorer Martin E. Johnson, who traveled with Jack London, born in Rockford 1884

Originator of Baby Ruth candy bar Otto Schnering born in Chicago 1891 *

Roger Touhy and six others escaped from Joliet and were free for two months, 1942 *

10 British flag raised at Fort de Chartres 1765

French flag removed at Fort de Chartres, ending French presence in what would become the U.S., in 1765

A locomotive moved 5 miles out of Chicago on the Galena and Chicago Union Railroad tracks 1848

Popcorn machine inventor Charles Cretors received a patent 1893 *

Basketball Hall of Fame contributor Louis G. Wilke born Chicago 1896

Chicago received its all-time heaviest rainfall — 7 inches in 24 hours, 1954

11   First Illinois State Fair, at Springfield, opened 1853
      Child-care writer Frances Lillian Ilg born in Oak Park
         1902
      Actress Joan Cusack born in Evanston 1962
12   Virden mining riot 1898 *
      Innovative columnist and Pulitzer Prize winner Stan
         Delaplane born Chicago 1907 *
      Broadcast journalist Chris Wallace born 1947 in Chicago
      Dresden Nuclear Power Plant at Morris, first private plant
         in U.S., dedicated 1960
13   Sixth debate between Lincoln and Douglas held at Quincy
         1858 *
      Pulitzer Prize-winning political cartoonist Herblock (real
         name: Herbert Block) born in Chicago 1909 *
      Puppeteer Burr Tillstrom born Chicago 1917 *
      Oscar-winning costume designer Bill Thomas born
         Chicago 1921
      4-cent Kosciusko stamp issued at Chicago 1933
      Basketball player Glenn Anton "Doc" Rivers born
         Maywood 1961
      Cellular phone introduced, in Chicago, 1983
14   White Sox won Chicago's only subway World Series,
         1906 *
      NFL's longest losing streak ends at 29 games 1945
15   Seventh and last Lincoln-douglas debate, held at Alton
         1858 *
      Editor/publisher Alicia Patterson born 1909 in Chicago
16   Lincoln called for the emancipation of slaves in a speech
         at Peoria 1854
      Hall of Famer and American League president Will
         Harridge born Chicago 1881
      The new Chicago subway system opened up to riders
         1943
17   Dancer/choreographer Doris Humphrey born 1895 in Oak
         Park
      Negligence in meeting safety standards caused mine
         explosion at Royalton killed 52 in 1914
      Gangster and murderer Al Capone found guilty of income
         tax evasion 1931 *
18   Editor-journalist Katherine Woodruff Fanning born 1927
         in Chicago
19   Creator of influential *American Spectator* magazine,
         Benjamin O. Flower, born in Albion 1858
      The 2-cent Ohio River stamp was issued at Cairo 1929
      Actor Robert Reed (real name: John Robert Rietz) born
         1932 in Chicago
20   Ellen Hardin Walworth, one of the founders of the DAR,
         born in Jacksonville 1832
      James R. Mann, author of White Slave Act, born near
         Bloomington 1856 *
      Cork-centered baseball first used in World Series play in
         Chicago 1910
      Football player Zeke Bratkowski born in Danville 1931
21   Musician Lee Loughnane of the group Chicago born 1946
         in Chicago
      Stephen Jones sets new marathon world record of 2 hrs., 8
         min., 5 sec. in Chicago 1984
22   Feminist-suffragette Abigail Jane Scott Duniway born
         1834 in Groveland
      Nobel Prize chemist Clinton Joseph Davisson born
         Bloomington 1881
      Philosopher and theologian Paul Tillich died in Chicago
         1965
23   Buildings of the Columbian Exposition dedicated by
         President Cleveland 1892 *
      Gangster Joey Aiello killed by Capone's men, ending
         local opposition, 1930 *
      Author/film director Michael Crichton born 1942 in
         Chicago
      Football player Mike Tomczak born in Calumet City 1962

24   George Hancock's plan for softball was solidified in rules
         accepted 1889 *
25   Symphony conductor and composer Grant Fletcher born
         in Hartsburg 1913
      Basketball player Dan Issel born in Batavia 1948
26   Postum and Grape-Nuts creator Charles William Post
         born in Springfield 1854 *
      TV Wheel of Fortuner Pat Sajak born in Chicago 1946
      First Lady Hillary Rodhan Clinton born in Park Ridge
         1947
27   Steamer *Stonewall* burned on Mississippi River below
         Cairo in 1869, 200 killed
      Astronaut Steven Nagel born in Canton 1946
      Actress Carrie Snodgrass born in Chicago 1946
28   Chicago Mayor Carter Harrison assassinated last day of
         Columbian Exposition in 1893 *
29   Baseball player Jesse Barfield born in Joliet 1959
30   Fictional Professor Farrell started Orson Welles' great
         Halloween hoax *
      Illinois Central railway accident in Chicago killed 45 in
         1972
      100th game in rivalry between Aurora East and Aurora
         West 1992 *
31   Singer-musician-songwriter Tom Paxton born 1937 in
         Chicago
      Actor David Ogden Stiers of "M*A*S*H" born in Peoria
         1942

NOVEMBER

1   Young adult novelist Mildred Elwood Lawrence born
         1907 in Charleston
      Author Richard Martin Watt born 1930 in Berwyn
      Broadcast journalist Mike Jensen born 1934 in Chicago
2   Abraham Lincoln lost senatorial race to Stephen A.
         Douglas 1858
      First auto "race" run from Chicago to Waukegan 1895 *
3   Congressman Philip M. Crane born in Chicago 1930
      Actor-dancer Ken Berry born in Moline 1930
      Pulitzer Prize dramatist David Alan Mamet born 1947 in
         Chicago *
      Journalist Tom Shales born in Elgin 1948
      Chicago Tribune published its famous but wrong headline
         saying Dewey beat Truman in the presidential elec-
         tion of 1948
      Actor Mandy (Mandel) Patinkin born in Chicago 1952
      Comedian Roseanne (Barr) Arnold born in Moline 1952
      Illinois elected first black woman to Senate (Carol
         Moseley Braun) and first Hispanic from Midwest to
         the House of Representatives (Luis Gutierrez) 1992 *
4   Abraham Lincoln and Mary Todd married by Ninian
         Edwards in Springfield 1842
      James Thompson elected to fourth term as governor, a
         state record, 1986
5   Pulitzer historian Odell Shepard born 1884 in Sterling *
      Dramatist/actor Sam Shepard (Samuel Shepard Rogers)
         born 1943 at Fort Sheridan
      CTA "L" collided with a North Shore electric train,
         killing 8, 1956
6   First Republican and first Illinoisan elected president,
         Abraham Lincoln, 1860 *
      Author Noel Gerson born 1914 in Chicago
      From Here to Eternity author James Jones born in
         Robinson 1921 *
      Broadcast journalist (and wife of Arnold Schwarzenegger)
         Maria Shriver born 1955 in Chicago
      Mrs. Earle B. Searcy, first woman elected to statewide
         office in Illinois, elected 1956
      First black female judge, Edith Sampson, elected as
         municipal judge Chicago 1962

7 Abolitionist editor Elijah P. Lovejoy murdered in Alton 1837 *

Publisher of the *Washington Post,* Eleanor Medill Patterson, born in Chicago 1884

Football game between Cardinals and Tigers "decide" franchise 1920 *

8 Judge Kenesaw Mountain Landis appointed baseball commissioner after Black Sox scandal 1920 *

Singer Minnie Riperton born 1948 in Chicago

Jazz singer Rickie Lee Jones born in Chicago 1955

9 Pulitzer Prize-winning poet James Schuyler born in Chicago 1923

Baseball player Whitey Herzog born in New Athens 1931

10 Poet Vachel Lindsay born Springfield 1879 *

Dion O'Banion killed by Al Capone's gang in Chicago 1924 *

11 Actor Robert Ryan born in Chicago 1913

Wisconsin senator known for "Golden Fleece"waste awards, William Proxmire, born 1915 in Lake Forest

Football player Otis Armstrong born Chicago 1950

12 Composer Richard A. Whiting was born Peoria 1891 *

Supreme Court justice Harry Blackmun born in Nashville 1908

The first drive-up window in a bank opened in Chicago's Exchange National Bank 1946

Scott Turow, lawyer-turned-novelist, born in Chicago 1949

13 Nobel Prize chemist Edward Doisy born in Hume 1893

St. Paul Mine disaster kills 259 miners near Cherry in 1909 *

14 Opera singer Jean Madeira born in Centralia 1918

Actor McLean Stevenson of "M*A*S*H" born 1929 in Bloomington

Basketball player Jack Wayne Sikma born in Kankakee 1955

Illinois became the first state to ratify 24th Amendment, prohibiting poll tax, 1962

15 Journalist/humorist Franklin P. Adams (writing as F.P.A.) born in Chicago 1881 *

Chicago cartoonist Bud Fisher introduced"A. Mutt," which later became "Mutt and Jeff" 1907 *

16 Lecture in Springfield by Lincoln's law partner, William Herndon, starts story of Lincoln-Rutledge romance, in 1866 *

Radio performer Jim Jordan of "Fibber McGee & Molly" born 1896 in Peoria

Astronaut Carl J. Meade born at Chanute Air Force Base in 1950

17 Actor Rock Hudson born in Winnetka 1925 *

Fashion designer and artist Michaele J. Vollbracht born in Quincy 1947

Actress Mary Elizabeth Mastrantonio born in Lombard 1958

18 Voters ratified the fourth state constitution 1970

19 Murderer Nathan Leopold of the Leopold and Loeb case born 1904 in Kenwood *

Author David Ely born in Chicago 1927

TV journalist Garrick Utley, son of newsman Clifton Utley, born in Chicago 1939

20 Brooklyn baseball pitcher Leon J. Cadore born in Chicago 1891

Big band singer June Christy born in Springfield 1925 *

Labor leader/socialist Eugene V. Debs died in Elmhurst 1926

21 Geneticist Alfred Sturtevant born in Jacksonville 1891

Hall of Fame third baseman Fred Lindstrom born in Chicago 1905

Female jockey Barbara Jo Rubin born in Highland 1949

Conviction of the Chicago 7 overturned 1972 *

22 Baseball player Greg "The Bull" Luzinski born in Chicago 1950

24 Marshal of Dodge City, Kansas, Bat Masterson, born in Iroquois County (maybe) 1853 *

27 Rock Island Independents sell future Hall of Famer Healey for $100 1922 *

The Blackhawks, the Chicago hockey team, played their first game, against the Toronto St. Patricks, who they beat, 4-1, 1926

Actor Marshall Thompson born in Peoria 1926

Gangster Baby Face Nelson shot 17 times and escaped near Barrington 1934 *

28 Designer of Lincoln Memorial, architect Henry Bacon, born Watseka 1866

Ernie Nevers scored 40 points in one football game 1929 *

29 Silent film actor Rod LaRocque born in Chicago 1898

DECEMBER

1 Illinois constitution ratified by Congress, enabling statehood, 1818 *

Vandalia declared capital of state for next 20 years 1820 *

Abraham Lincoln of New Salem took his seat in the Illinois House of Representatives 1834

Journalist Frazier "Spike" Hunt born in Rock Island 1885

Grammy-winning singer Lou(is) Rawls born 1936 in Chicago

Actor and Grammy-winning comedian Richard Pryor born 1940 in Peoria *

Actress Marcia Warfield of "Night Court" born in Chicago 1955

Ninety children and nuns killed in Our Lady of the Angels school fire Chicago 1958

2 Oscar-winning composer Harry Sukman born in Chicago 1912

Artist James Valerio born in Chicago 1938

Enrico Fermi succeeded in creating the first controlled nuclear reaction at Chicago 1942 *

Montgomery Ward's "Rudolph the Red-nosed Reindeer" hit the top of the pops 1949 *

Illinois gets a no-fault divorce law 1983

3 Illinois was admitted to the Union as a state 1818 *

Third state capitol building at Vandalia occupied, 1836 *

The Iroquois Theatre fire killed about 600 people 1903*

Radio performer Don McNeill born 1907 in Galena *

4 Pere Marquette landed at Grosse Point and wintered at Chicago 1674 *

Legislature met for first time at Vandalia's new capitol building 1820 *

Tennis star Marty Riessen born in Hinsdale 1941

5 Educator Hugh Stewart Magill born in Auburn 1868

Gum-maker and owner of the Chicago Cubs Philip K. Wrigley born Chicago 1894 *

Journalist and current events writer Vincent Sheean born Pana 1899

Animated film producer Walt Disney born 1901 in Chicago *

Poet Vachel Lindsay committed suicide in Springfield 1931 *

6 British held a court session in Illinois for first time at Fort de Chartres 1768

Abraham Lincoln took his seat in Washington in the U.S. House of Representatives 1846

Cornelia Meigs,1934 Newbery Medal win for *Invincible Louisa,* born in Rock Island 1884

Hall of Fame baseball umpire Jocko Conlan born Chicago 1899 *

Football Hall of Famer Otto Graham born in Waukegan 1921 *

Mass murderer Richard Speck born Kirkwood 1941 *

8 Creator of "Popeye," cartoonist Elzie Crisler Segar, born 1894 in Chester *

United Airlines 737 crashed near Chicago's Midway Airport killed 45, 1972 *

9 Illinois officially became a county of Virginia when it was annexed in 1778 *

The second capitol building at Vandalia burned, 1823 *

Levant Richardson received patent for ball-bearing roller skates 1884

Hall of Fame Chicago Bear and actor Dick Butkus born 1942 in Chicago *

Actor John Malkovich born 1953 in Christopher

10 Soap opera crator Agnes Nixon born in Chicago 1927 *

TV actress Susan Dey born in Pekin 1952

Playboy magazine went on sale for the first time in 1953 *

Basketball player Mark Aquire born in Chicago 1959

11 Actress Donna Mills born in Chicago 1944

12 Buffalo Bill Cody arrived in Chicago to start a theatrical career 1872 *

Playwright Rachel Crothers, author of *Susan and God,* born in Bloomington 1878

Architect John Lloyd Wright, son of Frank Lloyd, born in Oak Park 1892

Quiz show producer Louis Cowan born Chicago 1909 *

Voters overwhelming rejected the proposed new constitution 1922

13 Constitutional convention began in Springfield 1869

Broadcast and newspaper journalist Drew Pearson born 1897 in Evanston

Light-heavyweight boxing champ for a decade, Archie Moore, might have been born in Collinsville

14 Pianist Rosalyn Tureck born 1914 in Chicago

Comedian and gagwriter Morey Amsterdam, the first talk-show host, born Chicago 1914 *

15 Automotive pioneer Charles Duryea born in Canton 1862*

Physician William A. Hinton, first black professor at Harvard, born Chicago 1883 *

Voters ratified the new state constitution 1970

16 Science fiction writer Philip K. Dick born in Chicago 1928

17 TV announcer and game-show host Gene Rayburn born in Christopher 1917

Actor Richard Long born in Chicago 1927

Journalist-editor Marilyn (Mohr) Beck born 1928 in Chicago

Chicago Bears win first NFL championship against New York Giants in 1933 *

Roger "The Terrible" Touhy, just released from prison, shot on Chicago street 1959 *

18 First interscholastic high school basketball game in Illinois, 1896 *

Basketball Hall of Famer DePaul coach Ray Meyer born Chicago 1913 *

Singer Anita O'Day (Colton) born 1919 in Chicago

19 Humorist H. Allen Smith, author of *Life in a Putty Knife Factory,* born in McLeansboro 1907

TV actor Tim Reid was born in Harvey 1944

Actress Jennifer Beals born 1963 in Chicago

20 Actress Audrey Totter born in Joliet 1918

21 William "Willie" Wallace Lincoln, third son of Abraham Lincoln, who died in the White House, born in Springfield 1850

Mine disaster killed 119 at West Frankfort in 1951

Patricia Roberts Harris, born Mattoon, sworn in as first black female cabinet member 1976 *

22 Inventor of first radio telescope Grote Reber born Wheaton 1911 *

Mother Cabrini, who would later be named first American saint, died in Chicago 1917 *

Actor Frankie Darro born 1917 in Chicago

About 500 KKK members were sworn in as Prohibition enforcement agents in Carbondale 1923

Bodies of seven young men discovered buried at John Wayne Gacy, Jr.'s home in Norwood Park 1978 *

23 Poet and creator of *Poetry* magazine Harriet Monroe born in Chicago 1860 *

Medal of Honor winner and vice presidential candidate James Stockdale born Abingdon 1923 *

Runner Richard C. Wohlhuter born in Geneva 1945

24 Creator of Raggedy Ann and Andy, Johnny Gruelle, born in Arcola 1880 *

Christmas Eve mine disaster at Moweaqua entombed 54 men 1932 *

25 Union Stock Yards opened in Chicago in 1865 *

Oakland A's leadoff batter Rickey Henderson born in Chicago 1958

26 Labor Secretary Lynn Martin, under President Bush, born in Chicago 1939

31 Guitarist/ singer/poet Patti Smith born in Chicago 1936

Chicago Bears win NFL championship defeating New York Giants 14-0 in 1963

INDEX OF PEOPLE, PLACES, AND ORGANIZATIONS

PHOTO CREDITS

Photo Courtesy of the Arcola Chamber of
 Commerce: 104
Argonne National Laboratory: 87, 88
The Bettman Archive: 126 (top)
Carol Moseley Braun: 50
Caterpillar, Inc.: 159
The Champaign-Urbana News-Gazette: 110
Chicago Bears: 131, 133
Chicago Bulls: 129
City of Chicago/Peter J. Schulz: 93
Chicago Historical Society: 74, 134
L.R. Clarke: 162
Cold Spring Harbor Laboratory Archives: 89
Deere & Company: 157
DePaul University/Department of Athletics: 128
Courtesy Field Museum of Natural History: 26
 (top), 92
Galatin National Company: 29
The Goodman Theatre: © Lascher: 103
Handgun Control Inc.: 145
Paul Harvey: 166 (bottom)
Illinois Department of Conservation: 16, 17,
 21, 22, 36
Illinois Endangered Species Protection Board:
 26 (bottom)
Photo Courtesy of the Illinois Historic
 Preservation Agency: 4, 8, 32, 71, 72, 100
 (right)
Illinois Secretary of State/Communications
 Department: 9
Courtesy of the Illinois State Historical
 Library: 33, 34, 37, 41 (both), 51, 65

(both), 69 (top), 70, 99 (both), 100 (left),
 143, 147 (both), 155, 167, 168, 169
JJK & Associates/Tony Duff: 137
Johnson Publishing Company, Inc.: 165 (both)
McDonald's Corporation: 161
The Merchandise Mart: 171
The Metropolis Planet: 69 (bottom)
Dana Montana: 166 (top)
Montgomery Ward: 170
National Aeronautics and Space
 Administration: 63
National Baseball Library, Cooperstown, NY:
 125, 126 (bottom), 127
Courtesy NRAO/AUI: 84 (both)
The Olney Daily Mail: 25
Photo courtesy of the Ottawa Silica Company
 Foundation: 28
The Randolph County Herald Tribune: 95
Ronald Reagan Home Preservation
 Foundation: 52, 122
Springfield Illinois Convention & Visitors
 Bureau: 13
U.S. Army Corps of Engineers, Memphis
 District: 62
U.S. Navy: 76
Harold Washington Library: 67
Wisconsin Center for Film and Theater
 Research: 106, 136
The Frank Lloyd Wright Archives: 94
Courtesy of the William Wrigley Jr. Company:
 156
Yerkes Observatory/University of Chicago: 83